David Cross

Self-Development Guide Proven Success Strategies

Part 1

2024

Copyright

© 2024 David Cross. All rights reserved.

No part of this book may be reproduced, distributed, or transmitted in any form or by any means, including photocopying, recording, or other electronic or mechanical methods, without the prior written permission of the publisher, except in the case of brief quotations embodied in critical reviews and certain other noncommercial uses permitted by copyright law.

This book is a work of nonfiction. The names, characters, places, and incidents are the product of the author's experience and research. Any resemblance to actual events, locales, or persons, living or dead, is entirely coincidental. The advice provided in this book is for informational purposes only and should not be taken as legal, financial, or professional advice. The author and publisher assume no responsibility for any actions taken based on the content of this book.

Disclaimer Notice:

Please note the information contained within this document is for educational and entertainment purposes only. All effort has been executed to present accurate, up to date, and reliable, complete information. No warranties of any kind are declared or implied. Readers acknowledge that the author is not engaging in the rendering of legal, financial, medical or professional advice. The content within this book has been derived from various sources. Please consult a licensed professional before attempting any techniques outlined in this book.

By reading this document, the reader agrees that under no circumstances is the author responsible for any losses, direct or indirect, which are incurred as a result of the use of the information contained within this document, including, but not limited to, — errors, omissions, or inaccuracies.

The book partially incorporates elements related to artificial intelligence.

Content

Introduction **6**
1. Goal Setting **8**
- 1.1 Introduction and Context 8
- 1.2 Main Theory 11
- 1.3 Problematic Situations and Examples 13
- 1.4 Practical Advice and Solutions 18
- 1.5 Daily Implementation Plan 23
- 1.6 Reflection and Conclusions 29

2. Morning Rituals **33**
- 2.1 Introduction and Context 33
- 2.2 Main Theory 35
- 2.3 Problematic Situations and Examples 39
- 2.4 Practical Advice and Solutions for Implementing Morning Rituals 42
- 2.5 Daily Implementation Plan 48
- 2.6 Reflection and Conclusions 52

3. The Pomodoro Technique **55**
- 3.1 Introduction and Context 55
- 3.2 Main Theory 57
- 3.3 Problematic Situations and Examples 60
- 3.4 Practical Advice and Solutions for Implementing the
     Pomodor Technique 62
- 3.5 Daily Implementation Plan 67
- 3.6 Reflection and Conclusions 70

4. Goal Visualization **74**
- 4.1 Introduction and Context 74
- 4.2 Main Theory 75

- 4.3 Problematic Situations and Examples 77
- 4.4 Practical Advice and Solutions for Implementing
  the Visualization Technique 82
- 4.5 Daily Implementation Plan 83
- 4.6 Reflection and Conclusions 86

5. Journaling 90
- 5.1 Introduction and Context 90
- 5.2 Main Theory 91
- 5.3 Problematic Situations and Examples 97
- 5.4 Practical Advice and Solutions for Journaling 98
- 5.5 Daily Implementation Plan 106
- 5.6 Reflection and Conclusions 111

6. Meditation and Mindfulness 115
- 6.1 Introduction and Context 115
- 6.2 Main Theory 117
- 6.3 Problematic Situations and Examples 119
- 6.4 Practical Advice and Solutions for Meditation and Mindfulness 122
- 6.5 Daily Implementation Plan 130
- 6.6 Reflection and Conclusions 133

7. Energy Management 138
- 7.1 Introduction and Context 138
- 7.2 Main Theory 139
- 7.3 Problematic Situations and Examples 144
- 7.4 Practical Advice and Solutions for Energy Management 146
- 7.5 Daily Implementation Plan 154
- 7.6 Reflection and Conclusions 157

8. Planning and Prioritization 161
- 8.1 Introduction and Context 161
- 8.2 Main Theory 162
- 8.3 Problematic Situations and Examples 165
- 8.4 Practical Advice and Solutions for Planning and Prioritization 167
- 8.5 Daily Implementation Plan 174
- 8.6 Reflection and Conclusions 177

9. Building a Supportive Environment 181
- 9.1 Introduction and Context 181
- 9.2 Main Theory 182
- 9.3 Problematic Situations and Examples 185
- 9.4 Practical Advice and Solutions for Developing
  Support and Environment 196
- 9.5 Daily Implementation Plan 197
- 9.6 Reflection and Conclusions 201

10. Principles of Continuous Learning 205
- 10.1 Introduction and Context 205
- 10.2 Main Theory 206
- 10.3 Problematic Situations and Examples 209
- 10.4 Practical Advice and Solutions for Continuous
  Learning and Development 214
- 10.5 Daily Implementation Plan 218
- 10.6 Reflection and Conclusions 222

Epilogue 227
About the Author 229
Additional Materials 230

Introduction

In today's world, where the pace of life is increasing every day, the idea of self-development is becoming increasingly important. The desire to achieve success, find a balance between work and personal life, and maintain mental and physical health are key goals for many of us. However, achieving these goals often seems challenging, especially when we face daily challenges, stress, and a lack of time. How can one find a path to stable personal and professional growth? How can ambitions be turned into reality? The answer to these questions lies in a conscious approach to organizing one's life and using effective self-development techniques.

This book is a practical guide that brings together ten key self-development techniques, each of which has the potential to significantly boost your productivity, improve your quality of life, and help you achieve your goals. We explore such important topics as goal setting, morning rituals, the Pomodoro technique, visualization, journaling, meditation and mindfulness, energy management, planning and prioritization, support networks, and continuous learning. Each chapter contains not only theoretical knowledge but also practical recommendations that will help you implement these techniques into your daily life.

Goal setting is the foundation of any successful development plan. We will examine the principles of SMART (Specific, Measurable, Achievable, Relevant, Time-bound) that will help you create clear and realistic goals that align with your life priorities. Without proper goal setting, it is difficult to build an effective strategy for success.

Morning rituals are the next important step on the path to increasing productivity. They help you tune in to a positive mindset, focus on important tasks, and start the day with calmness and confidence. Successful people know that the beginning of the day sets the tone for the entire day, so they carefully plan their morning rituals, including physical exercise, meditation, or day planning.

The Pomodoro Technique, which we also explore in this book, is an effective tool for time management and enhancing concentration. It allows you to break down the work process into short intervals, which promotes better focus on tasks and reduces the risk of burnout. This method will help you use your time as efficiently as possible and achieve results.

Visualization is a powerful tool that helps create a mental image of your success. It activates the subconscious mind, helping you move towards your goals with greater confidence and motivation. We will discuss how to properly use the visualization technique to achieve desired results in various areas of life.

Journaling is another important technique that helps you systematically analyze your progress, set new goals, and maintain motivation. A journal is a tool for self-reflection that allows you to gain a deeper understanding of your emotions, thoughts, and actions, as well as adjust your behavior according to your goals.

Meditation and mindfulness help reduce stress levels and improve overall mental well-being. They contribute to the development of inner stability and harmony, which is extremely important in today's world, where stress is becoming increasingly common.

Energy management is a key aspect that is often overlooked. We will examine how to properly allocate your resources throughout the day, taking into account natural productivity cycles, to achieve maximum results with minimal effort.

Planning and prioritization are what help you avoid chaos and focus on the most important tasks. We will look at effective planning methods that will help you set priorities and make the most of your time.

Support networks are an integral part of success. We will discuss how your environment influences your achievements and how to build relationships that contribute to your development.

Finally, continuous learning is the key to ongoing growth and development. We will explore how to stay open to new knowledge and skills to continuously enhance your competence and reach new heights.

This book is designed to help you step by step approach your best self. It combines practical tools and inspiration necessary to turn your dreams into reality. Regardless of the stage of life you are at, these ten techniques will provide you with the support and direction needed to make your life more conscious, productive, and harmonious.

Chapter 1: Goal Setting

Introduction and Context

Goal Setting: The Foundational Principle of Success

Goals are what define our path in life; they help us understand where we are going and what we want to achieve. This is not just a popular trend or psychological trick, but a key principle that allows us to systematically move forward toward results. Just as a map helps you reach your destination during a journey, in life, goals serve as a guide, indicating the right direction and helping plan our actions.

Goals play a critical role in all aspects of our lives. In the professional realm, clearly defined goals contribute to growth and development, creating a clear plan to reach career heights. For example, a goal to achieve a certain level within a company or become an expert in your field helps focus on important tasks and develop the necessary skills, leading to success.

In personal life, goals can be even more diverse, ranging from mastering new skills and hobbies to achieving personal ambitions or improving the quality of life. For example, the desire to learn to play a musical instrument or to study a new language can become a powerful motivator for self-improvement. This not only broadens your horizons but also enriches your experience and contributes to personal development.

In the area of health, goals can relate to physical exercise, dietary changes, or improving mental well-being. For instance, a goal to improve physical fitness might include regular workouts, dietary changes, or participation in sports events. These goals not only strengthen physical health but also enhance overall well-being and improve quality of life.

Goals also hold immense importance in relationships. Shared goals can improve understanding and harmony between partners. For example, setting financial goals or planning a family vacation can strengthen the relationship, creating a closer bond and reducing conflicts. Working together to achieve goals helps partners understand each other better and fosters healthy, supportive relationships.

Psychological Benefits of Goal Setting

Clearly defined goals allow people to experience more satisfaction and less stress. Scientific studies confirm that having goals positively impacts psychological and emotional well-being. Psychologist Gary Locke found that individuals with specific, measurable goals exhibit higher levels of motivation and productivity. When you have a clear understanding of what you are striving for and a plan of action to achieve it, this creates clarity and reduces stress and anxiety.

For example, a study at the University of California showed that people who keep journals of their goals and regularly track progress experience less anxiety and more satisfaction with life. Writing down goals helps structure thoughts, focus on important tasks, and celebrate achievements. This not only reduces uncertainty but also provides a sense of control and progress.

Having goals also fosters positive thinking and enhances self-esteem. Achievable goals and their accomplishment boost confidence in one's abilities. For instance, completing a project or reaching a personal milestone can inspire and motivate, leading to further achievements.

Goals as a Tool for Self-Regulation

Goals are a powerful tool for self-regulation, helping control behavior and maintain discipline. They create a clear plan of action and provide a structure for achieving desired outcomes. For example, if your goal is to improve skills in a certain area, setting specific goals allows you to organize your time and resources for learning and practice, making the process of achieving the goal more systematic and focused.

Methodologies such as SMART (Specific, Measurable, Achievable, Relevant, Time-bound) are effective tools for goal setting. The SMART methodology helps shape goals that are specific, measurable, achievable, relevant, and time-bound. It allows you to break down large tasks into smaller, attainable stages, providing a clear understanding of what needs to be done for success.

For example, if your goal is to improve physical fitness, the SMART methodology might include steps such as identifying the type of physical activity (Specific), setting the number of workouts per week (Measurable), ensuring the goal is realistic (Achievable), checking the goal's relevance to health (Relevant), and setting a timeline for achieving the goal (Time-bound). This approach helps clearly plan and implement your goals.

Goals also help develop skills in self-control and discipline. By setting goals, you learn to organize your time and resources, which positively impacts overall productivity and achievement in life. For example, if your goal is to complete a large project, creating a detailed plan and sticking to it fosters organization and discipline.

The Impact of Goals on Various Aspects of Life

Career: Setting career goals is critically important for professional success. People with clear career goals generally have more opportunities for growth. For example, a goal to become a leader in your field might include obtaining additional education, participating in professional seminars and conferences, and building a network of contacts. Such goals help maintain motivation and provide a clear plan for achieving success. Research shows that employees with specific goals demonstrate higher levels of productivity and job satisfaction.

Personal Development: Goals in personal development might include learning new skills or mastering a new hobby. For example, a goal to learn a new language or play a musical instrument can broaden your horizons and improve your quality of life. Acquiring new skills not only enriches your life but can also be highly satisfying and inspiring. It allows you to develop creative abilities and boost self-esteem.

Health: Setting health-related goals can include physical exercise, healthy eating, or improving mental well-being. For example, if your goal is to lose weight or improve fitness, you might set goals for regular workouts, dietary changes, or participation in sports events. These goals help focus on a healthy lifestyle and provide motivation to form healthy habits. Setting health goals can significantly improve the quality of life and overall well-being.

Relationships: Shared goals in relationships can help improve understanding and harmony. For instance, joint financial planning or vacation organization can strengthen the bond between partners. Working together to achieve goals helps partners better understand each other and foster supportive relationships. This can also help resolve conflicts and improve communication, positively impacting the quality of the relationship.

Section Overview

In this chapter, we will explore the importance of goal setting, its psychological benefits, and its role as a tool for self-regulation. You will learn how goals impact various aspects of life, such as career, personal development, health, and relationships. The aim of this chapter is to provide you with a clear understanding of why goals are important, how they influence your life, and how to effectively set them.

The main methods of goal setting include the SMART methodology and other approaches. SMART (Specific, Measurable, Achievable, Relevant, Time-bound) is an effective tool for setting goals. This approach allows you to shape goals that are specific, measurable, achievable, relevant, and time-bound, providing a clear plan of action and enabling effective achievement of desired results. Other methods, such as OKR (Objectives and Key Results), focus on setting ambitious goals and measuring progress through key results. Studying these methods will help you create an effective action plan and implement it in your life.

Main Theory

Goal Setting as a Powerful Tool for Success

The SMART methodology is an indispensable tool for those who strive for a systematic approach to achieving their goals. It provides clarity, structure, and efficiency, helping avoid misunderstandings and misinterpretations that can arise from vaguely defined or unrealistic goals. Let's delve into each component of the SMART methodology in detail and understand how this approach contributes to effective goal setting.

Specific

Specificity is the foundation of the SMART methodology. Clearly formulated goals provide clarity and focus, helping avoid confusion and misunderstandings. Defining specific goals allows you to concentrate efforts on achieving a clear outcome.

- **Example of a specific goal:** Instead of a general statement like "improve health," specify your goal as "exercise three times a week for the next three months." Such specificity provides a clear understanding of what needs to be done and when.

- **Benefits of specificity:** Specificity helps avoid vague tasks and allows for the creation of a clear action plan by identifying necessary resources. This contributes to more efficient time and effort management, reducing the likelihood of distractions.

- **Strategies for defining specific goals:** To make your goal specific, ask yourself: "What exactly do I want to achieve?" "What actions do I need to take to achieve this goal?" and "What resources do I need?" For example, instead of "becoming more successful," specify "complete a project management course by the end of the quarter."

Measurable

Measurability is a key component of the SMART methodology that allows you to assess progress in achieving goals. It is important to know how close you are to reaching the goal so you can adjust your actions if necessary.

- **Example of a measurable goal:** If your goal is to "improve physical fitness," make it measurable, for instance, "lose 5 kg in three months" or "increase endurance to 30 minutes of running without stopping." Such metrics make it easy to track progress and make timely adjustments.

- **Benefits of measurability:** Measuring progress maintains motivation and provides feedback on achievements. It also helps identify problems early and adjust the strategy for better results.

- **Methods for measuring progress:** Use quantitative or qualitative indicators to assess progress. For example, keep a journal to track physical exercises or use mobile apps to monitor your activities.

Achievable

Achievability ensures that the goal is realistic considering your resources, capabilities, and limitations. This helps maintain motivation and avoid disappointment.

- **Example of an achievable goal:** If you haven't exercised for a long time, a goal of "exercising three times a week" may be achievable. However, if you don't have time for regular workouts, a goal of "training professionally five times a week" might be too ambitious.

- **Benefits of achievability:** Setting realistic goals helps avoid stress and demotivation, as your efforts will align with real possibilities. It allows you to create a plan that is feasible within your resources and time.

- **Analysis of achievability:** Before setting a goal, assess your capabilities, resources, and limitations. This includes analyzing your time, skills, financial resources, and other factors that might influence the achievement of the goal.

Relevant

Relevance determines the significance of the goal for your life and its alignment with your life priorities. A goal should not only be important but also correspond to your personal or professional aspirations.

- **Example of a relevant goal:** If you aspire to career growth, a goal like "take professional development courses to get a new position" would be relevant. It is connected to your career goals and will help you achieve professional development.

- **Benefits of relevance:** Relevant goals ensure that your efforts are directed toward achieving something that matters to your life and development. This maintains high motivation and satisfaction from achievements.

- **Evaluation of relevance:** Consider how the goal will impact your life values, career aspirations, and personal ambitions. Ensure that the goal truly aligns with your interests and will help you achieve the desired result.

Time-bound

Time-boundedness is an important element that helps set clear deadlines for achieving the goal. It provides structure and helps avoid procrastination, creating a sense of urgency.

- **Example of a time-bound goal:** A goal like "improve English to B2 level within six months" provides a clear timeline for achieving the result. This allows you to plan your learning and evaluate progress regularly.
- **Benefits of time-boundedness:** Setting deadlines helps avoid delays and maintain discipline. It creates a sense of urgency and encourages regular task completion, enabling goals to be achieved within the established timeframe.
- **Strategies for meeting deadlines:** Break down a large goal into smaller tasks with their own deadlines. Use planners or mobile apps to monitor deadlines and organize work.

Scientific Justification of SMART Goals

Scientific research supports the effectiveness of the SMART methodology. People who set SMART goals have higher achievement levels compared to those who do not use clearly defined goals. This is confirmed by several studies showing that:

- **Level of motivation:** Studies show that people with clearly defined and measurable goals demonstrate higher levels of motivation and focus on achieving results. They exhibit more enthusiasm and willingness to put in the effort to achieve their goals.
- **Structure and organization:** SMART goals help create a clear plan of action and identify necessary resources. This ensures effective organization of time and effort, enabling results to be achieved more efficiently and quickly.
- **Feedback and adjustments:** Setting specific and measurable goals allows for feedback on progress and timely adjustments to the strategy. This helps avoid disappointment and provides an opportunity to respond promptly to any challenges.

The SMART methodology is an important tool for achieving success because it provides clarity, measurability, achievability, relevance, and time-boundedness for setting and achieving goals. Using this approach helps effectively plan, organize, and implement tasks, contributing to the achievement of desired results and success in various aspects of life.

Problematic Situations and Examples: How SMART Goals Can Improve Your Life

The lack of clear goals can be a source of chaos and uncertainty in various areas of life. Let's take a look at typical situations where setting goals can significantly change your situation, and how the SMART methodology can help find the optimal solution.

Situation 1: Lack of Clear Life Goals

• **Problem:** A person without clearly defined goals often feels lost and lacks direction. This leads to feelings of failure, stress, and a lack of motivation. For example, if you are working in a position that does not satisfy you and have no clear vision of your next step, you may spend time on secondary tasks that bring neither satisfaction nor development.

• **Solution with SMART Methodology:**

♦ **Specific:** Instead of a general desire to "improve life," formulate the goal as "find a job that aligns with my values and interests within three months." This allows for a clear understanding of what needs to be done.

♦ **Measurable:** Set specific criteria for assessing progress, such as "send 20 resumes in two weeks and attend two networking events within a month."

♦ **Achievable:** Ensure the goal is realistic given your experience and capabilities. If you have the relevant skills, focus on finding a job in your field.

♦ **Relevant:** Ensure the goal aligns with your life priorities. For example, a new job that matches your interests can restore your motivation and improve job satisfaction.

♦ **Time-bound:** Set a specific timeframe to achieve the goal, such as "find a new job within three months."

Situation 2: Career Development Without a Clear Plan

• **Problem:** Without clear career goals and a development plan, you may find yourself stagnating. For example, working in a position that does not promote your growth can become an obstacle to further career advancement.

• **Solution with SMART Methodology:**

♦ **Specific:** Set a clear career development goal, such as "obtain project management certification within a year."

♦ **Measurable:** Establish clear criteria for measuring progress, such as "complete three project management courses and pass the certification exam by the end of the year."

♦ **Achievable:** Ensure the goal is realistic given your capabilities and resources. If you have experience in project management, obtaining certification is a logical step.

♦ **Relevant:** Ensure the goal is important for your career growth. For example, certification can help you reach a new professional level.

♦ **Time-bound:** Set a deadline to achieve the goal, such as "obtain certification by the end of the year."

Situation 3: Lack of Shared Goals in Relationships

• **Problem:** The absence of shared goals between partners can lead to misunderstandings and conflicts. For example, if one partner wants to buy a new apartment and the other is against it, this can become a source of tension.

• **Solution with SMART Methodology:**

♦ **Specific:** Set specific shared goals, such as "jointly plan the family budget and save a certain amount of money each month."

♦ **Measurable:** Determine how you will measure success, for example, "save $500 a month for the next six months."

♦ **Achievable:** Ensure the goal is achievable for both partners. Joint budget planning can be achievable if both partners are willing to work together.

♦ **Relevant:** Ensure the goal is important for both partners. For example, joint budget planning can strengthen financial stability and reduce conflicts.

♦ **Time-bound:** Set specific deadlines to achieve the goal, such as "create a budget plan by the end of the month and review it every three months."

Situation 4: Lack of Goals in Education and Personal Development

• **Problem:** Without clear goals in education, you may feel lost and not know how to develop further. For example, if you want to learn a new skill but don't have a concrete plan, it can be difficult to achieve the desired results.

• **Solution with SMART Methodology:**

♦ **Specific:** Define a clear goal for learning, such as "learn the basics of Python programming within three months."

♦ **Measurable:** Set criteria for measuring progress, such as "complete 10 online lessons and finish three practical projects by the end of the course."

♦ **Achievable:** Ensure the goal is realistic, such as learning the basics of programming can be achievable if you spend three hours a week studying.

♦ **Relevant:** Ensure the goal is important for your personal and professional aspirations; for example, knowing Python can help in your career.

♦ **Time-bound:** Set deadlines to achieve the goal, such as "complete the course within three months."

Situation 5: Time Management Problems

• **Problem:** The lack of clear goals can lead to time management issues. For example, spending excessive time on minor tasks instead of focusing on important ones can reduce your productivity.

- **Solution with SMART Methodology:**

♦ **Specific:** Set specific goals for time management, such as "create a daily task plan and follow it for a week."

♦ **Measurable:** Establish criteria for evaluating effectiveness, such as "complete all major tasks by 5:00 PM each workday."

♦ **Achievable:** Ensure the goal is realistic given your workload; for example, planning tasks can be achievable if you spend 15 minutes each morning drafting them.

♦ **Relevant:** Ensure the goal is important for improving your time management, such as creating a daily plan to help you become more organized.

♦ **Time-bound:** Set deadlines to achieve the goal, such as "implement the daily plan over the next week."

Situation 6: Financial Problems

- **Problem:** Without clear financial goals, you may struggle with managing finances and achieving desired financial outcomes. For example, if you don't have a savings or investment plan, it can lead to financial difficulties.

- **Solution with SMART Methodology:**

♦ **Specific:** Define clear financial goals, such as "save $2,000 for an emergency fund within six months."

♦ **Measurable:** Determine how you will measure progress, such as "save $333 a month."

♦ **Achievable:** Ensure the goal is realistic given your income; for example, if you can save a certain amount each month, this can be an achievable goal.

♦ **Relevant:** Ensure the goal is important for your financial well-being, such as creating an emergency fund to help ensure financial stability.

♦ **Time-bound:** Set deadlines to achieve the goal, such as "save $2,000 within six months."

Situation 7: Issues with Physical Activity and Health

- **Problem:** The lack of clear goals in physical activity can reduce your motivation and lead to a decline in physical fitness. For example, if you want to exercise but don't have a specific plan, it can hinder achieving your fitness goals.

- **Solution with SMART Methodology:**

♦ **Specific:** Define specific goals for physical activity, such as "run three times a week for the next two months."

♦ **Measurable:** Set criteria for measuring progress, such as "run 5 km during each workout and gradually increase the distance."

♦ **Achievable:** Ensure the goal is realistic given your physical condition; for example, start with shorter distances and gradually increase the load.

♦ **Relevant:** Ensure the goal is important for improving your health; for example, regular workouts can help increase endurance.

♦ **Time-bound:** Set deadlines to achieve the goal, such as "run three times a week for two months."

Situation 8: Problems with Work-Life Balance

• **Problem:** Without clear goals for maintaining work-life balance, it can be difficult to find harmony and avoid burnout. For example, if you are constantly working overtime and not spending enough time on your hobbies, it can lead to stress and loss of motivation.

• **Solution with SMART Methodology:**

♦ **Specific:** Define specific goals to improve balance, such as "spend at least two hours a week on hobbies and relaxation."

♦ **Measurable:** Set criteria for measuring progress, such as "plan and execute one leisure or hobby activity each weekend."

♦ **Achievable:** Ensure the goal is realistic given your schedule; for example, allocate time for hobbies through effective delegation of duties.

♦ **Relevant:** Ensure the goal is important for improving your quality of life; for example, spending time on hobbies can help reduce stress.

♦ **Time-bound:** Set deadlines to achieve the goal, such as "dedicate two hours a week to hobbies over the next three months."

Examples of Successful Application of SMART Goals

1. Personal Development:

♦ **Situation:** You want to learn a new language for personal development.

♦ **SMART Goal:** "Complete an A1 level Spanish course within three months, attending classes twice a week and practicing the language daily for 30 minutes."

2. Healthy Lifestyle:

♦ **Situation:** You want to improve your physical fitness and health.

♦ **SMART Goal:** "Lose 10 kg in 6 months by exercising three times a week and following a diet with a calorie limit of 2,000 per day."

3. Career Growth:

♦ **Situation:** You want to enhance your qualifications for career advancement.

♦ **SMART Goal:** "Complete a project management course and obtain certification within a year, finishing one module every two weeks and passing the final exam by year-end."

4. Financial Goals:

♦ **Situation:** You want to create an emergency fund for unexpected expenses.

♦ **SMART Goal:** "Save $2,000 for an emergency fund within six months, setting aside $333 per month."

5. Personal Balance:

♦ **Situation:** You want to better manage your time between work and personal life.

♦ **SMART Goal:** "Spend at least two hours a week on hobbies and relaxation, planning time for this each week."

Applying the SMART methodology helps turn abstract dreams into achievable goals, making the process of reaching them more realistic and structured. This significantly improves your motivation, effectiveness, and overall satisfaction with life.

Practical Advice and Solutions

To successfully implement the SMART methodology in your life, it is necessary to follow several key steps. These will help you achieve the desired results, and real-life examples will make the process clearer and more practical.

Goal Formulation

Formulating goals is a critical stage in implementing the SMART methodology. Clearly defining a goal allows you to create a clear action plan and focus efforts on achieving a specific result. Let's look at this through examples of specific situations and characters.

Example 1: Improving Physical Fitness

- **Character:** Emily, 32 years old, a sales manager at an IT solutions company, lives in New York City. She spends most of her day at the computer, and her physical activity is limited. Emily loves dessert cafes and often dines out with colleagues, which affects her health. Lately, she has been feeling low on energy and gaining weight. She decided to change her lifestyle to improve her fitness and well-being.
- **Main Goal:** "Improve physical fitness."
- **SMART Formulation:**

  ♦ **Specific:** "Exercise three times a week for 30 minutes. The workouts will include cardio (running on a treadmill or using an exercise bike) and strength exercises (weight training). Emily also decided to add more vegetables and fruits to her diet, replacing high-calorie snacks with healthier alternatives."

  ♦ **Measurable:** Emily will log her workouts in a fitness app to track the number of workouts, their duration, and the exercises performed. She will also measure her weight and body measurements weekly to monitor progress.

  ♦ **Achievable:** Emily signed up for fitness classes at a gym near work. She has received support from friends who also work out and has scheduled her workouts at convenient times-early in the morning before work or late in the evening.

  ♦ **Relevant:** Improving physical fitness is important to Emily because she feels tired and low on energy. She aims to improve her well-being, reduce stress, and strengthen her health.

  ♦ **Time-bound:** Emily plans to achieve her goal within three months. She has set intermediate goals: to feel improved fitness and endurance after one month and to notice significant weight loss and overall well-being improvement after three months.

Example 2: Mastering a New Language

- **Character:** Andrew, 27 years old, a marketing specialist, lives in San Francisco. He works at an international company where he frequently communicates in Spanish. Andrew has always wanted to improve his language skills, but his attempts to learn Spanish have been inconsistent. He believes that his lack of confidence in speaking limits his career opportunities.
- **Main Goal:** "Learn Spanish."
- **SMART Formulation:**

  ♦ **Specific:** "Achieve B2 level in Spanish through online courses and regular practice with native speakers. Andrew plans to take a Spanish course, attend conversation clubs, and use mobile apps to learn new words and grammar structures."

♦ **Measurable:** Andrew will take language proficiency tests every two months. He will also attend conversation clubs once a week and track his activity in language learning apps.

♦ **Achievable:** Andrew can dedicate half an hour daily to studying the language thanks to his flexible work schedule and support from colleagues who also help him practice speaking.

♦ **Relevant:** Improving his Spanish proficiency is crucial for his career prospects. Andrew hopes for promotion and the opportunity to work on international projects.

♦ **Time-bound:** Andrew plans to reach B2 level within six months, reviewing his progress monthly and adjusting his study plan as needed.

Example 3: Starting a Business

• **Character:** Sarah, 40 years old, works in interior design in Los Angeles. She has always dreamed of owning a business related to her hobby—making handmade items. Sarah decided to create an online store to sell her creations. She has a clear vision of what her store should look like and the products she wants to sell, but she has never run a business professionally.

• **Main Goal:** "Launch an online store."

• **SMART Formulation:**

♦ **Specific:** "Create an online store to sell handmade products. Include at least 20 unique items, such as handmade home decor. Develop a website, organize an order processing system, and launch a marketing campaign through social media."

♦ **Measurable:** Sarah will track the number of products on the site, analyze traffic and sales, and monitor the effectiveness of advertising campaigns.

♦ **Achievable:** Sarah has basic knowledge of website design and has already hired a freelancer to develop it. She has a budget for purchasing materials and advertising.

♦ **Relevant:** Launching a business is important to Sarah, as it is her long-held dream and an opportunity to combine her hobby with professional activity.

♦ **Time-bound:** Sarah plans to complete the website development within one month, start the marketing campaign within two months, and officially launch the online store within three months.

Common Mistakes to Avoid

1. Unrealistic Goals

Character: Jack, 35 years old, owner of a small café in Chicago, plans to "triple the profits of his business within a month." His café has a low customer flow, and he doesn't consider that such rapid growth might be unrealistic for a small business.

Problem: Unrealistic goals can lead to significant stress and disappointment. Jack does not account for seasonality and market competition, making his goal overly ambitious.

Solution: Jack should reassess his goals and set more realistic targets. For example, "increase profits by 20% over three months." He could introduce a new menu, organize promotions, or improve customer service to achieve this gradual growth.

2. Lack of Measurability

Character: Maria, 29 years old, a lawyer at a large company, wants to "become a better leader." She wrote this goal in her journal but did not define how she will measure her progress.

Problem: Without clear criteria for assessing progress, Maria may not understand how far she has come in achieving her goal. Her progress will be difficult to evaluate without specific metrics.

Solution: Maria should set specific criteria for assessing her leadership skills. For example, she could evaluate her progress in leadership through feedback from her team, the number of successfully completed projects, or improved employee satisfaction metrics.

3. Lack of a Deadline

Character: Alex, 45 years old, an IT project manager, plans to "improve project management skills." He wants to take several courses and apply new knowledge at work, but he has not set a specific deadline for achieving this goal.

Problem: The lack of a deadline may result in Alex not feeling a sense of urgency in achieving his goal and delaying starting work on it.

Solution: Alex should set a specific deadline for achieving his goal, such as "complete two project management courses within the next six months." This will help him organize his schedule and focus on achieving the goal within the specified time.

Chapter 1: Goal Setting

4. Unclear Goals

Character: Jessica, 26 years old, a freelance designer from Los Angeles, wants to "improve her career." She doesn't know how to achieve this or what specific steps to take.

Problem: Unclear goals make planning and executing necessary tasks difficult. Jessica doesn't know what to focus on or what specific actions she needs to take.

Solution: Jessica should define specific sub-goals, such as "secure three new projects from major clients within a year," "improve portfolio by adding ten new works by the end of the quarter," or "participate in three design exhibitions by the end of the year." This will allow her to create a clear action plan and track her progress.

5. Lack of Support

Character: Mark, 31 years old, an accountant from Chicago, decided to "improve his financial skills." He didn't discuss his plans with colleagues or friends and lacks support in achieving his goal.

Problem: The lack of support and feedback can complicate the goal achievement process. Mark may feel isolated in his pursuit and lack a source of motivation.

Solution: Mark should find like-minded people or a mentor who can support him in achieving his goals. For example, he could enroll in financial planning courses, join a support group, or discuss his goals with friends and family to receive feedback and motivation.

6. Task Overload

Character: Rachel, 33 years old, owner of a small furniture store in Atlanta, plans to "significantly expand the product range and increase sales." She tries to manage everything at once, leading to stress and overload.

Problem: Task overload can result in a loss of focus and reduced efficiency. Rachel may feel overwhelmed and unable to achieve the desired outcome.

Solution: Rachel should break her goal into smaller, achievable steps. For example, "introduce new products to the range by the end of the month," "launch a social media advertising campaign within two weeks," "conduct a sales analysis and identify the most popular products within three months." This will allow her to gradually achieve the goal and avoid overload.

7. Ignoring Feedback

Character: Daniel, 38 years old, a CTO at a startup in Boston, plans to "improve his communication skills." He does not pay attention to feedback from colleagues and friends, making it difficult for him to develop.

Problem: Ignoring feedback can lead to misguided efforts in achieving the goal. Daniel may not realize his weaknesses and not know how to improve them.

Solution: Daniel should actively seek feedback and use it to adjust his skills. For example, he can ask colleagues and mentors to evaluate his communication and make adjustments based on the advice received. He should also organize regular meetings with the team to discuss communication challenges and improve approaches to communication.

Conclusion

The SMART methodology is a powerful tool for achieving goals when implemented correctly. Formulating goals according to SMART principles, avoiding common mistakes, and applying practical advice will help you create a clear action plan and realize your ambitions. It is important to remember that success depends on your approach to goal setting and your willingness to adapt to changing life circumstances.

Daily Implementation Plan for the SMART Methodology

Day 1: Identify General Goals for Different Life Areas

- Task: Identify general goals for different areas of your life.
- Details:

1. Life Areas Analysis:

- Sit in a quiet place with a notebook or computer. Assess different aspects of your life, including career, personal relationships, health, education, finances, personal development, and hobbies.
- Write down general goals for each area without trying to detail them at this stage. The main task today is to record the general directions that interest you.

2. Example:

- **Career:** "Enhance professional qualifications."
- **Personal Relationships:** "Improve relationships with loved ones."
- **Health:** "Lose 10 kg."
- **Education:** "Learn a new language."
- **Finances:** "Save a certain amount of money."
- **Hobbies:** "Learn to play a musical instrument."

Chapter 1: Goal Setting

3. **Potential Issues:** You may find it challenging to identify general goals. If so, start by analyzing your current responsibilities and tasks, considering which are most important and how they may impact your life overall.

Day 2: Formulate SMART Goals for Each Area

- **Task:** Formulate specific SMART goals for each area of your life.
- **Details:**

1. Applying SMART:

- Take the general goals identified on Day 1 and turn them into specific SMART goals. Use the SMART principles: Specific, Measurable, Achievable, Relevant, Time-bound.

2. Example:

- **Career:** "Complete a project management certification course by the end of this quarter."
- **Personal Relationships:** "Plan one shared activity with each family member over the next month."
- **Health:** "Lose 10 kg over the next 3 months by exercising three times a week and changing diet."
- **Education:** "Learn the basics of Spanish by the end of the year by taking a course for 2 hours a week and practicing with native speakers."
- **Finances:** "Save $2,000 over the next 6 months by setting aside $300 monthly."
- **Hobbies:** "Learn to play basic chords and songs on the guitar within three months by practicing 30 minutes daily."

3. **Potential Issues:** You may find it difficult to determine specific criteria for each goal. Try using SMART as a tool to test your goals, ensuring they are realistic and achievable.

Day 3: Break Down Goals into Subtasks and Assign Deadlines

- **Task:** Break each SMART goal into smaller subtasks and assign deadlines for their completion.
- **Details:**

1. Decomposition:

- Break each SMART goal into smaller, more manageable subtasks. For example, if your goal is to complete a certification course, the subtasks might include enrolling in the course, creating a study plan, completing assignments, and preparing for the exam.

2. Assigning Deadlines:

- Assign specific deadlines for each subtask. Write them down in your planner or on your calendar.

3. Example:

- **Career:** "Register for the course by the 15th of this month. Complete assignments and review materials weekly. Finish exam preparation by the 30th."
- **Health:** "Sign up with a trainer by the 5th. Establish a diet plan by the 7th. Start training by the 8th."

4. **Potential Issues:** You might be tempted to set too many tasks in a short period of time. Remember that the plan should be realistic and achievable.

Day 4: Assess the Necessary Resources for Achieving Goals

- **Task:** Assess the resources needed to achieve your goals.
- **Details:**

1. Resource Assessment:

- Identify the resources you will need to achieve each goal. These may include financial resources, time, skills, tools, or help from others.

2. Resource List:

- Make a list of all the necessary resources and think about how you can obtain them.

3. Example:

- **Career:** "Need to pay for the course, have time for studying, and access to the internet."
- **Education:** "Need access to an online course, language learning apps, and time for practice."

Chapter 1: Goal Setting

4. **Potential Issues:** If you feel that the necessary resources are lacking, consider possible alternatives or ways to obtain them.

Day 5: Create a Visual Goal Board

- **Task:** Create a visual goal board that will motivate you to achieve your goals.
- **Details:**

1. Creating the Board:

- Use large sheets of paper, a board, or digital tools (such as Canva or Pinterest). Place images, words, and phrases on it that symbolize your goals.

2. Decorating:

- Add images that symbolize your goals. These can be photographs, magazine cutouts, or printouts from the Internet.

3. Example:

- **Career:** "Photos of diplomas and certificates, images of an office."
- **Health:** "Pictures of healthy foods, photos of fitness activities."

4. **Potential Issues:** You might find it difficult to find motivating images. Focus on what truly inspires you and aligns with your goals.

Day 6: Analyze Potential Obstacles and Develop Strategies to Overcome Them

- **Task:** Analyze potential obstacles to achieving your goals and develop strategies to overcome them.
- **Details:**

1. Obstacle Analysis:

- Think about potential difficulties that may arise on the path to achieving your goals. These can be internal barriers (e.g., fear, laziness) or external (e.g., lack of time, financial constraints).

2. Strategy Development:

- Develop a strategy for overcoming each obstacle. Think about ways to avoid or minimize these problems.

3. Example:

- **Health:** "Obstacle: Lack of time for workouts. Strategy: Sign up for classes at a convenient time or develop a quick workout plan."
- **Finances:** "Obstacle: Lack of money for courses. Strategy: Find free resources or choose more affordable courses."

4. **Potential Issues:** You may encounter obstacles that initially seem insurmountable. Focus on finding flexible and creative solutions.

Day 7: Develop a Detailed Action Plan

- **Task:** Create a detailed action plan for each SMART goal.
- **Details:**

1. Creating a Schedule:

- Create a detailed schedule that outlines all steps, deadlines, and responsible parties (if any). Use a calendar or specialized planning programs.

2. Assigning Tasks:

- Assign specific dates and times for completing each subtask.

3. Example:

- **Career:** "1st-15th: Register for the course. 16th-30th: Study the first modules. 1st-7th of the next month: Prepare for the exam."
- **Health:** "1st-7th: Sign up with a trainer. 8th-14th: Change diet. 15th-30th: Train 3 times a week."

4. **Potential Issues:** You might find it difficult to create a realistic schedule. If this happens, return to the analysis of your resources and adjust the schedule to make it achievable.

Day 8: Set Rewards for Achieving Intermediate Goals

- **Task:** Set rewards for yourself for achieving each intermediate goal.
- **Details:**

1. Choosing Rewards:

- Identify small but meaningful rewards that you will receive for achieving each intermediate goal.

Chapter 1: Goal Setting

2. Recording Rewards:

- Write down what specific rewards you will receive and when.

3. Example:

- **Career:** "Reward: Purchase a new book or attend a seminar after completing the course."

- **Health:** "Reward: A delicious healthy dessert or a visit to the spa after each week of training."

4. **Potential Issues:** You might find it difficult to choose rewards that truly motivate you. Make sure they align with your interests and priorities.

Day 9: Review and Adjust Goals as Needed

- **Task:** Review your goals and adjust them as needed.
- **Details:**

1. Progress Evaluation:

- Review your goals and progress over the past few days. Assess how well you are moving toward achieving them.

2. Goal Adjustment:

- If you find that some goals no longer meet your needs or are too challenging, adjust them.

3. Example:

- **Health:** "You may need to adjust your workout plan if you can't exercise three times a week."

4. **Potential Issues:** It might be difficult to admit that some goals need to be changed. Remember that adaptability is key to success.

Day 10: Evaluate Progress and Prepare New Goals for Continued Growth

- **Task:** Evaluate your progress and prepare new goals for further growth.

- **Details:**

1. **Results Evaluation:**

    ■ Assess what you have achieved over the past 10 days. Consider the results you have obtained and the skills or knowledge you have gained.

2. **Setting New Goals:**

    ■ Based on your experience, define new goals or review existing ones. Create a plan for further development.

3. **Example:**

    ■ **Career:** "If you completed the course, consider earning a new certification or pursuing a promotion."

    ■ **Health:** "If you achieved your weight loss goal, set a new goal for maintaining results or improving fitness."

4. **Potential Issues:** You may find it hard to part with already achieved goals. Remember that development always requires moving forward.

This plan will help you effectively implement the SMART methodology into your life. Don't be afraid to make adjustments and adapt it to your needs. Success depends on your perseverance and readiness for change.

Reflection and Conclusions

Evaluating the Success of Goal Implementation

Achieving goals is only part of the journey to success. To ensure long-term personal and professional development, it is important to periodically assess achievements, analyze strategies, and refine approaches. Reflection, obtaining feedback, and reviewing goals are key steps in this process. Let's take a closer look at each of these stages.

The Importance of Reflection

Reflection is the process of deeply analyzing your experiences, which helps you understand not only what succeeded or failed but also why. It allows you to recognize your strengths, identify weaknesses, and find ways to address them.

1. The Secret to Success through Reflection

♦ Reflection allows you to focus on strategies that led to success or failure. For example, John, a project manager, after successfully completing a large project, decided to reflect. He realized that effective communication within the team was a key factor in the project's success. This insight allowed John to improve his management skills and apply them to future projects.

2. Methods of Reflection

♦ **For effective reflection, various methods can be used:**

■ **Keeping a Journal:** Record your achievements, challenges, and solutions. This helps you see the bigger picture, identify patterns, and understand which strategies were effective.

■ **Analyzing Results:** Regularly review your successes and failures. Analyze why some aspects worked well while others did not. This allows you to refine approaches and discover new ways to achieve your goals.

Feedback

Receiving feedback from others is an important element in assessing progress. It helps you get an objective evaluation of your achievements, discover new perspectives, and obtain ideas for further improvement.

1. Examples of Receiving Feedback

♦ Emily, a junior analyst, after completing an important report, decided to get feedback from senior colleagues. They suggested ways to improve the report's formatting, making her work more understandable and valuable to the team. As a result, Emily was able to improve her skills and gain new knowledge.

2. How to Effectively Receive Feedback

♦ **Ask Specific Questions:** Instead of a general "Did you like my report?" ask, "What specifically could be improved in the report in terms of data structuring?" This will help you get more concrete and useful recommendations.

♦ **Accept Constructive Criticism:** Listen carefully and use the advice to improve your skills. Constructive criticism is a tool for your growth, not a reason for disappointment.

Reviewing and Adjusting Goals

Life is dynamic, and your goals may need adjustment. Regular reviews allow you to adapt plans to new circumstances or changes in priorities, ensuring their relevance and achievability.

1. Example of Goal Adjustment

♦ James set a goal to improve his physical fitness, but due to an injury, he had to review his workout plan. Instead of regular exercises, he added recovery training and adjusted his diet, which allowed him to continue moving toward his goal, albeit in a different format.

2. How to Effectively Review Goals

♦ **Regular Reviews:** Set specific times to review and adjust goals, such as monthly or quarterly. This helps to timely identify the need for changes and keep your goals relevant.

♦ **Analyze Life Changes:** Assess how changes in your life or career have impacted your goals. For example, a change in work schedule or new responsibilities may require a revision of plans and adaptation to new conditions.

Final Recommendations

1. Continue Developing

♦ Achieving one goal is not the end of the journey. Continuously set new challenges to maintain motivation and continue personal development. For example, when Sarah, an experienced accountant, completed training in a new accounting program, she decided to learn new skills in financial analysis to stay competitive in the job market.

2. Use the Experience Gained

♦ The knowledge and skills acquired while achieving previous goals can be valuable for new tasks. If you found certain strategies to be successful, apply them to new projects. For example, successful work organization methods can be adapted to new situations.

3. Be Flexible

♦ Flexibility allows you to adapt to changes and seize new opportunities. This means being open to change and ready to adjust your plans according to new circumstances. For example, when Jennifer got a new job that required moving to another city, she adapted her goals by including new social and professional networks in her development plan.

Practical Advice

1. How and When to Reflect

♦ It's best to reflect regularly, such as once a week or month. This can be in the form of weekly summaries or monthly reviews of achievements and challenges. Include planning for future steps in this process. For example, consider whether your goals are still relevant, whether additional training is needed, or whether changes in strategy are necessary.

2. Historical Context

♦ History shows that a systematic approach to goal setting and evaluation has helped many outstanding individuals. For example:

■ **Benjamin Franklin:** One of the Founding Fathers of the United States, Franklin used reflection as part of his daily routine. He created a list of personal virtues he sought to develop and checked his progress in achieving them every day. His method of reflection helped him succeed in various areas of life, from scientific discoveries to political activities.

■ **Winston Churchill:** The British Prime Minister during World War II regularly reflected on and analyzed strategies and tactics for conducting the war. This allowed him to adapt his plans to changing conditions and ensure strategic advantages for the United Kingdom.

3. Practical Tips

♦ **Keeping a Reflection Journal:** Record your thoughts and conclusions. This can be in a diary or digital document. It's important that the entries are regular and structured. Use visual elements like graphs and charts to better track progress.

♦ **Discussing with Mentors:** Regularly discuss your achievements and challenges with mentors. This helps to gain external perspective and additional motivation. They can help you refocus on your plan and provide new ideas for achieving your goals.

Reflection and Success Evaluation as a Path to Continuous Development

Reflection and success evaluation are critically important for personal and professional development. They not only help assess achievements but also identify ways for further improvement. Through continuous reflection, feedback, and goal review and adjustment, you can reach new heights and ensure sustainable progress in your life.

Chapter 2: Morning Rituals

Introduction and Context

Morning rituals are the foundation of a productive day. They help set a positive tone, boost energy levels, and focus on important tasks. How you start your day can significantly affect your productivity, mood, and overall well-being throughout the day.

Many successful people acknowledge that their success largely depends on how they start their day. Morning rituals can vary from physical exercises and meditation to reading and planning the day. Regardless of the specific ritual you choose, the key is that it helps you achieve your goals and improve your quality of life.

The Importance of Morning Rituals

Morning rituals create the foundation for productivity throughout the day. They help you start the day with calm and focus rather than chaos and stress. Morning habits can influence your mood, energy levels, and ability to concentrate.

- **Starting the Day Right:** Instead of jumping out of bed and immediately diving into the chaos of work or other activities, you create a space for yourself that allows you to start the day consciously and focused.

- **Habit Formation:** It is important that morning rituals become a habit. This means that you automatically start your day on a positive note, contributing to long-term changes in your life.

- **Emotional Balance:** Practices such as meditation or journaling can help stabilize your emotional state, which is important for managing stress and maintaining psychological well-being.

How Morning Rituals Affect Success

People who practice morning rituals typically experience increased productivity, better concentration, and overall improvement in well-being. Morning rituals help prioritize tasks and focus on what matters, contributing to success in both personal and professional life.

- **Boosting Productivity:** Morning rituals, such as planning the day or setting goals, help organize tasks and focus on priorities. This allows you to work more efficiently throughout the day.

Chapter 2: Morning Rituals

• **Reducing Stress:** Rituals that include meditation or physical activity can significantly reduce stress levels. Starting the day with a clear mind makes it easier to handle challenges that arise throughout the day.

• **Improving Health:** Morning exercises not only strengthen the body but also improve mental health by releasing endorphins-the body's natural "feel-good" hormones.

• **Strengthening Motivation:** A clear understanding of your goals and progress can greatly enhance motivation. Keeping a success journal, for example, helps you stay focused on achievements rather than failures.

Examples from the Lives of Famous Individuals

1. Tim Cook, CEO of Apple: Tim Cook starts his day very early, waking up at 4:30 AM. He uses this time for gym workouts and reading emails. This morning ritual helps him stay focused and energetic throughout the workday.

2. Oprah Winfrey, Media Mogul: Oprah starts her day with meditation, which helps her set a calm and focused tone. After meditation, she spends time exercising and having breakfast, allowing her to maintain a high energy level throughout the day.

3. Richard Branson, Founder of Virgin Group: Branson begins his day with physical activities like kite surfing or tennis, which help him stay fit and maintain high productivity. Morning activity is an essential element of a successful start to his day.

Purpose of the Chapter

This chapter aims to help you develop effective morning rituals that will improve your life. We will examine examples of successful morning routines and provide practical recommendations for creating your own ritual that meets your needs and goals.

• **Analyzing Existing Rituals:** Before implementing new practices, it is important to understand what you are already doing and how it affects your day. Are you satisfied with your morning routine? Are there things you would like to change?

• **Developing Personalized Rituals:** We will explore various approaches to creating rituals that fit your unique needs and goals. These can range from short practices to more detailed rituals that encompass different aspects of your life.

• **Implementation and Adaptation:** Successfully implementing rituals requires discipline and flexibility. We will discuss how to stay motivated, adapt rituals to life changes, and evaluate their effectiveness.

• **Practical Examples:** We will provide examples of morning routines from famous successful people, as well as simple practices that you can adapt for yourself. From the simplest exercises to more complex rituals-there is something for everyone.

In this chapter, we strive to help you not only understand the importance of morning rituals but also provide tools for their effective implementation. Remember, the key to success is gradual but consistent implementation of changes that work for you.

Main Theory

Morning rituals can include a variety of activities that help set the tone for a successful day. The key is to create a ritual that suits you and takes into account your individual needs. To be effective, rituals must be personalized and align with your unique goals, preferences, and life circumstances.

The Importance of Starting the Day

The start of the day sets the tone for the entire day. How you begin your morning can affect your mood, energy level, and productivity throughout the day. Morning rituals help you focus, set a positive tone, and avoid distractions. A well-structured morning can significantly improve your efficiency and mood.

• **Focus and Concentration:** Taking time in the morning to focus helps you avoid distractions that may interfere during the day. For example, meditation can serve as a tool for developing inner focus and stability.

• **Psychological Comfort:** Instead of rushing and feeling stressed from the morning, rituals allow you to create a sense of calm and control. This can reduce stress and anxiety levels.

• **Physical Activity:** Starting the day with physical exercises promotes the release of endorphins, which boost mood and create a positive emotional background.

Examples of Successful Morning Routines

Let's look at specific examples of morning rituals practiced by successful people:

Physical Exercise

Many successful people start their day with physical exercise, which boosts energy levels and improves physical fitness. Morning physical activity stimulates blood circulation, increases energy levels, and enhances concentration throughout the day.

Chapter 2: Morning Rituals

- **Life Example:**

♦ Tim Ferriss, author of the bestseller "The 4-Hour Workweek," is known for his detailed approach to morning rituals. He wakes up at 5:00 AM every day and starts the day with 20 minutes of meditation, which helps him achieve calm and focus. After that, Tim spends 30 minutes at the gym, where he performs intense workouts. According to him, this helps boost his energy and set the tone for a productive day.

Meditation

Meditation helps you focus, relieve stress, and improve concentration. It can be a short but effective part of your morning ritual. Meditation promotes inner calm and focus, which is important for managing stress and maintaining mental stability.

- **Life Example:**

♦ Ray Dalio, founder of Bridgewater Associates and a renowned investor, practices transcendental meditation twice a day, starting with it in the morning. His morning meditation lasts about 20 minutes. Ray believes that this allows him to clear his mind, improve focus, and reduce stress. Thanks to this ritual, Dalio is able to make more thoughtful decisions throughout the day.

Reading

Reading inspires, develops thinking, and provides new knowledge. Many successful people include reading in their morning ritual to start the day with new ideas. Reading in the morning can be a stimulus for broadening horizons and inspiration for new projects.

- **Life Example:**

♦ Bill Gates, co-founder of Microsoft, considers reading an important component of his morning ritual. Every day he dedicates time to reading books and articles to keep his mind fresh and stay informed on various topics. Gates especially enjoys reading scientific publications and biographies, which help him broaden his worldview and learn about the successes of others.

Planning

Planning the day helps set priorities and focus on important tasks. This avoids chaos and provides a clear vision for the day. Planning helps optimize time and energy, ensuring structure and order.

- **Life Example:**

♦ Elon Musk, CEO of SpaceX and Tesla, is known for his extraordinary productivity. One of his key tools is planning. He divides his day into five-minute intervals, allowing him to focus on specific tasks and make the most of his time.

Musk starts his day by checking emails and identifying key tasks that need to be completed. This helps him organize work and focus on top priorities.

Scientific Basis for the Importance of Morning Rituals

Morning rituals have a significant impact on our lives. They can improve productivity, reduce stress, and enhance overall happiness. Here is a more detailed overview of several studies that support these claims.

1. Cornell University Study

- **Objective:** To investigate how morning planning affects productivity and stress levels.
- **Methodology:**
  - **Participants:** 200 employees from various professional fields, including IT, medicine, and education.
  - **Groups:**
    - The first group (100 participants) dedicated 15 minutes daily to planning tasks at the beginning of the workday.
    - The second group (100 participants) received no instructions and continued their usual routine.
  - **Process:** The first group wrote down their main goals and tasks for the day, prioritizing them and estimating the time needed for each task.
- **Results:**
  - **Productivity:** Participants who planned their day were 15% more productive. They completed tasks faster and had fewer distractions.
  - **Stress:** Participants in the first group reported a 20% reduction in stress levels compared to the second group, as they had a clear plan of action for the day.
- **Conclusion:** Morning planning helps organize the workday, reducing stress and increasing productivity.

2. University of California Study

- **Objective:** To study how morning physical exercises affect energy levels and concentration throughout the day.
- **Methodology:**
  - **Participants:** 150 university students from various specialties.
  - **Groups:**
    - The first group (75 participants) performed 30-minute morning physical exercises (e.g., yoga or jogging).

Chapter 2: Morning Rituals

- The second group (75 participants) did not perform physical exercises.
- **Process:** The first group trained daily for four weeks. Exercises included cardio, stretching, and strength training.

♦ **Results:**

- **Energy:** Participants in the first group noted a 30% increase in energy levels throughout the day. They felt more alert and experienced less fatigue.
- **Concentration:** Their ability to concentrate improved, leading to better academic performance and other activities.

♦ **Conclusion:** Morning physical activity significantly improves energy levels and concentration, contributing to overall improvement in quality of life.

3. Harvard Business School Study

♦ **Objective:** To evaluate the impact of meditation on cognitive functions and stress management.

♦ **Methodology:**

- **Participants:** 120 office workers from various industries.
- **Groups:**
- The first group (60 participants) practiced 20-minute morning meditation for eight weeks.
- The second group (60 participants) continued their usual morning routine without meditation.
- **Process:** The first group used meditation techniques to calm the mind and enhance mindfulness, including breathing exercises and visualization.

♦ **Results:**

- **Cognitive Functions:** Participants who meditated showed a 25% improvement in attention and focus.
- **Stress:** They also reported reduced stress levels, as confirmed by lower cortisol (stress hormone) levels in their blood.

♦ **Conclusion:** Morning meditation positively impacts cognitive abilities and effectively reduces stress.

These studies suggest that morning rituals such as planning, physical exercises, and meditation have a significant positive impact on our physical and mental health. They can help us become more productive, energetic, and happier. Choose the practices that suit you best and incorporate them into your morning routine to improve your quality of life.

Thus, implementing morning rituals can become an important tool for improving the quality of life and enhancing personal effectiveness. Choose the practices that best fit your needs and goals, and make them an integral part of your morning routine.

Problematic Situations and Examples

In life, there are often situations where the absence of a clear morning routine can lead to stress, reduced productivity, and dissatisfaction. Let's explore a few typical scenarios with fictional characters where morning rituals could have significantly improved the situation, but their absence resulted in negative consequences.

Situation 1: Morning Stress and Anxiety

Story:

Emily is a young marketing manager in New York. Every morning, she wakes up feeling anxious and tense, afraid of being late for work and not finishing all her tasks. Her mind is overwhelmed with thoughts of deadlines and assignments even before she gets out of bed. The lack of a structured start to the day leads her to feel overwhelmed and exhausted.

Consequences:

Due to this chaos, Emily often feels anxious and cannot concentrate at work. Her productivity decreases, she misses important deadlines, and begins to doubt her professional competence. The lack of ways to cope with stress affects her mental health and her relationships with colleagues.

How to Change the Situation:

Emily decided to implement a few morning rituals to improve her start to the day. She began with simple breathing exercises and a short 10-minute meditation to help her calm down and set a positive tone. She also started creating a brief list of priorities for the day to avoid feeling overwhelmed. After a few weeks of these changes, Emily noticed that her stress levels had significantly decreased, and her work productivity increased.

Situation 2: Chaotic Mornings and Fatigue Throughout the Day

Story:

Michael is a programmer in San Francisco who works on complex projects. His mornings often start in a rush as he tries to get ready and make it to work on time. Because of the hustle, he often skips breakfast and leaves home feeling tired even before the day begins.

Chapter 2: Morning Rituals

Consequences:

Due to a lack of energy, Michael finds it difficult to concentrate on his work, leading to coding errors. He begins consuming large amounts of coffee to keep himself alert, which causes irritability and nervousness. The chaotic start to the day leaves him exhausted and unmotivated by the end of the day.

How to Change the Situation:

Michael decided to start getting up 30 minutes earlier to avoid the morning rush. He incorporated light physical exercises into his routine, such as stretching or a short run, which helps him wake up and energize. He also started preparing a healthy breakfast to provide his body with essential nutrients. Over time, Michael noticed that his energy and concentration levels improved, and he became less dependent on caffeine.

Situation 3: Distractions and Procrastination Due to an Unplanned Start to the Day

Story:

Sarah is a graphic designer working from home in Los Angeles. Her mornings usually start with checking social media and the news, which often takes more time than she planned. Because of this, she feels overwhelmed and cannot focus on her work.

Consequences:

The lack of a clear plan leads Sarah to constantly delay work, procrastinate, and often fail to complete important tasks. This negatively affects her professional reputation, causing her stress and dissatisfaction. She loses confidence in her abilities and begins to feel like a failure.

How to Change the Situation:

Sarah decided to change her morning routine to avoid distractions and procrastination. She started her day by making a plan where she outlines the most important tasks and priorities. Additionally, Sarah established a rule not to check social media until the first hour of work is completed. She also started using the Pomodoro technique, breaking her work into short intervals with breaks, which helped her maintain focus and productivity throughout the day. Over time, Sarah noticed that her workflow became more organized and productive, and her self-confidence increased.

Situation 4: Lack of Time for Personal Development

Story:

Jake is a sales manager in Chicago. He is constantly busy with work and meetings, so he rarely finds time for personal development or learning. His days begin with checking emails and rushing to get ready for work, leaving him little time for self-improvement.

Consequences:

Jake feels stuck and unable to develop his professional skills. He loses motivation and feels like he is not achieving his career goals. This causes him to feel dissatisfaction and anxiety about the future.

How to Change the Situation:

Jake decided to dedicate 30 minutes in the morning to reading professional literature or watching educational videos. This helps him feel more knowledgeable and confident in his field. He also started planning his days, allocating time for developing new skills, which positively impacted his career and overall life satisfaction.

Situation 5: Negative Mood and Lack of Motivation

Story:

Lisa is a primary school teacher in Boston. Every morning she wakes up feeling irritated and in a bad mood. Her day starts with endless tasks and worries, leaving her little time for personal needs.

Consequences:

Due to constant stress and a negative mood, Lisa loses motivation for work and begins neglecting her responsibilities. This affects her relationships with colleagues and students, causing additional stress and dissatisfaction.

How to Change the Situation:

Lisa decided to introduce short gratitude and visualization practices into her morning. She starts her day by writing down three things she is grateful for, which helps her focus on the positive. Additionally, she uses visualization to set a positive tone and motivation to achieve her goals. Gradually, Lisa began to feel more satisfied with her work and improved her relationships with students and colleagues.

Conclusion

In each of these cases, the absence of morning rituals led to negative consequences that affected the quality of life and work of the characters. Implementing simple but effective rituals can lead to significant positive changes, helping to maintain calm, energy, and focus. This highlights the importance of a structured start to the day for improving well-being and achieving success.

Chapter 2: Morning Rituals

Practical Tips and Solutions for Implementing Morning Rituals

Implementing morning rituals can significantly improve your productivity, mood, and overall well-being. Below are detailed steps and tips to help you successfully integrate morning rituals into your life.

1. Identifying What Energizes You

Before changing your morning routine, it's essential to understand what makes you feel energized and ready for the day. Take time to reflect on which activities or habits fill you with energy. Your task is to identify those elements that help you wake up with a positive mindset and a desire to take action.

Steps:

- Analyze Your Mornings: Reflect on how you feel after different morning activities. Which actions boost your mood and energy?

- Try Different Approaches: If you're unsure what suits you best, experiment with various activities-try exercise, yoga, reading, or meditation.

- **Keep a Journal:** Record your observations about how different activities affect your mood and energy levels.

Example: You might start your morning with a short jog if you find that physical activity awakens your mind and body and charges you with positivity for the day.

2. Planning Your Morning Routine

Creating a personalized morning routine is the key to an effective start to the day. It should cater to your individual needs and preferences.

Steps:

- **Identify Core Elements:** Choose 3-5 key activities you enjoy and want to include in your morning routine.

- **Consider Your Schedule:** Ensure your routine fits your daily schedule and doesn't overwhelm you.

- **Be Realistic:** Start with simple activities that you can easily perform, and gradually add new ones.

Example: Your ideal morning routine might include a 10-minute meditation, a cup of coffee with a book, and 20 minutes of yoga.

3. Introducing a New Ritual

Begin with one new ritual that you want to add to your morning routine. This will help you gradually adjust to the changes and avoid feeling overwhelmed.

Steps:

- **Choose a Practice You Enjoy:** Pick a ritual that excites you.
- **Start Gradually:** Begin with a few minutes and gradually increase the time devoted to the new ritual.
- **Be Persistent:** Regularity is key to successfully incorporating new habits.

Example: If you want to start your morning with meditation, begin with 5 minutes daily and gradually increase to 15 minutes.

4. Adding Meditation

Meditation is a powerful tool for calming the mind and setting a positive tone. It helps with focus and stress reduction.

Mindful Breathing Meditation Instructions:

1. Sit Comfortably: Find a quiet place where you won't be disturbed. Sit with a straight back, with your hands resting on your knees or a table.

2. Close Your Eyes: Focus on your breathing. Slowly inhale through your nose while counting to four, hold your breath for four counts, and exhale through your mouth, also counting to four.

3. Observe Your Breath: Pay attention to the sensations during the inhale and exhale. If your mind wanders, gently bring your focus back to your breath.

4. Conclude the Meditation: After 5-10 minutes, slowly open your eyes, feel your body, and reflect on how you feel.

Visualization Instructions:

1. Sit Comfortably: Choose a quiet place where you won't be disturbed. Sit with a straight back, with your hands relaxed.

2. Close Your Eyes: Imagine a place or situation that calms and inspires you, like a beach or a forest.

3. Focus on Details: Concentrate on the details—sounds, smells, colors. Imagine yourself in this place and feel its atmosphere.

4. Hold the Visualization: Continue visualizing this place for 5-10 minutes, allowing yourself to feel peace and harmony.

Meditation Apps: Headspace, Calm, or Insight Timer can be helpful in your initial attempts at meditation.

5. Reading Motivational Material

Reading motivational books or articles can inspire you to achieve new goals and give you the strength to pursue your ambitions.

Chapter 2: Morning Rituals

Steps:

- **Choose Inspirational Material:** These could be self-development books, biographies of successful people, or inspiring articles.

- **Set Aside Time:** Dedicate 10-15 minutes daily to reading.

- **Take Notes:** Keep a journal of ideas that inspire you so you can revisit them later.

Examples of Books:

- **"Atlas Shrugged" by Ayn Rand:** A classic novel that encourages readers to reflect on goals, values, and success.

- **"The Power of Your Subconscious Mind" by Joseph Murphy:** Offers practical advice on harnessing the power of the subconscious to achieve desired outcomes in life.

- **"The 7 Habits of Highly Effective People" by Stephen Covey:** Helps develop personal effectiveness and leadership skills.

6. Preparing a Healthy Breakfast

A healthy breakfast provides you with the energy and nutrients needed for a productive day.

Steps:

- **Plan Ahead:** Prepare ingredients or meals in advance to save time in the morning.

- **Focus on Nutrition:** Choose foods rich in proteins, vitamins, and minerals.

- **Experiment:** Find recipes you enjoy and incorporate them into your routine.

Examples of Healthy Breakfasts:

- **Oatmeal with Fruits and Nuts:** Rich in fiber and antioxidants, oatmeal helps keep you full for longer and provides sustained energy.

- **Green Smoothie:** A quick way to get vitamins and minerals at the start of the day. A smoothie with spinach, banana, and almond milk energizes the body and helps with hydration.

- **Eggs with Avocado:** Eggs are an excellent source of protein, supporting muscle mass and helping with satiety. Avocado is rich in healthy fats that support heart health and provide energy.

- **Greek Yogurt with Berries and Honey:** Greek yogurt is high in protein and probiotics, supporting digestion. Berries offer antioxidants, while honey adds natural sweetness.

Morning Supplements:

• **Turmeric Water:** Turmeric has powerful anti-inflammatory properties. Drinking a glass of water with half a teaspoon of turmeric helps boost the immune system and improve digestion.

• **Lemon Water:** A glass of warm water with lemon helps hydrate the body, supports digestion, and detoxifies. It also provides a dose of vitamin C.

• **Ginger Tea:** Ginger has antioxidant and anti-inflammatory properties. Ginger tea aids digestion, reduces inflammation, and boosts immunity.

7. Evaluating Your Morning Routine

Regularly assess your morning routine to ensure it's working for you.

Steps:

• **Pay Attention to Your Feelings:** Reflect on how you feel after performing the rituals are they really helping you?

• Make Adjustments: If something isn't working, don't hesitate to change or replace it.

• **Listen to Yourself:** Your routine should be flexible and adapt to your needs.

Example: You might notice that certain elements of your routine aren't producing the desired results and decide to replace them with other practices that suit you better.

8. Planning Your Day

Briefly planning your day helps you prioritize and focus on important tasks.

Steps:

• **Set Aside 10 Minutes in the Morning:** This allows you to calmly assess what needs to be done during the day.

• **Identify Three Main Tasks:** Focus on the most important things you want to accomplish.

• **Be Realistic:** Don't overload yourself with tasks to avoid feeling stressed.

Example: You can create a morning list of three priority tasks, helping you stay focused and productive.

9. Practicing Gratitude

Practicing gratitude helps you focus on the positive aspects of life and increases your overall happiness.

Chapter 2: Morning Rituals

Steps:

- **Start a Gratitude Journal:** Write down three things you're grateful for every day.

- **Reflect on the Past Day:** Think about the positive moments that happened to you.

- **Share Your Gratitude:** Exchange gratitude with friends or family.

Example: Every morning, write down three things you're grateful for to help you start the day with positive thoughts.

10. Reviewing Results

Regularly analyze the impact of your new rituals on your life and note the positive changes.

Steps:

- **Keep Records:** Note positive changes and feelings after implementing the rituals.

- **Analyze Progress:** Reflect on how the rituals are impacting your life.

- **Be Flexible:** Don't be afraid to change your routine if it stops working for you.

Example: You might notice that your new morning routine has helped you become more focused and productive, positively impacting your work and personal life.

Implementing Morning Rituals

Implementing morning rituals can be an important step toward improving your life, but this process may involve some challenges. Let's explore how to avoid common pitfalls and what you can do to make your new habits as beneficial as possible.

Common Mistakes to Avoid When Implementing Morning Rituals

Overloading Your Routine

When you decide to change your morning, there may be a temptation to try everything at once. You add meditation, yoga, planning, reading, and so on-all in one day. But this can quickly become overwhelming.

What to Do: Start small. Choose one or two rituals that interest you most and try to implement them. Once they become a regular part of your day, you can add another element. This approach helps you avoid feeling overwhelmed and stressed.

Unrealistic Expectations

Many people expect that implementing new rituals will instantly change their lives. The reality is that change takes time, and it may take several weeks or months to see results.

What to Do: Be realistic. Don't expect all your problems to disappear overnight. Instead, enjoy the process of change and celebrate small victories along the way to your big goal.

Lack of Regularity

If you only perform rituals occasionally, they are unlikely to become a habit. Regularity is the key to success.

What to Do: Set a clear schedule for your rituals and stick to it. Even if it seems like you have more time to relax on weekends, try to maintain your routine to strengthen your habits.

Practical Tips for Implementing Morning Rituals

Record Your Routine

Keeping a journal is a great way to structure your mornings and track progress.

How to Do It: Write down each day which rituals you performed, how you feel, and what changes you notice. This will help you see what works and what doesn't, and make timely adjustments.

Visualize Your Rituals

Visualization can be a powerful tool for motivation.

How to Do It: Create a visual board where you place images that symbolize your rituals, such as a photo of a beautiful place for meditation or your favorite activity. This will serve as a daily reminder of why you are doing it.

Collaborate

Involving others in your process can greatly enhance motivation.

How to Do It: Tell your friends or family about your plans. This can provide support and an opportunity to perform some rituals together. A joint run or morning yoga can be a great way to spend time together and support each other.

Conclusion

Implementing new habits takes time and effort, but if you avoid common mistakes and follow these tips, you can significantly improve your quality of life. Remember that every small step toward change is already a success. Be patient, experiment, and enjoy the positive changes in your life.

Implementing morning rituals is an effective way to boost your productivity and improve well-being. Here's a 10-day step-by-step plan to help you integrate these rituals into your life, along with potential challenges that may arise and ways to overcome them.

10-Day Implementation Plan

Day 1: Identifying Energy Sources

Before diving into new habits, it's essential to understand which morning activities already make your day better. This day is dedicated to observing and analyzing what brings you the most energy and motivation at the start of the day.

Task:

- **Morning Analysis:** Note which morning activities evoke positive emotions. It could be a walk, exercise, or a cup of aromatic coffee.

- **Journaling:** Record your observations about what brings you the most satisfaction and energy.

Example: You notice that after a 10-minute walk in the fresh air, you feel more energetic and ready to work.

Possible Problems and Solutions:

- **Problem:** Lack of clear ideas about what energizes you.

- **Solution:** Observe how different activities affect your mood and energy throughout the day. You might discover something new that you genuinely enjoy.

Day 2: Planning the Ideal Routine

Having understood what energizes you, you can start forming your ideal morning routine. At this stage, it's crucial to select a few key elements that best suit your needs and lifestyle.

Task:

- **Make a List:** Choose the rituals you want to implement, such as 10 minutes of meditation, 20 minutes of exercise, and a cup of green tea.

• **Time Allocation:** Dedicate specific time slots for each ritual in your schedule.

Example: Your ideal routine could look like this: 7:00 — wake up, 7:10 — meditate, 7:30 — exercise, 7:50 — breakfast, 8:00 — reading.

Possible Problems and Solutions:

• **Problem:** An unrealistic schedule that's hard to maintain daily.

• **Solution:** Start small and gradually add new elements. Make sure you consider your current schedule and avoid overloading yourself.

Day 3: Implementing a New Ritual

Now that you have a clear plan, it's time to start implementing it. Choose one ritual you want to try first and begin incorporating it into your life.

Task:

• **Choose a Ritual:** Select the ritual that seems most appealing and beneficial to you.

• **Execution:** Dedicate time to this ritual every morning.

Example: You decide to start with morning exercise. Each morning, you perform a simple set of exercises such as stretching, squats, and push-ups.

Possible Problems and Solutions:

• **Problem:** Lack of motivation to perform the new ritual.

• **Solution:** Remember your goals and the benefits of this ritual. Try involving a friend or family member for support and motivation.

Day 4: Adding Meditation

Exercise has become a part of your morning, so now it's time to add another element-meditation or reflection. This will help you focus and set a positive tone for the day.

Task:

• **Find a Quiet Spot:** Choose a place where you won't be disturbed.

• **Meditate:** Start with 5 minutes and gradually increase the time to 10 minutes.

Example: You find a comfortable spot in your home, sit with a straight back, close your eyes, and focus on your breathing.

Possible Problems and Solutions:

• **Problem:** Your mind constantly wanders during meditation.

Chapter 2: Morning Rituals

• **Solution:** This is normal for beginners. When you notice your mind wandering, gently bring your attention back to your breath.

Day 5: Reading Motivational Material

Meditation helps you focus, and now it's time to get inspired by new ideas and motivation through reading. This can become a source of inspiration and new knowledge.

Task:

• **Choose a Book or Article:** Select material that interests and motivates you.

• **Set Time for Reading:** Dedicate 10-15 minutes every morning.

Example: You choose to read "The 7 Habits of Highly Effective People" by Stephen Covey and read a few pages each morning.

Possible Problems and Solutions:

• **Problem:** Lack of interest in the chosen material.

• **Solution:** Try different genres or topics to find something that genuinely captivates you.

Day 6: Preparing a Nutritious Breakfast

A healthy breakfast is the foundation of a productive day. It provides you with the energy and nutrients needed.

Task:

• **Plan Your Menu:** Choose foods rich in proteins, vitamins, and minerals.

• **Preparation:** Prepare breakfast in advance to save time in the morning.

Example: You decide to prepare oatmeal with berries and nuts every morning to energize yourself for the day.

Possible Problems and Solutions:

• **Problem:** Lack of time to prepare breakfast.

• **Solution:** Prepare ingredients the night before or choose meals that can be made quickly.

Day 7: Evaluating the Morning Routine

Today, it's important to assess how your new routine affects you. Consider what's working well and what might need adjustment.

Task:

- **Evaluation:** Reflect on which rituals bring you the most satisfaction and energy.

- **Adjustment:** Make necessary changes to better align the rituals with your needs.

Example: You notice that exercise gives you the most energy, but reading in the morning takes more time than expected. You decide to move reading to the evening.

Possible Problems and Solutions:

- **Problem:** You don't notice significant changes or improvements.

- **Solution:** Don't rush to conclusions. Give yourself more time and don't hesitate to experiment with different approaches.

Day 8: Planning the Day

Planning helps you focus on important tasks and avoid chaos throughout the day.

Task:

- **Set Aside 10 Minutes:** Dedicate time to planning your day.

- **Create a Priority List:** Identify the 3-5 most important tasks for the day.

Example: You use a planner to list the most important tasks for the day and rank them by priority.

Possible Problems and Solutions:

- **Problem:** Feeling overwhelmed by tasks.

- **Solution:** Choose only 3-5 key tasks and avoid trying to tackle everything at once.

Day 9: Practicing Gratitude

Practicing gratitude helps you focus on the positive aspects of life and increases happiness.

Task:

- **Write Down 3 Things You're Grateful For:** Focus on the positive aspects of your life.

- **Reflect:** Think about these things throughout the day.

Example: Every morning, you write in a journal three things you're grateful for, such as health, family, and the support of friends.

Possible Problems and Solutions:

- **Problem:** Difficulty finding new things to be grateful for.

- **Solution:** Consider the small joys in life-like a warm morning, good mood, or friendly support.

Day 10: Reviewing

Results It's time to review the results of your efforts and note the positive changes in your life.

Task:

- **Analysis:** Reflect on how your well-being and productivity have changed over the past 10 days.

- **Choosing Future Rituals:** Identify which rituals you want to keep and which to add.

Example: You notice that you've become more energetic and focused and decide to keep exercise, meditation, and a healthy breakfast as permanent elements of your routine.

Possible Problems and Solutions:

- **Problem:** Difficulty assessing results or noting changes.

- **Solution:** Pay attention to even the smallest improvements. Ask for feedback from close friends or family.

Conclusion This 10-day plan will help you gradually and stress-free integrate morning rituals into your life. Follow these steps to create a routine that brings you joy and boosts your productivity. Remember, change takes time, but it's worth the effort.

Reflection and Conclusions

Implementing morning rituals can be a significant step toward increasing productivity, improving well-being, and achieving personal goals. However, to make these changes truly effective and sustainable, it's important to regularly evaluate their impact and seek ways to improve them further. This section focuses on the importance of reflection, feedback, and the review and adjustment of rituals.

The Importance of Reflection Reflection allows you to pause and analyze your experience, evaluate your achievements, and understand what can be improved. It's a crucial step that helps you identify successes and mistakes, draw conclusions, and develop new strategies to achieve your goals. Without proper analysis, it's difficult to understand which rituals work best and which need adjustment.

How to Reflect:

- **Allocate Time:** Set aside time at the end of each week or month for self-analysis. This could be 30 minutes on a Saturday or Sunday.

- **Ask Questions:** Ask yourself, what exactly have you achieved during this period? Which rituals helped you feel better? What needs to be changed?

- **Record Observations:** Keep a journal of your reflections to track your progress and identify trends.

Example: At the end of the month, you review your journal and notice that meditation significantly reduced your stress, but morning reading didn't yield the expected results.

Feedback Communicating with others can provide you with objective feedback and help you evaluate your achievements from a different perspective. Friends, colleagues, or mentors can offer valuable advice or suggest better ways to implement your plan.

How to Get Feedback:

- **Communicate Openly:** Share your morning rituals and their impact on your life with friends or colleagues.

- **Ask Specific Questions:** Request feedback on specific aspects of your routine that concern you.

- **Be Open to Criticism:** View constructive criticism as an opportunity for improvement.

Example: You share your success in implementing exercise with a friend, who then suggests adding more cardio exercises to boost your overall energy level.

Review and Adjustment of Rituals Life circumstances can change, and it's important to be ready to adapt your plans according to new challenges and opportunities. Regular review and adjustment of rituals allow you to maintain their relevance and effectiveness.

How to Adjust Rituals:

- **Review Your Goals:** Ensure that your rituals align with your current goals and needs.

- **Be Flexible:** Don't be afraid to make changes if a ritual no longer delivers the desired results.

- **Experiment:** Try new approaches or methods to improve your routine.

Example: If your job becomes more demanding and you find that you don't have time to complete all the planned rituals, consider moving some to another time of day or shortening their duration.

Final Recommendations

1. Continue Developing Your Morning Rituals Don't stop at what you've achieved. There is always room for improvement. Remember that your rituals should evolve with you.

♦ **Continuous Improvement:** Seek new ideas and approaches to make your rituals even more effective.

♦ **Adaptation to Change:** Be ready to adapt your rituals if your circumstances or goals change.

Example: In the summer, you add morning runs outdoors, while in the winter, you replace them with indoor yoga sessions.

2. Use the Experience Gained for Future Strategies The experience gained during the implementation of morning rituals can be invaluable for developing other areas of your life. Use this experience to develop effective strategies in the future.

♦ **Analyze Successes:** Consider which strategies were the most successful and apply them to other aspects of your life.

♦ **Learn from Mistakes:** Identify what didn't work and learn from those mistakes to avoid them in the future.

Example: If you found that planning evening tasks helped you better perform morning rituals, apply this approach to planning other important tasks.

3. Be Flexible and Open to Change Flexibility and openness to change will help you make the most of growth and development opportunities. Don't be afraid to experiment and change your habits if they no longer meet your needs.

♦ **Experiment with New Approaches:** Try different methods and techniques to find what works best for you.

♦ **Be Open to New Opportunities:** View changes as an opportunity for personal growth and development.

Example: You decide to try a new meditation technique or change the order of rituals to see how it affects your productivity.

Conclusion This section provided you with a deep understanding of the importance of morning rituals and practical tools for their effective implementation in your life. Implementing rituals is not a final destination but an ongoing process of improvement and adaptation. Through regular reflection, feedback, and adjustment of rituals, you will be able to achieve the desired results and grow as a person. Remember, your path to success begins with small steps, and each one brings you closer to your goal.

Chapter 3: The Pomodoro Technique

Introduction and Context

The Pomodoro Technique as a Tool for Enhancing Efficiency

The Pomodoro Technique is one of the most popular time management methods, designed to improve concentration, productivity, and reduce fatigue. Its primary concept involves breaking down work into intervals, usually 25 minutes long, called "pomodoros." After each interval, a short break follows, allowing you to recharge and avoid burnout.

History and Origin of the Pomodoro Technique

The Pomodoro Technique was proposed by Francesco Cirillo in the 1980s. As a student, Cirillo sought ways to improve his productivity and focus during study sessions. He used a kitchen timer shaped like a tomato to track his work intervals, hence the name "Pomodoro." This simple yet effective approach quickly gained popularity among students, freelancers, programmers, and many other professionals seeking to use their time more efficiently.

The Importance of Time Management

In today's world, we are often faced with an overwhelming number of tasks and distractions. Effective time management has become crucial for achieving success in both professional and personal spheres. The Pomodoro Technique helps focus on important tasks, increasing productivity and reducing stress. It teaches us to value our time and use it wisely, enabling us to complete tasks with less effort and better results.

How the Pomodoro Technique Affects Productivity

Breaking work into short intervals helps maintain high concentration throughout the work process. Each 25-minute "pomodoro" allows you to focus on completing a specific task without being distracted by other matters. The short breaks that follow each interval help you relax and recharge, making your work more effective.

This approach also helps identify tasks that take longer than expected and adjust the plan accordingly. Understanding the actual time required for

Chapter 3: The Pomodoro Technique

tasks helps prevent overload and burnout, as work time becomes more predictable and manageable.

Purpose of the Chapter

This chapter aims to teach you how to use the Pomodoro Technique to improve productivity and reduce stress. We will cover the basic principles of this technique, provide tips for implementing it in your life, and help you develop an effective work plan.

You will learn how to use a timer to plan work intervals, organize breaks, and adapt the technique to your needs. Our goal is to help you get the most out of each workday, ensuring a balance between work and rest. This approach will allow you to improve your quality of life by increasing your efficiency and reducing stress levels.

Chapter Structure

- **The Importance of Practice for Personal Development:** We will explore how the Pomodoro Technique contributes to the development of self-discipline, improved concentration, and increased productivity.

- **Overall Goals and Expected Outcomes from Implementation:** We will define the changes you can expect from applying this technique in your life.

- **History and Origin:** We will familiarize ourselves with the history of the technique's creation, its author, and its core principles.

- **Impact on Productivity:** We will examine in detail how breaking work into short intervals helps avoid burnout and increase efficiency.

- **Tips for Implementation:** We will provide practical recommendations for using the Pomodoro Technique in everyday life.

- **Implementation Plan:** We will offer a 10-day plan to integrate the technique into your daily routine.

- **Reflection and Conclusions:** We will summarize the results obtained and provide recommendations for further improving your productivity.

This chapter will equip you with all the necessary knowledge and tools for the successful application of the Pomodoro Technique, allowing you to use your time more efficiently and achieve your desired goals.

Core Theory

Concept of the Pomodoro Technique

The Pomodoro Technique is based on the simple yet effective idea of breaking work into short intervals called "pomodoros." Each "pomodoro" lasts 25 minutes, followed by a short 5-minute break. After four such intervals, a longer break of 15 to 30 minutes is recommended. This structure helps maintain high concentration and energy levels throughout the workday.

Key Principles of the Pomodoro Technique

1. Breaking Tasks into Intervals

Dividing work into short intervals is the key principle of the Pomodoro Technique. Each "pomodoro" lasts 25 minutes, during which you focus on completing a single task. After the interval ends, you take a short break, which allows you to recharge. This approach helps avoid overload and maintain high productivity throughout the day.

2. Focusing on a Single Task

During each "pomodoro," you concentrate on one specific task. This helps avoid distractions and improves the quality of your work. Focusing on a single task for a set time helps you delve into the process and achieve a deeper understanding of the work at hand.

3. Recording Results

After completing each "pomodoro," it is essential to record your results. This helps track progress, see how much time is needed to complete a task, and identify opportunities for improvement. Recording results also promotes self-awareness and self-organization.

4. Analyzing and Adjusting the Plan

After completing several "pomodoros," it is useful to analyze your productivity. Identify tasks that require more time and adjust the plan accordingly. This allows for more rational resource allocation and achieving set goals.

Scientific Basis for the Pomodoro Technique

The Pomodoro Technique has a scientific foundation supported by numerous studies demonstrating the positive impact of breaking work into short intervals on concentration and productivity.

Chapter 3: The Pomodoro Technique

Dividing Work into Intervals and Improving Concentration

Studies show that dividing work into short intervals can increase concentration and focus levels. For example, research conducted by scientists at the University of Illinois showed that short breaks can prevent a decrease in concentration during prolonged work. This is because the brain has limited resources for maintaining constant attention, and periodic breaks allow for the restoration of these resources.

Impact of Short Breaks on Brain Recovery

Short breaks between "pomodoros" help the brain restore its resources, which enhances work efficiency. Research conducted at Cardiff University confirmed that short breaks can increase productivity by reducing fatigue and stress.

Using a Timer and the Sense of Urgency

Using a timer during the Pomodoro Technique creates a sense of urgency that helps avoid procrastination. A study published in the Journal of Consumer Research showed that time constraints increase productivity by forcing focus on the task and reducing the likelihood of distractions.

Personal Story of Applying the Pomodoro Technique

As an entrepreneur involved in selling decorative items worldwide, I often face a large number of tasks that require attention and concentration. In the process of developing my own business, I realized how important it is to manage my time effectively.

Once, while preparing for an important presentation for potential investors, the amount of work seemed overwhelming. I needed to analyze the market, prepare a detailed business plan, and create a presentation that showcased all the strengths of my business. At that moment, I decided to try the Pomodoro Technique, which I had heard about from a colleague.

I divided my work into "pomodoros"- 25-minute intervals, each dedicated to a specific task. I started with market analysis, then moved on to strategy development, and finally, to creating the presentation. After each "pomodoro," I took short breaks, during which I could quickly walk around, drink water, or just look out the window. This helped me regain concentration and relieve tension.

Thanks to this technique, I not only managed to complete the work on time but also felt less exhausted and more confident. The presentation went well, and my investors were impressed with the quality of my preparation. Using the Pomodoro Technique was a revelation for me, allowing me to achieve my goals faster and more efficiently. Since then, I have regularly used this method in my daily schedule, helping me stay organized and productive in developing my business.

Scientific Basis for the Pomodoro Technique

Research on the Impact of Intervals on Concentration

One of the most well-known studies on the effectiveness of short work intervals was conducted at the University of Illinois. The study aimed to understand how short breaks affect productivity and concentration.

- **Participant Group:** The study involved 84 university students.
- **Methodology:** Participants were divided into two groups. One group worked without breaks for 50 minutes, while the other group followed a 50-minute work session divided into two "pomodoros" with a 5-minute break between them.
- **Results:** Participants who worked using the Pomodoro method showed a 15% higher level of concentration and task efficiency compared to those who worked without breaks. This study confirmed that short breaks can significantly enhance the ability to maintain attention.

Research on the Impact of Short Breaks on Brain Recovery

Cardiff University conducted a study that examined the impact of short breaks on brain recovery and overall productivity.

- **Participant Group:** The study involved 120 adults working in the IT sector.
- **Methodology:** Participants were divided into three groups. The first group had 5-minute breaks every 25 minutes, the second every 50 minutes, and the third worked without breaks.
- **Results:** Participants in the first group reported significant improvements in well-being and stress reduction. They demonstrated 20% higher productivity in solving complex tasks compared to participants without breaks. This study highlights that regular short breaks can help reduce fatigue and increase work efficiency.

Research on the Sense of Urgency and Procrastination

A study published in the Journal of Consumer Research examined how time constraints using a timer can affect the sense of urgency and the level of procrastination.

- **Participant Group:** The study covered 200 office workers from various industries.

- **Methodology:** Participants performed the same tasks during 25-minute intervals with and without a timer.

- **Results:** Participants who used a timer completed tasks 30% faster than those who worked without time constraints. They noted that the timer creates a sense of urgency that helps avoid procrastination and focus on the task.

Based on these studies, it can be concluded that the Pomodoro Technique is an effective time management method that increases productivity and improves work quality. Dividing work into short intervals with breaks helps maintain high concentration, reduce stress levels, and enhance overall efficiency. Using a timer contributes to creating a sense of urgency, which helps avoid procrastination.

Problematic Situations and Examples

In life, there are often situations where the lack of a clear plan and time management leads to stress and decreased productivity. Let's explore a few typical scenarios where the Pomodoro Technique can significantly improve the situation.

Situation 1: Constant Distractions at Work

Sarah's Story

Sarah works as a marketing manager in a large company. Her workday begins with a morning meeting where strategies for promoting new products are discussed. After that, she tries to focus on market analysis, but constant calls from colleagues and requests from other departments force her to frequently stop working. Continuous emails only complicate the situation further.

Midday, Sarah attempts to prepare a presentation for management, but distractions from phone calls and urgent tasks prevent her from focusing. She feels that she is losing control over her work time and is unable to complete important tasks. The constant stress and sense of overload begin to negatively impact her productivity and mood.

At the end of the workday, Sarah sees that she hasn't completed even half of the planned tasks, leading to frustration and dissatisfaction with herself. She begins to doubt her ability to manage her time effectively and achieve her goals.

Solution Using the Pomodoro Technique

Sarah decided to try the Pomodoro Technique to manage distractions. She started breaking her workday into 25-minute intervals during which she focused on one task, turning off notifications on her phone and computer. She established a rule to check emails and answer calls only during breaks. This allowed Sarah to concentrate on important tasks without constant interruptions.

Result

After a few weeks, Sarah noticed significant improvements in her productivity. She started accomplishing more tasks and felt less tired at the end of the day. The Pomodoro Technique taught her how to manage her time and avoid unnecessary distractions, significantly improving her efficiency and reducing stress levels. She felt that her workday became more structured and controllable, allowing her to regain satisfaction in her job.

Situation 2: Fatigue and Burnout Due to a Heavy Workload

Mike's Story

Mike is a young doctor working in a hospital. His workday begins early in the morning with patient rounds. Throughout the day, he conducts numerous consultations, fills out medical records, and advises colleagues on various issues. The constant flow of patients and the high responsibility for their health lead to accumulated fatigue.

In the evening, after his shift ends, Mike often stays late at the hospital to complete administrative work. He feels that he has no time for himself or his family, causing him constant stress and burnout. Mike knows that such a work rhythm negatively affects his health, but he doesn't know how to change the situation.

Each week becomes increasingly difficult for Mike, and thoughts of changing his profession start to arise more frequently. He realizes that he is losing enthusiasm for a job that once brought him joy.

Solution Using the Pomodoro Technique

Mike decided to try the Pomodoro Technique to better manage his work time. He began using a timer to divide his day into short intervals with breaks. For example, after 25 minutes of work, he allowed himself a 5-minute break to relax and recharge. He also learned to delegate some of his administrative tasks to colleagues, freeing up more time for rest.

Result

Over time, Mike noticed that he felt less tired and more focused during work. The short breaks helped him reduce tension and prevent burnout.

The Pomodoro Technique enabled Mike to find a balance between work and rest, which positively impacted his health and overall well-being. He rediscovered the joy of his work and could spend more time with his family.

Situation 3: Procrastination Due to a Lack of a Clear Action Plan

John's Story

John is a university student who often puts off important tasks until the last minute. He knows he needs to write his thesis, but he constantly finds other things to do to distract himself. Deadlines are approaching, and his work remains unfinished.

Every day, John plans to sit down and work on his thesis, but without a clear plan, he finds it difficult to concentrate. He often spends hours on social media or watching TV shows, feeling a constant sense of guilt for the unfinished work. The lack of progress causes him stress and anxiety, further complicating the situation.

He also feels pressure from his parents and professors, who expect high results from him. This makes John feel overwhelmed and incapable of handling the task.

Solution Using the Pomodoro Technique

John decided to apply the Pomodoro Technique to combat procrastination. He began breaking down the large task of writing his thesis into smaller parts and completing them in 25-minute intervals, with short breaks in between. This approach helped him overcome his fear of large projects and made the tasks more manageable.

Result

John noticed that he started completing tasks faster and with less effort. His stress level decreased, and his confidence grew. The Pomodoro Technique helped him find a clear action plan and overcome procrastination, positively impacting his studies and well-being. He was able to finish his thesis on time and received a high grade.

Examples of Successful Application of the Pomodoro Technique

The Pomodoro Method is a universal tool that can be effectively applied not only at work but also in everyday life. Let's explore a few examples of how this approach helps people in various fields.

1. Students

♦ Students often face a large amount of study material, especially during exam preparation. The Pomodoro Technique allows them to break down the material into smaller, more manageable parts. Short breaks help maintain high concentration and reduce stress. For example, during exam preparation, a student can work on one section for 25 minutes, then take a break to refresh. This reduces the likelihood of burnout and improves the quality of information retention.

2. Freelancers

♦ Freelancers who work from home often struggle with organizing their workday. A lack of structure can lead to overload and burnout. The Pomodoro Method helps structure work time by dividing tasks into intervals with breaks. This allows freelancers to work more efficiently, meet deadlines, and avoid overload. They can plan their workday by alternating 25-minute intervals with breaks, helping maintain a balance between work and rest.

3. Programmers

♦ Programmers often work on complex projects that require high concentration and focus. Breaking work into short intervals helps maintain productivity, with short breaks for recovery. This helps avoid fatigue and improves the quality of work. For example, a programmer can use this method to solve complex algorithmic problems, maintaining a clear focus throughout the workday.

4. Learning a New Language

♦ Many people struggle with learning new languages due to time constraints and the volume of material. Using the Pomodoro Method allows them to divide the learning process into short sessions, making it more effective. During a 25-minute interval, one can focus on learning new words or grammar rules, with short breaks helping to restore energy and avoid fatigue.

5. Physical Exercise

♦ For many people, regular physical exercise can seem exhausting and difficult to organize into a daily routine. Using this approach helps break workouts into short sessions, making them less daunting. For example, one can perform exercises for 25 minutes and then take a break to recover. This helps maintain regular workouts and improve physical fitness without excessive strain.

6. Cooking

♦ For those who love cooking but feel they don't have enough time for complex recipes, the Pomodoro Technique can be a revelation. Breaking

Chapter 3: The Pomodoro Technique

the cooking process into individual stages allows you to focus on each one separately. For example, preparing ingredients can take 25 minutes, followed by a break during which you can prepare for the next stage. This makes the cooking process more manageable and enjoyable, reducing stress and tension.

In each of these cases, the Pomodoro approach becomes a powerful tool for enhancing productivity and reducing stress. It helps find a balance between work and rest, positively impacting overall well-being and effectiveness in various areas of life.

Practical Advice and Solutions for Implementing the Pomodoro Technique

To successfully integrate the Pomodoro Technique into your life, it's essential to follow specific steps and consider potential pitfalls. Here's a practical approach that will help you use this time management method as effectively as possible.

Steps for Implementing the Pomodoro Technique

1. Preparation for Work Before you start, it's crucial to identify the tasks you plan to accomplish. Prepare all necessary materials and tools to avoid distractions during work. Break large tasks into smaller parts that can be completed within one interval.

Quote: "Preparation is the key to success." - Alexander Graham Bell

About the Author and Context: Alexander Graham Bell, a renowned inventor and scientist, emphasized the importance of preparation in engineering and science during one of his lectures. Bell, best known for inventing the telephone, always highlighted the significance of meticulous preparation before starting work on major projects. His approach to preparation was as revolutionary as his technological innovations. In his laboratory, he insisted that his team plan each experiment stage, which helped avoid mistakes and increased the chances of success.

2. Setting the Timer Set a timer for 25 minutes (or another duration that suits you) and start working on the task. Focus only on one task and try not to get distracted. If you feel that 25 minutes is too short, try increasing the interval to 30 or even 45 minutes.

Instructions: To set the timer, you can use a standard kitchen timer, a clock on your smartphone, or specialized apps such as "Pomodoro Timer" or "Focus Booster." Choose the tool that best fits your needs and is easy to set up.

3. Short Breaks After each interval, take a short 5-minute break. Use this time to relax, stretch, or take a short walk. This will help you recharge and return to work with renewed energy.

Self-Development Guide Proven Success Strategies

Quote: "A break is a moment to recharge your energy." — Virgil

About the Author and Context: Virgil, an ancient Roman poet, mentioned this in his work "Georgics," where he described the importance of rhythm in agricultural work. Virgil believed that nature itself dictates when to work and when to rest to achieve maximum productivity. In the modern context, this quote reminds us how important it is to take breaks to maintain energy and efficiency in daily tasks.

4. Long Breaks After four "Pomodoros," take a longer break lasting 15-30 minutes. Use this time to rest, have a snack, or engage in other relaxing activities. Long breaks allow your brain to fully recover and reduce the risk of burnout.

Quote: "Time spent in rest is not wasted." - Benjamin Franklin

About the Author and Context: Benjamin Franklin, one of the Founding Fathers of the United States, an inventor, and a philosopher, always considered rest an integral part of a productive life. This quote comes from his journals, where he described his schedule, which included time for rest and reflection. Franklin understood that overwork without rest could lead to exhaustion and reduced creative energy, so he always emphasized the balance between work and rest.

5. Keeping Records Record your work results after each interval. This helps track progress and see how much time is needed to complete tasks. Note how many "Pomodoros" you spent on each task.

Instructions: To keep records, you can use a simple notebook or task management apps like Todoist, Trello, or Notion. This will help you track your progress and plan your workday more effectively.

6. Analyzing Productivity After completing several intervals, analyze your productivity. Identify which tasks require more time and adjust your plan accordingly. This will help you distribute your efforts more effectively and achieve your goals.

Quote: "Track what you do to know how you do it." - Tyler Page

About the Author and Context: Tyler Page, a modern time management expert, stated this during a lecture on the importance of self-reflection in achieving high productivity. Page believes that regularly analyzing your work allows you to identify strengths and weaknesses, helping to improve processes and work methods continuously.

Common Mistakes to Avoid

- **Distractions During Intervals** Avoid distractions during work intervals. Turn off notifications on your phone and computer to focus on the task. Let your colleagues or family members know about your intention to use the Pomodoro method so they don't distract you during work.

- **Neglecting Breaks** Ensure you take breaks after each interval. This is crucial for recharging and maintaining productivity. Sometimes it might seem like you can continue working without a break, but this can lead to burnout.

- **Lack of Flexibility** Remember that the duration of intervals can vary depending on your needs. Don't be afraid to adjust the length of "Pomodoros" if it helps you concentrate better and complete tasks more effectively.

Practical Tips for Implementing the Pomodoro Method

- **Write Down Tasks** Keep a list of tasks you plan to complete and divide them into intervals. This helps structure your day and make it more efficient. Choose several tasks you want to complete during the day and distribute them across intervals.

- **Visualize Progress** Use visual elements like charts or graphs to track your progress and see how many "Pomodoros" you've completed. This can be a motivating factor and help you assess your productivity.

Instructions: Create a table or chart in Excel or Google Sheets to see how many tasks you've completed throughout the day or week. This will help you visualize your achievements and inspire you to accomplish more.

- **Collaboration** Involve colleagues or friends for support and motivation. Share your tasks with them to receive feedback and additional support. Using the Pomodoro method together can be a great way to improve teamwork and interaction.

Quote: "Together we are stronger." - Mary Kay Ash

About the Author and Context: Mary Kay Ash, founder of the well-known cosmetics company Mary Kay, always believed that collaboration and teamwork are key factors for success. She said these words at one of her company conferences, emphasizing the importance of mutual support and cooperation. Her business approach was always based on engaging and motivating the team to achieve common goals.

Additional Resources for Enhancing Efficiency

- **Books:** "The Pomodoro Technique" by Francesco Cirillo.

- **Apps:** "Forest" app for blocking distractions and increasing focus.

- Courses: Online time management courses on platforms like Coursera or Udemy.

Implementing the Pomodoro Technique can significantly boost your productivity and reduce stress levels. By following these practical tips, you'll be able to better manage your time, achieve your goals, and find a balance between work and rest. Remember, everyone is unique, so it's important to adapt the method to your needs and lifestyle.

10-Day Implementation Plan

Over the next 10 days, you can gradually integrate the Pomodoro Technique into your life. By following this plan, you will master the technique, adapt it to your needs, and achieve noticeable improvements in productivity.

Day 1: Preparation for Work

On the first day, it's important to clearly define the tasks you plan to complete. Take time to prepare all the necessary materials and tools to avoid distractions during work. Make a list of tasks you want to accomplish during the day. Divide them into 25-minute intervals, so each task can be completed in one "Pomodoro." This could be a large task broken into several stages or several smaller tasks.

Example: If you plan to conduct research for a report, start by identifying all the sub-tasks, such as gathering information, reading articles, drafting an outline, writing a draft, and editing. Then prepare all necessary materials, such as a computer, notebooks, pens, and access to online resources.

Goal of the Day: Create a clear plan for the day and prepare for effective work.

Day 2: Focus on One Task

Set a timer for 25 minutes and start working on the first task from your list. Focus only on one task and try not to get distracted by other things. Turn off notifications on your phone and computer to minimize the risk of distractions. This day will help you learn to concentrate on one task and improve your ability to focus.

Example: If you are working on creating a presentation, focus only on that task for one "Pomodoro." Don't get distracted by checking emails or social media. Complete one task at a time, such as creating the introductory slide or gathering images for illustration.

Goal of the Day: Practice concentration and focus on completing one task at a time.

Day 3: Importance of Short Breaks

Today, focus on the importance of taking short breaks after each interval. After the 25-minute interval, take a 5-minute break. Use this time to relax, stretch, or take a short walk. These breaks will help you recharge and return to work with renewed energy. It's important not to neglect these short breaks, as they help maintain high productivity.

Example: After finishing a 25-minute work interval on a project, take a short break to step out onto the balcony, drink water, or do a few stretching exercises. This will help you retain energy and focus for the next stage of work.

Goal of the Day: Master the habit of taking regular breaks to enhance work efficiency.

Day 4: Long Breaks for Recovery

After four "Pomodoros," take a longer break of 15-30 minutes. Use this time to rest, have a snack, or engage in other relaxing activities. Long breaks allow your brain to fully recover and reduce the risk of burnout. This day will help you find a balance between work and rest and understand the importance of extended rest.

Example: After completing several "Pomodoros," you can take a walk in the park, read a few pages of a book, or prepare a light meal. This will give your brain a chance to recover and get ready for the next stage of work.

Goal of the Day: Learn to take long breaks for full recovery and to prevent burnout.

Day 5: Keeping Records

Today, focus on keeping records of your work results after each interval. Record how many "Pomodoros" you spent on each task and note any difficulties you encountered. This will help you track your progress and see how much time is needed to complete tasks. Keeping records will also allow you to analyze the efficiency of your work and identify areas for improvement.

Example: Record in a notebook or electronic app the number of "Pomodoros" spent on writing an article and note which parts of the work caused you the most difficulty. This will help you better plan similar tasks in the future.

Goal of the Day: Learn to track progress for further analysis and improvement.

Day 6: Productivity Analysis

After completing several intervals, conduct an analysis of your productivity today. Identify which tasks require more time and adjust your plan accordingly. Some tasks may need more "Pomodoros" than you initially planned. This will help you better allocate your efforts and more effectively achieve your goals.

Example: You found that writing a report takes more time than you initially planned. Adjust your schedule to allocate more "Pomodoros" to complete this task in the coming days. This will help you be flexible in planning.

Goal of the Day: Master the skills of analyzing productivity to optimize planning.

Day 7: Varying the Duration of Intervals

Today, try varying the duration of intervals. If you feel that 25 minutes is not enough for some tasks, try increasing the interval to 30 or even 45 minutes. Conversely, for simple tasks, you can reduce the interval to 20 minutes. This will allow you to better adapt the Pomodoro method to your personal needs and work rhythm.

Example: If you are working on a task that requires deep concentration, such as programming, try increasing the interval to 45 minutes to have more time to focus on complex code, and take longer breaks.

Goal of the Day: Adapt the technique to individual needs to enhance efficiency.

Day 8: Visualizing Progress

Use graphical elements such as tables or charts to track your progress and see how many "Pomodoros" you have completed. Visualization can be a powerful motivator as it clearly shows your achievements. Create a table or chart where you will record the results of each day.

Example: Create a table in Excel or Google Sheets where you mark completed tasks and the number of "Pomodoros" spent. Use color codes to easily see which tasks were successfully completed and which need more attention.

Goal of the Day: Visualize progress to boost motivation and analyze achievements.

Day 9: Feedback

Communicate with colleagues or friends to get objective feedback on your tasks and progress. Open dialogue can provide you with new ideas for improving efficiency and help you better assess your strengths and weaknesses. Collaborating with others helps you see your achievements and shortcomings from another perspective.

Example: Ask a colleague to review your project or report and provide suggestions for improvement. Use their feedback to refine your work and increase productivity.

Goal of the Day: Get feedback to refine work methods and enhance efficiency.

Day 10: Summarizing

Today, review the results of implementing the Pomodoro Technique and note positive changes in your productivity. Draw conclusions about what worked well and what needs further refinement. Summarizing will help you assess the effectiveness of the Pomodoro method in your life and determine how you can continue using this technique to achieve your goals.

Example: Review your notes and visualizations from the past 10 days. Determine which tasks were completed faster than expected and which required more time. Use this data to improve planning and implement new approaches to work.

Goal of the Day: Evaluate results and determine a plan for future actions to maintain productivity.

Final Recommendations

Implementing the Pomodoro Technique in your life can significantly increase productivity and reduce stress. Over these 10 days, you've learned how to effectively manage your time, adapt the method to your needs, and use it to achieve your goals. Remember that it's important to continue practicing and refining your skills to stay on the path to success.

Reflection and Conclusions

Evaluating the success of implementing the Pomodoro Technique is a crucial step in the process of developing and refining your time management skills. In this section, we will explore the importance of reflection, feedback, and the need for continual review and adjustment of methods to ensure they remain relevant and aligned with your life priorities.

The Importance of Reflection

Reflection is the process of thinking critically about your experiences, which allows you to pause, evaluate your achievements, and identify areas for improvement. This is an essential stage that helps you recognize successes and mistakes, draw conclusions, and develop new strategies for achieving your goals.

Analyzing Achievements

Reflection enables you to acknowledge your accomplishments and recognize the successes achieved through the Pomodoro Technique. This could include increased productivity, reduced stress levels, or improved work-life balance. Consider asking yourself the following questions:
- What have I been able to accomplish using the Pomodoro Technique?
- What changes in my productivity have I noticed?
- What personal achievements have I attained?

Identifying Challenges and Opportunities

Reflection also allows you to identify what didn't go as planned and consider opportunities for improvement. These could be tasks that required more "Pomodoros" than expected or moments when it was challenging to stick to the schedule. Ask yourself:
- What difficulties arose while using the Pomodoro Technique?
- What could have been done better to achieve greater efficiency?
- What new strategies can be implemented to improve results?

Feedback

Communicating with others is an effective way to receive objective feedback on your tasks and achievements. Colleagues, friends, or mentors can offer valuable advice and suggestions on how to better implement your plans.

Objectivity and Tips

It's often difficult to evaluate yourself objectively, so it's important to get feedback from those around you. Others may see your successes and mistakes from a different perspective and provide useful recommendations. Ask the following questions:
- What aspects of my work do you see as strengths?
- Where can I improve my productivity?
- Do you have any tips for optimizing my use of the Pomodoro Technique?

Support and Motivation

Feedback not only helps improve productivity but also provides support and motivation. Knowing that your efforts are noticed and appreciated boosts your motivation to continue working toward your goals. Sharing thoughts and advice can be a powerful stimulus for further development.

Review and Adjustment of the Technique

Life circumstances can change, and it's important to be ready to adapt your plans according to new challenges and opportunities. Regular review and adjustment of the Pomodoro Technique will help keep it relevant and effective.

Evaluating Priorities

Periodically review your tasks and priorities to determine whether they align with your current life goals. Consider the following questions:
- Have my life priorities changed?
- What new challenges do I need to consider when planning?
- Do I need to change the structure of my day to better align with my goals?

Adapting Methods

If you feel that your current methods are not yielding the desired results, don't hesitate to adapt them. For example, you can adjust the duration of intervals or add new elements to your daily routine to better suit your needs.
- What aspects of the Pomodoro Technique should be adjusted to enhance its effectiveness?
- What new tools or strategies can help me achieve my goals?

Final Recommendations

1. Continue Developing Your Time Management Skills

♦ The Pomodoro Technique is just one of many tools for managing time. Keep exploring new methods and strategies to find the most effective approaches to organizing your work.

♦ Study new time management techniques and adapt them to your needs.

♦ Develop planning and task prioritization skills.

2. Use the Experience Gained to Develop Effective Strategies for the Future

♦ Utilize your experience with the Pomodoro Technique to develop new strategies that will help you succeed in the future. Analyze which approaches worked and which didn't to optimize your work.

♦ Draw conclusions from past achievements and failures.

♦ Develop new strategies based on experience to boost productivity.

3. Be Flexible and Open to Change

♦ Always be prepared to adapt your plans and methods in response to changes in your life. Flexibility and openness to change will help you make the most of opportunities for growth and development.

♦ Stay open to new ideas and methods.

♦ Approach changes as opportunities for improvement and growth.

Summary

This section provides a deep understanding of the importance of the Pomodoro Technique and offers practical tools for its effective implementation in your life. By doing so, you will be able to achieve your desired results and grow as an individual.

The Pomodoro Technique is not just a tool for boosting productivity but also a way to create a more balanced and controlled approach to work and life. Use this method as a foundation for developing effective strategies that will help you succeed in all areas of your life. Remember that the most important thing is continuous development and improvement, which will allow you to unlock your potential and achieve your goals.

Chapter 4: Goal Visualization

Introduction and Context

Goal visualization is a powerful tool that helps turn dreams into reality. It involves creating vivid mental images of your goals, allowing you to better understand what you want to achieve and how you plan to accomplish it. Visualization is a key component of success in many areas of life, from sports to business and personal development. It acts as a bridge between our present and future, motivating us to take action and helping us overcome internal obstacles.

The Importance of Visualization

Visualization helps focus attention on desired outcomes by creating a clear picture of what you want to achieve. When you see yourself crossing the finish line, your brain starts working towards making that image a reality. This fosters positive thinking and boosts self-confidence. Your imagination becomes a bridge between where you are now and where you want to be.

Imagine standing on a stage, receiving an award for an achievement you've long dreamed of. This is not just a fantasy—it's a visualization that inspires you to embark on your journey to success. Visualization not only helps define the end goal but also prompts your brain to develop strategies to achieve it.

In sports, visualization plays a key role in preparing athletes for competition. Michael Phelps, a renowned swimmer and Olympic champion, actively used visualization, imagining every move and turn, which allowed him to reach new heights. Each of his swims was mentally rehearsed beforehand. In business, entrepreneurs visualize themselves as leaders of successful companies, helping them make decisions geared towards achieving ambitious goals. By visualizing future success, they better understand the steps needed to reach it.

How Visualization Influences Goal Achievement

Visualization creates a sense of attainability and motivation, increasing the likelihood of realizing your goals. When you imagine yourself as successful, your brain begins searching for ways to achieve that success. This method helps activate imagination and the subconscious, allowing for better planning and the achievement of desired results.

Studies have shown that visualization can enhance productivity and effectiveness. It stimulates the brain to work more actively, improves concentration, and helps overcome internal barriers. By envisioning yourself at the pinnacle of success, you create an internal drive that leads you to take the necessary actions to achieve those goals.

The concept of success is not limited to professional achievements. Visualization can be beneficial in personal life as well, improving relationships, health, and overall well-being. For example, people who aim to improve their health might visualize themselves in good physical shape, enjoying an active lifestyle. This can motivate them to maintain healthy eating habits and engage in regular physical exercise.

Purpose of the Chapter

This chapter aims to teach you how to use visualization to improve your life. We will explore the basic principles of visualization, offer advice on how to incorporate it into your daily life, and help you develop an effective plan for achieving your goals. You will learn how visualization can become your best ally in overcoming difficulties and reaching personal and professional heights.

Imagine the moment when your dreams become reality. With visualization, that moment is closer than you think. Take the first step towards your goals and discover the power of visualization as an integral part of your success. Visualization is not just a technique but a way of life that helps you stay focused on what truly matters and move forward with confidence and enthusiasm.

Core Theory

Visualization is a technique that involves creating mental images of your goals and desired outcomes. It helps strengthen motivation, focus on what's important, reduce stress, and create a clear path to achieving your ambitions. This method allows you to see yourself in a successful future, awakening inner strengths and stimulating you to take active steps.

Key Principles of Visualization

1. Clarity of Images

♦ **Explanation:** Create the clearest possible mental images of your goals. Imagine how you achieve these goals, the emotions you feel, and the benefits you gain. Clarity helps your brain better understand what you are striving for and more easily find ways to achieve it.

♦ **Instruction:** Spend 5-10 minutes each day focusing on your goal. Sit in a quiet place, close your eyes, and start imagining yourself at the moment of achieving your goal. Pay attention to all the details: where you are, what you see, what sounds you hear, and what sensations you experience. Memorize these images and repeat them daily.

Chapter 4: Goal Visualization

♦ **Example:** If you dream of owning a successful business, visualize yourself in the office of your company. Feel the texture of the furniture under your hands, hear the hum of conversations among employees, and smell freshly brewed coffee. Imagine signing an important contract, realizing the success you've achieved.

2. Regular Practice

♦ **Explanation:** Visualization should be a regular practice. Set aside time for visualization every day to reinforce mental images and maintain motivation. This forms a habit that makes your dreams a constant part of your consciousness.

♦ **Instruction:** Set a reminder on your phone or use a regular time of day (such as morning or evening) for visualization. Follow this routine daily for 21 days to establish a strong habit.

♦ **Example:** If your goal is to learn a new language, visualize yourself traveling to another country and communicating freely with locals. Imagine reading books or watching movies without subtitles. Regular visualization practice will help you maintain motivation for daily learning.

3. Emotional Involvement

♦ **Explanation:** Incorporate emotions into your visualization to create a stronger connection with your goals. Emotions make visualization more vivid and stimulating, helping you stay on track.

♦ **Instruction:** During visualization, pay attention to your feelings. Try to experience the joy, pride, or satisfaction of achieving your goal. Use music or scents that evoke positive emotions to enhance the effect.

♦ **Example:** If you're working on improving your physical fitness, visualize yourself crossing the finish line of a marathon. Feel the rush of adrenaline as you cross the line, hear the applause of spectators, feel the sweat on your skin, and the pride in your accomplishments.

4. Realism

♦ **Explanation:** Visualize achievable goals that align with your capabilities and realities. This helps maintain self-confidence and reduces the risk of disappointment. Realism ensures a balance between ambition and feasibility.

♦ **Instruction:** Analyze your resources, skills, and circumstances before visualizing. Set intermediate goals that you can achieve on the way to your main goal, and visualize them in detail.

♦ **Example:** If your goal is to become a professional musician, start by visualizing yourself performing at local clubs or festivals. Realistically assess the time and effort needed to reach this level and gradually move toward more ambitious dreams.

Scientific Basis of Visualization

Visualization has garnered significant attention in the scientific community due to its impact on performance and success. Studies show that visualization activates the same areas of the brain used during task execution, enhancing confidence and improving task performance.

One well-known study in this field was conducted in 1996 by a psychologist from the University of Chicago who explored the impact of visualization on athletic performance. The experiment involved three groups of students playing basketball. The first group practiced shooting hoops daily, the second only visualized the process, and the third did neither. After a month, the performance of the first and second groups was almost identical, significantly outperforming the third group. This study demonstrated that visualization could be as effective as physical training in improving skills.

Another study conducted at Stanford University examined the impact of visualization on students preparing for exams. Students who visualized successful exam outcomes and the study process performed better than those who did not practice visualization. This suggests that visualization can help reduce stress and boost confidence during significant life events.

At a physiological level, visualization stimulates neural connections in the brain similar to those formed during actual activities. This means your brain prepares for the actions you imagine, making them less stressful and more natural when you actually perform them.

Additionally, visualization can contribute to forming positive habits. When you visualize yourself succeeding, your brain perceives it as a possibility, forming neural pathways that enhance your ability to act according to your visualizations.

The conclusion from scientific research is that visualization is an effective tool for improving personal performance and achieving goals. It not only boosts your motivation but also makes the process of achieving goals more structured and less stressful.

Problematic Situations and Examples

In life, there are often situations where the lack of a clear vision for goals can lead to confusion and decreased motivation. Let's explore several common scenarios where visualization can significantly improve the situation:

Situation 1: Jennifer and Her Career Growth

- **Background:**

Jennifer works as a manager in a mid-sized company but feels stuck in her current position. She wants to climb the career ladder but lacks a clear

Chapter 4: Goal Visualization

vision of her goals and the steps needed to achieve them. Jennifer often thinks about how others succeed, but her own path remains unclear.

- **Negative Scenario:**

Without a clear vision of her goals, Jennifer continues working in her current role, not developing new skills or seeking new experiences. Her motivation declines, and she begins to feel frustrated. Without understanding where she is headed, Jennifer loses interest in her work and starts doubting her ability to achieve something greater.

- **Positive Scenario with Visualization:**

Using visualization, Jennifer begins to imagine herself in a higher position — she sees herself as a project leader, making important decisions, and negotiating with clients. She identifies the skills she needs for this and creates a plan to develop them. Jennifer visualizes herself as a successful leader every day, which helps her maintain motivation and self-confidence. Over time, she actively works on developing her skills, participates in professional training, and eventually gets promoted.

Situation 2: Michael and His Loss of Motivation

- **Background:**

Michael is a young entrepreneur who founded his startup a few years ago. Initially, the business thrived, but over time, it began to decline. He feels like he's losing motivation because many of his efforts are not yielding the expected results. He starts to doubt the direction he has chosen.

- **Negative Scenario:**

Without a clear vision for the future, Michael becomes increasingly demotivated. His business begins to stagnate as he loses initiative and stops seeking new solutions. Eventually, the business suffers losses, and Michael decides to close his company, losing faith in his abilities.

- **Positive Scenario with Visualization:**

Michael decides to use visualization to regain his motivation. He starts imagining himself at the helm of a successful company that thrives on new ideas. By visualizing different aspects of a successful business — from satisfied customers to an inspired team — Michael begins to understand what steps he needs to take. This helps him find new opportunities for growth and focus on innovation. Gradually, his business recovers, and Michael feels a renewed sense of energy and confidence.

Situation 3: Sarah and Her Fear of Failure

- **Background:**

Sarah has always dreamed of writing a book, but her fear of failure has constantly held her back. She doubts her writing abilities and fears that her work will not be recognized. This fear prevents her from starting the project.

- **Negative Scenario:**

By not overcoming her fear, Sarah postpones her dream indefinitely. She continues to work at her regular job, feeling dissatisfied and constantly thinking about missed opportunities. Her fear of failure keeps her ideas unrealized, and Sarah feels like a failure.

- **Positive Scenario with Visualization:**

Sarah decides to use visualization to overcome her fears. She begins to imagine herself as a successful author — seeing her book on bookstore shelves, imagining the joy of readers discovering her stories. This helps her gain confidence in her abilities and start working on the book. Step by step, she creates her first manuscript, which eventually finds a publisher and receives positive reviews. Sarah feels inspired and fulfilled, having turned her dream into reality.

Situation 4: Tom and His Athletic Goals

- **Background:**

Tom is an ambitious runner who dreams of becoming a professional athlete. He trains daily but increasingly feels pressure due to high expectations. Tom begins to doubt his abilities and loses faith in his chances of success.

- **Negative Scenario:**

Without visualization and a clear plan, Tom starts skipping training sessions, feeling tired and frustrated. His performance declines, and his mood becomes depressive. He feels like he's losing his chance to become a professional runner and eventually decides to give up his athletic career.

- **Positive Scenario with Visualization:**

Tom begins to use visualization to maintain motivation and confidence. He imagines himself on the finish line of an important race, hearing the applause of the crowd, feeling the adrenaline, and seeing himself as the winner. This helps him develop a clear training plan and focus on improving his skills. Tom continues training with enthusiasm and a renewed belief in his abilities, achieving new personal records and receiving invitations to professional competitions.

Chapter 4: Goal Visualization

Situation 5: Lisa and Her Creative Block

- **Background:**

Lisa is an artist who has always found inspiration in the world around her. However, recently, she has been experiencing a creative block, unable to find new ideas for her work and starting to doubt her talent. This leads to despair and dissatisfaction.

- **Negative Scenario:**

Without using visualization, Lisa continues to feel blocked. She spends time on aimless attempts to start a new painting, but each attempt ends in failure. Over time, Lisa loses interest in painting and begins to consider changing her profession.

- **Positive Scenario with Visualization:**

Lisa decides to use visualization to unlock her creative potential. She starts imagining herself in her studio, where new ideas naturally come to her, visualizing herself creating vibrant and unique paintings. This helps her find inspiration again and start a new project. Lisa discovers new techniques and themes, feels a renewed interest in art, and creates a series of paintings that gain recognition at an exhibition.

These scenarios demonstrate how visualization can transform challenges into opportunities, helping individuals achieve their goals by fostering clarity, motivation, and confidence. By incorporating visualization into daily life, you can overcome obstacles and create a clear path toward success in various aspects of life.

Practical Tips and Solutions

Visualization is a powerful tool for achieving goals, but implementing it effectively requires preparation and effort. By following these steps, you can maximize the effectiveness of this technique.

Steps for Successful Visualization Implementation

1. Creating Visual Images

♦ **Explanation:** Start by defining your goal to create clear mental images. Imagine the end result you want to achieve. Engage all your senses: imagine what you see, hear, and feel. For example, if you dream of a promotion at work, visualize yourself walking into a new office, interacting with colleagues, and feeling satisfied with your work. Make these images as vivid as possible so that they feel real.

♦ **Instruction:** Find a quiet place where you can relax and focus. Close your eyes, take a few deep breaths, and begin visualizing your goal. Use relaxation techniques like deep breathing or soft music to help concentrate on your images. Repeat this practice daily to reinforce the images in your mind.

2. Allocating Time

♦ **Explanation:** Regularity is key to successful visualization. Dedicate a few minutes each day when you can fully focus on your goals. This could be in the morning when you wake up or in the evening when you are preparing for bed. It's important that you are not distracted during this time.

♦ **Instruction:** Set a reminder on your phone or mark the time for visualization in your calendar. Start with 5 minutes a day and gradually increase to 10-15 minutes. Observe how your images become clearer with each practice. If you miss a day, don't worry-just return to the practice the next day.

3. Emotional Engagement

♦ **Explanation:** Emotions make visualization more powerful. Include thoughts about how you will feel when you achieve your goal. This could be joy, pride, calmness, or any other positive emotions that arise within you.

♦ **Instruction:** As you visualize yourself achieving your goal, pay attention to the emotions these images evoke. Allow yourself to fully experience these emotions. If you struggle with emotional engagement, try recalling a situation where you experienced similar feelings. This can help you recreate those sensations in your visualizations.

4. Realism

♦ **Explanation:** It's important to imagine goals that are truly within your reach. This helps avoid disappointment and maintain self-confidence. Realism doesn't mean limiting your ambitions, but it's crucial that your dreams are achievable in real life.

♦ **Instruction:** Before you start visualizing, assess your resources, time, and capabilities. Set intermediate goals that can serve as milestones on your way to the main goal. For example, if you want to write a book, start by visualizing the completion of each chapter rather than the entire manuscript at once. This helps you stay focused and motivated.

5. Keeping a Journal

♦ **Explanation:** A visualization journal can be a useful tool for tracking your progress and maintaining motivation. Record your visualizations, noting details and changes you observe in your life.

♦ **Instruction:** Choose a format for your journal that suits you—this could be a regular notebook or a digital document. Write down dates, visualization themes, and your feelings after each practice. Periodically review your entries to see how far you've come and what changes have already occurred in your life.

Common Mistakes to Avoid

1. Unrealistic Images

♦ **Explanation:** Sometimes people imagine themselves in situations that are too far removed from reality. This can lead to disappointment if expectations are not met. It's important to remember that visualization should be realistic.

♦ **Example:** Mark, a young entrepreneur, imagined himself becoming a millionaire within a year of launching his startup. He created images of a luxurious lifestyle without considering the need for gradual business growth. When his company didn't achieve quick success, he felt disappointed and lost motivation. After reassessing his goals, Mark began visualizing gradual growth, which allowed him to stay motivated and work on realistic tasks.

2. Lack of Regularity

♦ **Explanation:** Regular practice is an essential component of visualization. Without regularity, visualization may become less effective, as mental images don't get reinforced.

♦ **Example:** Sarah decided to use visualization to improve her physical fitness. However, due to her busy schedule, she practiced visualization only a few times a month. This didn't yield the desired results. After implementing regular practices every morning before her workout, Sarah noticed significant progress in her results and felt a renewed sense of motivation.

3. Insufficient Emotional Engagement

♦ **Explanation:** Emotions make visualization more vivid and powerful. Without emotions, visualization can be less effective and less motivating.

♦ **Example:** Lisa dreamed of a career in design, but her visualizations were dry and emotionless. She imagined her goals as mere steps without attention to feelings and experiences. She decided to try visualizing herself at a moment of triumph-when her work is presented at a major exhibition, and she feels pride and joy. This changed her approach and increased her motivation to work.

Practical Tips for Implementing Visualization

• **Record Your Visualizations:** Keeping a journal helps structure thoughts and track progress. Research shows that writing down goals increases the likelihood of achieving them by 42%. A journal can also be a source of inspiration when you have doubts.

- **Visualize Results:** Creating graphical elements such as tables or charts helps track your progress. Visual representations of achievements stimulate the brain and maintain motivation by reminding you how far you've already come.
- **Collaboration:** Share your visualizations with friends or family. Studies show that support from loved ones increases the likelihood of achieving goals. They can provide valuable feedback and support during difficult moments.
- **Meditation:** Integrating visualization into a meditative practice helps you focus more deeply on mental images. Meditation calms the mind and enhances your ability to concentrate on the details of visualization.
- **Mentorship:** Working with a mentor can help you better understand how visualization can be integrated into your goals. A mentor can offer new methods and approaches that may be beneficial in your process.

By following these guidelines and avoiding common pitfalls, you can make visualization a powerful ally in your journey toward achieving your goals.

10-Day Visualization Implementation Plan

Day 1: Creating Clear Mental Images

- **Task:** Create vivid and detailed images of your goals. Imagine achieving these goals by engaging all your senses to form a clear picture of success. This helps you clearly define what you want to achieve and create a specific image of success in your mind, making your goals more real and attainable.
- **Possible Challenges:** Difficulty in creating clear images.
- **Solution:** If you find it difficult to create clear images, start small. Imagine simple things that are easy to visualize and gradually add details. Focus on specific aspects of the goal that you can easily imagine, such as what your workspace looks like or what you are doing at the moment of achieving your goal.

Day 2: Allocating Time for Visualization

- **Task:** Set a specific time in your schedule for visualization and stick to it daily. This could be a few minutes in the morning or before bed. Allocating time helps to form a habit and ensures the regularity of practice, which is key to successfully integrating visualization into your daily life.
- **Possible Challenges:** Lack of time in the schedule.
- **Solution:** If you feel that you don't have time for visualization, try combining it with other rituals, such as morning exercise or evening meditation. Even

Chapter 4: Goal Visualization

5 minutes a day can have a positive impact if used effectively. Remember, regularity is more important than duration.

Day 3: Emotional Engagement

- **Task:** Add emotions to your visualizations to make them more realistic and motivating. Imagine the feelings you experience when you achieve your goals. Emotional engagement strengthens the connection to your goals, making visualization more powerful and motivating.

- **Possible Challenges:** Difficulty in evoking emotions.

- **Solution:** If you struggle to evoke emotions, try recalling real situations where you felt similar feelings. Use these memories to enhance emotional engagement in your visualization. Listening to music or watching inspiring videos can also help you get into the right emotional state.

Day 4: Realistic Goals

- **Task:** Imagine achievable goals that match your capabilities. Break them down into smaller steps to make the process more manageable. Imagining realistic goals helps avoid disappointment and maintains your confidence, making the goal achievement process more structured.

- **Possible Challenges:** Goals seem too ambitious.

- **Solution:** If your goals seem unattainable, break them down into smaller, achievable steps. This helps maintain motivation and allows you to focus on specific actions. Remember that great success is made up of small victories.

Day 5: Keeping a Journal

- **Task:** Record your visualizations and feelings afterward in a journal. This helps structure your thoughts and track progress. Keeping a journal allows you to see your progress and note changes in your life, keeping you focused on your goals.

- **Possible Challenges:** Loss of interest in journaling.

- **Solution:** To maintain interest in journaling, turn it into an enjoyable ritual. Use a beautiful notebook or your favorite pen to make the process more engaging. Also, try different recording methods, such as drawings, stickers, or colored markers, to make it visually appealing.

Day 6: Creating Visual Elements

- **Task:** Create visual elements that help track your progress and see how you're moving closer to your goals. Visual elements make your progress more tangible and stimulate motivation, allowing you to clearly see your achievements and inspire further efforts.

- **Possible Challenges:** Uncertainty about creating visual elements.
- **Solution:** If you're unsure how to create visual elements, try using online tools or mobile apps to create charts and diagrams. You can also use colored pens or markers to manually create tables and charts, making the process more creative and personal.

Day 7: Receiving Feedback

- **Task:** Communicate with friends or family about your visualizations and progress. Receive feedback and support from loved ones. This helps you see your progress from a different perspective and gain support during difficult moments, inspiring new ideas and solutions.
- **Possible Challenges:** Lack of support or interest from others.
- **Solution:** If you don't receive support from your surroundings, try finding a group of people with similar goals or interests. These could be online forums or interest groups where you can share your achievements and get inspiration from others.

Day 8: Using Visualization for Preparation

- **Task:** Use visualization to prepare for important events or tasks. Imagine yourself successfully completing tasks and achieving your goals. This helps reduce stress and increase confidence, allowing you to better focus on the task and achieve the best results.
- **Possible Challenges:** Nervousness before important events.
- **Solution:** Combine visualization with relaxation techniques, such as deep breathing or meditation, to calm your nerves and increase your effectiveness. You can also imagine how you have successfully handled similar tasks in the past, which helps to reinforce your confidence.

Day 9: Evaluating and Adjusting Visualizations

- **Task:** Evaluate your visualizations and make changes if necessary. Think about what works for you and what doesn't, and adjust your images according to your needs. This helps maintain the relevance and effectiveness of visualizations, allowing you to focus on aspects that truly help you achieve your goals.
- **Possible Challenges:** Doubts about the effectiveness of visualization.
- **Solution:** If you have doubts about the effectiveness of visualization, analyze the changes you've noticed in your life over the past 9 days. Focus on

the positive changes, even if they are small. This helps you realize that visualization is working and supporting you on your path to your goal.

Day 10: Summarizing

• **Task:** Review the results of your visualization practice and note positive changes in your life. Reflect on what you've achieved over the past 10 days and what new visualizations you want to maintain for the future. Summarizing helps you realize your progress and motivates you to continue practicing visualization, allowing you to see how it positively impacts your life.

• **Possible Challenges:** Underestimating achievements.

• **Solution:** If you underestimate your achievements, compare your initial state with where you are now. Note even small successes, as they are important steps toward more significant achievements. Remember that every step forward is part of your journey to success.

Reflection and Conclusions

Implementing visualization is a dynamic process that requires constant attention and improvement. Assessing the success of this process is a crucial step in your development as it allows you to pause and analyze achievements, understand what can be improved, and adapt to new challenges. This section provides a deep understanding of the importance of reflection, receiving feedback, and adjusting visualizations to maximize their potential.

The Importance of Reflection

Reflection is a process of self-discovery that allows you to evaluate your experience and draw conclusions. It helps you understand which strategies work and which need adjustment. Reflection provides the opportunity to track progress, notice successes and failures, and determine the direction of future actions.

How to Reflect Effectively:

1. Set Aside Time for Reflection: Regularly set aside time to evaluate your visualizations and progress. This could be a weekly or monthly session where you review your achievements and analyze what is working and what is not.

2. Record Your Thoughts: Keep a reflection journal where you write down your thoughts about visualizations and results. This helps structure your thoughts and notice changes over time.

3. Questions for Reflection: Ask yourself: What have I achieved through visualization? Which strategies were effective? What can I improve? Answers to these questions will help identify your strengths and weaknesses.

Feedback

Receiving feedback from others is an important step in the visualization process. Others can provide valuable advice and help you see your achievements from a different perspective. Feedback helps identify blind spots that you might have missed on your own.

How to Receive Feedback:

1. Communicate with People You Trust: Talk to friends, colleagues, or mentors about your visualizations and achievements. They can provide an objective view of your progress.

2. Be Open to Criticism: Remember that constructive criticism can be beneficial for your development. Don't be afraid to ask what can be improved.

3. Record Feedback: Write down the feedback you receive and consider it in the context of your goals. This will help you better understand which changes may be beneficial.

Reviewing and Adjusting Visualizations

Life circumstances change, and it is important to be ready to adapt your visualizations to new challenges and opportunities. Regularly reviewing and adjusting visualizations allows you to stay on track and maximize your potential.

How to Adjust Visualizations:

1. Analyze Changes: Regularly review your visualizations and assess how they align with your current life circumstances. If certain goals have become less relevant, adjust them accordingly.

2. Adapt Strategies: If certain strategies are not working, don't hesitate to change them. Experiment with different approaches to find what works best for you.

3. Be Flexible: It's important to be open to changes and ready to adapt your visualizations to new challenges and opportunities.

Final Recommendations

To successfully implement visualization in your life, it is important to follow certain recommendations. They will help you use visualization as a powerful tool for achieving your goals and personal growth.

Chapter 4: Goal Visualization

1. Continue Developing Your Visualization Skills: Visualization is a skill that requires continuous improvement. Keep exploring new methods and approaches to make your visualizations more effective.

2. Use Your Experience for Future Strategies: The experience you gain while implementing visualization can be valuable for developing new strategies in the future. Use it to better prepare for new challenges.

3. Be Flexible and Open to Change: Life is constantly changing, and it's important to be ready to adapt your plans according to new circumstances. This will help you make the most of opportunities for growth and development.

The Role of Visualization in Personal Development

Visualization is a powerful tool that can significantly impact your personal development. It helps not only to achieve goals but also to develop self-confidence, improve planning and adaptation skills, and stimulate the search for new opportunities.

Visualization helps to form a positive outlook, which is critically important for personal growth. When you visualize your goals, it fosters self-discipline and concentration as you constantly keep your priorities in focus. This, in turn, boosts your confidence as you see yourself steadily moving towards achieving your ambitions.

This process also enhances your ability to think creatively, as visualization often requires an unconventional approach to problem-solving. You learn to seek new paths and opportunities that may open up if you remain open to change.

Moreover, visualization contributes to developing emotional resilience. When faced with difficulties, the ability to imagine a successful outcome helps maintain calm and confidence, even in the most challenging situations. This makes you more flexible and capable of adapting to uncertainty.

Overall, visualization is an important tool that helps you not only achieve your goals but also grow as a person, improving your ability to learn, adapt, and overcome challenges.

Here are some recommendations for sources, books, and practices for those who want to learn more about visualization techniques and explore them in more detail:

Books

1. **"Psycho-Cybernetics" by Maxwell Maltz** This classic book offers practical advice on using visualization to improve self-perception and achieve success in various areas of life.

2. "Creative Visualization" by Shakti Gawain The book contains simple yet effective visualization methods that can be used to achieve personal and professional goals.

3. "The Law of Attraction" by Michael J. Losier This book helps to understand how positive thinking and visualization can influence the achievement of desired results in life.

Practices

1. Visualization Meditation Practice meditation that includes elements of visualization. Find a quiet place, close your eyes, and visualize your goals, focusing on details and feelings.

2. Keeping a Visualization Journal Regularly write down your visualizations, their impact on your life, and the changes you notice. This helps structure your thoughts and track progress.

3. Group Sessions or Workshops Join group sessions or workshops on visualization. Collective practice can be very motivating and inspiring.

Online Resources

1. Courses on Platforms like Udemy or Coursera Many online platforms offer visualization courses that cover various aspects of this technique.

2. Podcasts and Videos on YouTube Look for podcasts or videos dedicated to visualization where experts share their advice and experiences.

These sources and recommendations will help you delve deeper into visualization techniques and effectively apply them in your life. If you have any questions or need more recommendations, feel free to ask!

Chapter 5: Journaling

Introduction and Context

Journaling is an effective tool for developing self-awareness, emotional well-being, and enhancing productivity. This practice allows individuals to structure their thoughts, analyze life situations, and track personal progress. Journaling helps you focus on your goals and values, providing a better understanding of yourself. It's not just about recording daily events; it's a way of engaging in a dialogue with yourself that fosters inner growth.

In today's world, where information overload and external influences can cause stress, journaling becomes a crucial means of maintaining emotional stability. It allows you to pause, reflect on your actions and thoughts, and find the right solutions and new approaches. Regular journaling can significantly improve the quality of life, as it is a practice that develops critical thinking and the ability to self-analyze.

The Importance of Journaling

Journaling has a profound impact on self-discovery and personal development. It helps you better understand your emotions, track behavioral changes, and analyze life situations. Additionally, journaling reduces stress levels by allowing you to "release" negative emotions onto paper instead of holding them inside. It's an effective way to find balance in life and improve your emotional health.

Journaling also fosters creative thinking. It helps uncover new ideas and find unconventional solutions. In your journal, you can experiment with thoughts, explore different perspectives, and form new approaches to problem-solving. This practice also helps organize information, which can be useful for achieving specific goals in various areas of life.

The Impact of Journaling on Personal Development

Regular journaling influences personal development by helping you better understand yourself and your life priorities. It's a practice that enhances self-awareness, allowing for more conscious decision-making. Journaling fosters emotional intelligence - you learn to better recognize your emotions, analyze them, and find effective ways to manage them. This approach helps avoid emotional outbursts and better control reactions in challenging situations.

Moreover, journaling boosts productivity. By recording your plans and ideas, you better structure your actions, enabling you to achieve your goals more effectively. Journaling helps you focus on important tasks, track progress, and analyze results, contributing to continuous improvement.

The Purpose of This Chapter

This chapter aims to teach you how to use journaling to improve your quality of life. We will explore the main principles of journaling, provide practical advice on incorporating it into your daily routine, and help you develop a plan to maximize the benefits of this practice. You will learn how to turn journaling into an effective tool for self-development, enhancing self-awareness, and strengthening emotional health.

The main objectives of this chapter are:

1. Understanding the Importance of Journaling: You will learn why journaling is an essential part of personal development and how it can help you achieve your goals.

2. Learning the Key Principles of Journaling: We will explain how to journal effectively to gain the most benefit from this practice.

3. Providing Practical Tools for Implementing Journaling: We will offer specific recommendations and advice to help make journaling a regular and beneficial habit.

4. Helping to Develop a Personalized Journaling Plan: You will create your own journaling plan that suits your needs and life goals.

Journaling in the Modern World

In today's fast-paced world, where life often runs on autopilot, journaling becomes an essential tool for maintaining inner balance. It's a practice that helps you focus on yourself, find answers to important questions, and build a more conscious life. Regular journaling allows you to disconnect from external distractions, concentrate on your thoughts and emotions, and achieve harmony and peace.

Journaling is particularly useful during times of change or life challenges. It helps analyze the situation, find a way out of a crisis, and set new goals. This practice allows you to structure your thoughts and emotions, facilitating sound decision-making and ensuring successful navigation through life's challenges.

Core Theory

Journaling is a technique that involves regularly writing in a diary with the aim of self-reflection, personal development, and enhancing emotional well-being. It's a practice that helps structure thoughts, analyze life events, and track progress. Journaling promotes the development of emotional intelligence and reflective abilities, making it an important component of self-development.

Key Principles of Journaling

1. Regularity

Regularity is one of the key principles of journaling. To gain the most benefit from keeping a diary, it is important to do it systematically. Regular practice solidifies the habit, helps you dive deeper into the process of self-reflection, and ensures continuous development.

Example: A person who journals every evening before bed may notice that over time, these entries help them better understand their thoughts and emotions. For instance, daily entries might include a brief review of the day's events, an analysis of emotional reactions to certain situations, and thoughts on how to improve responses in the future. Such regular practice not only strengthens the habit but also allows for a gradual deepening of self-analysis, which eventually contributes to the development of emotional intelligence.

2. Openness

Openness with yourself is a crucial aspect of journaling. Journaling is a private space where you can be honest with your thoughts and emotions. The more open you are in your entries, the more benefits you will derive from this practice. Openness in writing helps uncover internal conflicts and seek ways to resolve them.

Example: Imagine you are dealing with constant stress at work but can't pinpoint the exact cause. Starting a journal might reveal that this stress is linked to specific situations or people. For instance, if you note your thoughts after each work meeting, you might notice that negative emotions arise when you are interrupted or not given a chance to speak. Understanding this allows you to develop strategies to address it, such as learning to express your thoughts more confidently or approaching your manager for support.

3. Focus on Positivity

Focusing on positive aspects of life is important for maintaining optimism and motivation. Include in your entries moments for which you are grateful, positive events, achievements, and successes. This helps foster a positive outlook, which in turn reduces stress and enhances emotional well-being.

Example: A person who writes down three things they are grateful for each day might find that their overall mood improves over time. These could be simple things like gratitude for a friend's support, satisfaction from achieving a small work goal, or the good feeling after a walk in the fresh air. Focusing on positive aspects of life helps maintain optimism even during difficult periods and boosts overall life energy.

4. Analysis and Reflection

Analysis and reflection are key goals of journaling. Reflection helps you understand the causes and effects of your actions and recognize patterns in your behavior. This allows you to identify recurring problems and find ways to overcome them.

Example: Imagine you regularly jot down your thoughts after important meetings or events. Over time, you may begin to notice that certain situations trigger similar emotional reactions or problems. For instance, if you often encounter conflicts at work, by recording your reactions and thoughts after each incident, you might discover that these conflicts frequently arise due to unclear communication or inadequate preparation.

5. Flexibility and Adaptability

Journaling is a flexible practice that can be adapted to your individual needs and circumstances. The format of the entries, the frequency of journaling, and the length of each session can vary depending on your mood, time, and life events.

Example: On days with a busy schedule, you might limit yourself to brief notes about your thoughts and emotions. This could be a few sentences about what you're feeling at the moment or what's bothering you. On days when you have more time, you might write more detailed entries that include reflections on past events, an analysis of what happened, and plans for the future.

This flexibility allows you to maintain the journaling habit even during busy or emotionally draining periods. The key is to maintain regularity and interest in the process, even if the format of the entries changes depending on the circumstances.

Scientific Basis of Journaling

Journaling has a strong scientific basis, supported by numerous studies. This practice helps reduce stress, improve mood, and develop emotional intelligence.

1. Stress Reduction

A key study conducted in 1997 by Professor James Pennebaker demonstrated that journaling can significantly reduce stress levels. The study involved people who regularly wrote about their emotional experiences for 20 minutes a day, 3-5 times a week. The results showed that participants who practiced journaling experienced reduced stress levels, improved mood, and overall mental health. Writing allowed them to better understand and process their emotions, leading to reduced anxiety and depressive symptoms.

2. Mood Improvement

In 2006, researchers at the University of California, San Francisco, conducted a study on the impact of gratitude journaling on happiness levels. Participants were asked to write down daily events or things they were grateful for. After a few weeks, the study found that these individuals experienced significant improvements in mood, increased optimism, and life satisfaction. This study highlighted the importance of focusing on positive aspects of life during journaling.

3. Development of Emotional Intelligence

In 2010, researchers from Harvard Medical School conducted a study on the impact of journaling on the development of emotional intelligence. Participants who kept a journal and analyzed their emotions and reactions showed improved self-reflection and self-regulation abilities. The study found that journaling fosters a deeper understanding of one's emotions, allowing for more effective management and improved interpersonal relationships. Participants who engaged in journaling became more mindful in their decisions and interactions with others.

Conclusions from Scientific Research

Scientific research confirms that journaling is an effective tool for maintaining emotional well-being and personal development. Regular journaling helps reduce stress, improve mood, and develop emotional intelligence. Journaling also enhances self-awareness, making it valuable for people in various areas of life.

Due to its flexibility and adaptability, journaling can be easily integrated into daily life, ensuring continuous development and improvement in quality of life. This practice is suitable for both beginners and those with experience in journaling, as it can be tailored to individual needs.

Challenging Situations and Examples

In life, there are often situations where a lack of clarity about your thoughts and emotions can lead to stress, loss of motivation, and general disorientation. Journaling is a powerful tool that helps you cope with these challenges and fosters personal development. Below are five typical situations where journaling can significantly improve a person's life.

Situation 1: Feeling Overwhelmed by Too Many Thoughts

Problem Description:

A person constantly feels that their thoughts are scattered, unable to focus on important tasks, and experiences stress due to uncertainty. The overwhelming number of unfinished tasks and chaotic thoughts make it difficult to concentrate and make rational decisions, leading to feelings of confusion and dissatisfaction with oneself.

Example:

Imagine trying to complete several tasks at once, but finishing none of them. For instance, you start writing a report, but get distracted by thoughts about an unfinished project, then switch to a new idea, leaving the report unfinished. In the end, you feel frustrated by the lack of progress.

Solution:

Journaling helps to structure your thoughts and prioritize tasks. By writing down all your tasks and thoughts, you can visually see what is truly important and what can be set aside. This allows you to focus on completing one task at a time, reducing stress and increasing efficiency.

Situation 2: Loss of Motivation Due to Lack of Clear Progress

Problem Description:

A person feels demotivated because they do not see the results of their efforts. They may be working toward their goals, but the inability to measure progress makes them feel like they are standing still.

Example:

Imagine you are trying to lose weight. You change your diet, start exercising, but after some time, you feel there is no progress. The lack of visible results leads to a loss of motivation, and you gradually revert to old habits.

Solution:

Journaling allows you to track small steps on the way to a big goal. By recording your daily achievements, even if they seem insignificant, you can see that progress is being made, however small. This helps maintain motivation and keeps you moving forward.

Situation 3: Inability to Understand Your Emotions

Problem Description:

A person feels emotional chaos, unable to understand why they feel a certain way. Frequent mood swings make it difficult to focus on work and interact with others.

Example:

You notice that you become irritable and can't understand why. For example, minor annoyances at work provoke disproportionately strong reactions, and you can't control your emotions, leading to conflicts with colleagues and a deteriorating work atmosphere.

Solution:

Keeping a journal helps track emotional triggers and analyze what causes certain reactions. By regularly recording your emotions and the circumstances under which they arise, you can better understand yourself and learn to manage your emotions, leading to improved interpersonal relationships and overall emotional well-being.

Situation 4: Feeling Stuck in Your Career

Problem Description:

A person feels that their career is not progressing, having been in the same position for several years without seeing opportunities for growth. The lack of professional development causes feelings of frustration and reduces motivation to work.

Example:

Imagine working in the same position for five years, performing the same duties without seeing prospects for promotion. Each day feels like a repeat of the previous one, and you lose interest in your work. You begin to doubt your abilities and feel uncertain about the future.

Solution:

Journaling can help you reassess your professional goals and find new paths for development. By writing down your thoughts and ideas about your career, you can better understand what you truly want to achieve. Analyzing these entries can help you identify learning opportunities, develop a professional growth plan, and start moving toward new goals.

Situation 5: Feeling Socially Isolated and Lonely

Problem Description:
A person feels lonely, disconnected from others, and finds it difficult to connect with people. Social isolation leads to lower self-esteem and can cause depression.

Example:
You notice that you are communicating less with friends and loved ones. For example, you used to meet regularly with friends, but now you rarely leave home and spend most evenings alone. This begins to evoke feelings of loneliness, and you feel misunderstood and unsupported.

Solution:
Journaling can help you understand your social needs and develop a plan to improve your social life. By recording your feelings and analyzing what led to social isolation, you can determine what needs to change in your life. You can create a plan to reconnect with old friends or make new ones, and start taking steps to improve your social life.

Examples of Successful Journaling Practices

Journaling is an essential tool for many well-known individuals who have achieved success in their fields through regular diary-keeping practices. Here are a few examples:

1. Emma Watson (Actress and Activist)

Emma Watson is known not only for her acting career but also for her active involvement in social and political life, particularly in issues of gender equality. Journaling has become an important tool for her in developing her career and self-awareness. She regularly writes about her emotions, thoughts, and plans, which helps her better understand herself and stay in harmony with her values.

Journaling helps Emma maintain a balance between her career and personal life. For example, she uses her diary to plan her time, set priorities, and evaluate her achievements. This allows her to manage her time more effectively and focus on what is truly important to her. She also notes that journaling helps her cope with societal pressures and maintain mental health amid high demands and public life.

2. Sheryl Sandberg (COO of Facebook, Author of "Lean In")

Sheryl Sandberg, known for her leadership role at Facebook and authorship of the bestseller "Lean In," also actively uses journaling for personal and professional development. For Sandberg, journaling has become a way to analyze her thoughts, priorities, and achievements. She writes about her decisions, emo-

Chapter 5: Journaling

tions, and plans for the future, which helps her stay focused on her goals and not lose motivation.

Sheryl uses journaling as a tool for reflection after challenging workdays or important meetings. For example, after delivering a key presentation or holding a significant meeting, she might jot down her impressions, allowing her to analyze her successes and mistakes and plan further steps for improvement. This approach helps her better understand how she handles challenges and which aspects of her professional life require focus.

3. Tim Ferriss (Author of "The 4-Hour Workweek")

Tim Ferriss, author of the popular book "The 4-Hour Workweek," is a strong advocate of journaling, which he actively uses as a tool for planning, self-reflection, and improvement. Ferriss is known for his pursuit of efficiency and life optimization, and journaling plays a key role in his approach to achieving these goals.

Ferriss uses his journal daily to record his thoughts, ideas, and goals. He applies journaling as a way to analyze his achievements and plans for the future, allowing him to stay focused on important tasks. Moreover, Ferriss notes that journaling helps him reduce stress levels and maintain emotional balance. For instance, he often writes about his successes and failures, analyzes what can be improved, and how to avoid mistakes in the future. This approach enables him to maintain high productivity and stay motivated in achieving his goals.

Conclusions

In each of these situations, journaling proves to be an effective tool for improving the quality of life and achieving positive changes. Through regular entries, a person can better understand their emotions, thoughts, and behavior, which allows them to cope more effectively with challenges, maintain motivation, and achieve their goals.

Journaling helps to structure thoughts, reduce stress, and maintain a positive mindset. It is a versatile tool that is suitable for both personal development and professional growth. Journaling can be adapted to your needs and circumstances, making it an effective and accessible practice for everyone.

Practical Tips and Solutions

To successfully incorporate journaling into your life and reap the maximum benefits from this practice, it's essential to follow a few key principles and tips. This section offers step-by-step instructions and solutions that will help make journaling an effective tool for personal development.

1. Choosing the Format: Paper or Digital Journal?

Description:

Before starting a journal, it's important to choose the format that suits you best. Today, there are many options available, from classic paper journals to digital apps.

Example:

If you enjoy the feel of paper and the process of writing by hand, a paper journal might be the perfect choice for you. Writing by hand allows you to focus on the process, reduce the influence of technology, and find satisfaction in the act of writing. On the other hand, if you frequently use gadgets, a digital journal might be more convenient. Using specialized apps, you can store your entries in the cloud, access them anytime, and easily edit them.

Solution:

Choose the format that fits your needs and lifestyle. If you're unsure, try both options and select the one that feels most comfortable. Remember, the key is convenience and comfort while journaling.

2. Regularity of Entries: Establishing a Habit

Description:

Journaling will only be effective if it is practiced regularly. Regularity helps establish a habit and ensures a continuous process of self-reflection.

Example:

Imagine deciding to journal every morning before starting your workday. It might only take 10-15 minutes, but it's important to do it daily. For instance, you could start your day by writing down three things you're grateful for and a brief outline of your plans for the day. This practice will not only help you set a productive tone for the day but also reduce stress and improve your mood.

Solution:

Set aside a specific time for journaling and stick to that schedule. It could be in the morning, before bed, or during lunch. The main thing is to maintain regularity to make journaling a part of your daily routine.

3. Openness: Be Honest with Yourself

Description:

For journaling to be truly effective, it's important to be open in your entries. Don't be afraid to express your true feelings and thoughts.

Chapter 5: Journaling

Example:

You're going through a difficult period at work but hesitate to openly discuss it with colleagues or management. Instead of bottling up your emotions, you decide to write everything down in your journal. For example, you might write about how you're concerned about your work being undervalued, your fear of losing your job, and the stress and fatigue you're feeling. These entries help you analyze the situation and find the inner strength to take the first step toward solving the problem.

Solution:

Keep your journal with maximum openness. Remember that this is your space, free from judgment or criticism. By expressing your thoughts and emotions, you'll better understand yourself and make more informed decisions.

4. Focus on the Positive: Cultivating Optimism

Description:

One of the key aspects of journaling is focusing on the positive moments in life. This helps maintain an optimistic outlook and increases life satisfaction.

Example:

You decide to end each day by writing about three things that brought you joy or for which you're grateful. For instance, this could include gratitude for a pleasant conversation with a friend, successfully completing a project at work, or simply enjoying good weather that lifted your spirits. This approach helps shift your perspective on life and focus on the positives, even on challenging days.

Solution:

Include moments of gratitude in your daily entries. These can be small things that bring you joy. Over time, you'll notice that your thinking becomes more positive, and your stress levels decrease.

5. Analysis and Reflection: Tracking Progress and Growth

Description:

It's important not only to write down your thoughts and emotions but also to analyze them. This helps identify patterns in your behavior, track progress, and find new ways to grow.

Example:

You decide to review your entries weekly and analyze them. For instance, you might notice that you frequently write about feeling anxious before important meetings. Analyzing these entries, you realize that this anxiety stems from inadequate preparation or a fear of failure. You decide to focus on better preparing for meetings and learning stress management techniques, which helps you gain better control over your emotions.

Solution:

Periodically review your entries to identify patterns and trends in your life. This will help you understand what changes are occurring and what you can do to improve the situation.

6. Using Visualization: Creating Graphical Elements

Description:

Visualization is a powerful tool that helps you better understand your progress and structure information. Using graphical elements in your journal can enhance your ability to analyze your entries.

Example:

You decide to create a mood chart for the month. Each day, you rate your mood on a scale of 1 to 10 and record these data in a table or graph. At the end of the month, you can see how your mood fluctuated and identify the events or circumstances that influenced these changes. This will help you understand what positively or negatively affects your emotional state.

Solution:

Use graphs, tables, or charts to visualize your data in your journal. This could involve tracking progress toward goals, changes in mood, or analyzing the frequency of certain events in your life.

7. Collaboration: Using Support from Others

Description:

Although journaling is typically a personal practice, sometimes involving others can be beneficial. Sharing your entries with trusted people or receiving their support can significantly enhance the effectiveness of this practice.

Example:

You decide to tell a friend about your journaling experience and share some of your entries with them. For instance, you discuss your career goals with your friend and receive advice and support from them. This collaboration helps you better understand your goals and gain additional motivation to achieve them.

Solution:

Don't be afraid to share your journaling experience with others. Involving friends or family members can help you gain valuable advice, support, and a new perspective on your entries. Collaboration can also strengthen your relationships with these people.

8. Using Journaling for Planning

Description:

Journaling can be not only a tool for reflection but also an effective way to plan your time and tasks. Keeping a journal helps structure your plans and allocate resources effectively.

Example:

You decide to use your journal for weekly planning. At the start of each week, you write down all the important tasks you need to complete and assign them to specific days. At the end of each day, you analyze what was accomplished and what was not, adjusting your plan for the next day. This allows you to better organize your time and increase productivity.

Solution:

Use your journal to plan tasks, allocate time, and track progress. This will help you better organize your life and achieve greater productivity.

9. Using Journaling to Increase Productivity

Description:

Journaling can help you increase your productivity by not only recording your thoughts but also outlining specific steps to achieve your goals.

Example:

You decide to write down your most important tasks for the day in your journal and track their completion. For instance, each morning, you write down the three most important tasks for the day and set reminders to complete them by the end of the day. In the evening, you analyze what was done and what wasn't and make adjustments for the next day. This allows you to focus on the most important tasks and avoid distractions.

Solution:

Record your key tasks for the day and analyze their completion. This will help you increase your productivity and achieve more in less time.

10. Monthly Reflection

Description:

In addition to daily entries, it's also important to periodically review and analyze your entries over longer periods, such as monthly.

Example:

At the end of each month, you review all the entries made during that period and analyze them. You might highlight key moments noted in your journal, assess your progress in achieving your goals, and draw conclusions for the future. For example, if you notice that certain tasks are consistently not being completed, this might signal the need to review your planning or change priorities.

Solution:

Make it a habit to review your entries monthly. This will allow you to better understand your progress, identify recurring issues, and find new opportunities for personal growth.

Common Mistakes to Avoid When Implementing Journaling

Even the most beneficial practices can lose their effectiveness if common mistakes are not avoided. Journaling is no exception. Here are a few mistakes to avoid to get the most out of this method.

1. Irregular Journaling

Description:

One of the most common mistakes is journaling sporadically without consistent regularity. Journaling becomes effective only when it turns into a habit.

Consequences:

Irregular entries can cause you to lose context and miss identifying patterns in your life. This reduces journaling's effectiveness as a tool for reflection and personal growth.

How to Avoid:

Set a specific time for journaling, such as in the morning or before bed, and stick to that schedule daily. If you miss a day, don't be discouraged-just continue the next day.

2. Unrealistic Expectations from Journaling

Description:

Some people start journaling with the expectation of immediate changes in their lives. However, journaling is a gradual process, and results may only become apparent over time.

Consequences:

If you expect immediate changes that don't occur, it can lead to disappointment and a desire to quit the practice.

How to Avoid:

It's important to understand that journaling is a long-term development tool. Give yourself time and don't expect instant results. Focus on the process rather than immediate outcomes.

3. Lack of Analysis of Entries

Description:

Another common mistake is failing to analyze your entries. Simply writing down thoughts and events is not enough; it's also important to review and analyze them.

Consequences:

Without analysis, you won't be able to identify patterns, understand what works and what doesn't, and make appropriate improvements to your life.

How to Avoid:

Set regular periods for analyzing your entries, such as weekly or monthly. This will help you better understand your thoughts, emotions, and behavior, as well as find new ways to grow.

4. Lack of Openness in Entries

Description:

It's important to be honest with yourself when journaling. If you're not open in your entries, you won't get the full benefit of journaling.

Consequences:

Concealing your true feelings and thoughts can prevent you from better understanding yourself and finding solutions to your problems.

How to Avoid:

Don't be afraid to express your true thoughts and feelings in your journal. Remember that it's your personal space where you can be yourself without fear of judgment.

5. Trying to Create the Perfect Journal

Description:
Some people try to make their journal entries perfect, which can hinder spontaneity and authenticity.

Consequences:
This approach can turn journaling into a routine task done out of obligation rather than inspiration, reducing motivation and making the practice less effective.

How to Avoid:
Allow yourself to make entries in the way that feels right to you, without excessive control over the format or style. Remember, the content of your entries matters more than their form.

6. Ignoring Positive Moments

Description:
Some people use their journal exclusively to record negative events or emotions, ignoring positive moments.

Consequences:
Focusing only on the negative can amplify feelings of anxiety and depression, creating the impression that there's nothing good in life.

How to Avoid:
Try to write something positive you're grateful for each day. Even small things can help you maintain balance and remember the good things in your life.

7. Too Rigid Boundaries

Description:
Setting rigid rules for journaling can make the process too formal and uncomfortable.

Consequences:
If you strictly adhere to specific rules, it can reduce your motivation and turn journaling into a routine task.

How to Avoid:
Be flexible in your approach to journaling. Allow yourself to deviate from the plan occasionally, write down what comes to mind, and not get caught up in formal rules.

Chapter 5: Journaling

These recommendations will help you avoid common mistakes and make journaling an effective and enjoyable practice that contributes to your personal growth and development.

10-Day Journaling Implementation Plan

To successfully incorporate journaling into your life, use this 10-day plan, which will help you gradually develop the habit of keeping a journal and make this practice an integral part of your daily routine.

Day 1: Choosing Your Journal Format

Task:

Choose a journal format that suits you-paper or digital.

Example:

Someone decides to use a paper journal because they enjoy the physical process of writing down their thoughts. They purchase a beautiful notebook and pen, which adds motivation to keep journaling. If you prefer digital formats, you can use journaling apps like Day One or Journey.

Possible Challenge:

You can't decide on a journal format.

Solution:

Try using both formats for a few days and see which one works best for you. You might find a compromise, such as using a digital format for quick notes and a paper journal for deeper reflection.

Reflection:

Consider which format suits you best and why. Note how you feel about choosing your tool, as this is the first step in establishing a new habit.

Day 2: Setting Aside Time for Journaling

Task:

Determine a time in your daily schedule dedicated to journaling.

Example:

A person decides to journal every morning before starting their workday. They set aside 10-15 minutes for writing, which helps them prepare for a positive and productive day.

Possible Challenge:

You struggle to find a suitable time for journaling due to a busy schedule.

Solution:

Start with brief entries at a convenient time, such as during a lunch break or before bed. Over time, you'll find the optimal moment for longer reflections.

Reflection:

Write down your feelings after your first day of journaling. Note how it affected your mood and plans for the day. Was it easy to find time for this practice?

Day 3: Openness and Honesty in Entries

Task:

Begin writing with maximum openness and honesty.

Example:

A person writes about their doubts and fears that they previously hesitated to acknowledge. They find relief in understanding that the journal is a safe space to express any thoughts and emotions.

Possible Challenge:

You find it difficult to be honest with yourself due to fear of negative emotions or self-criticism.

Solution:

Remember that your journal is a private space where you can be yourself. If certain thoughts feel too heavy, start with less painful topics and gradually move to deeper reflections.

Reflection:

Assess how you feel after openly expressing your thoughts. Did it bring relief? Did new thoughts or realizations emerge that you hadn't noticed before?

Day 4: Focusing on Positivity

Task:

Record the positive moments of each day for which you are grateful.

Example:

A person notices that after a tough day at work, they still found time for a walk with friends, which brought them joy. They record this in their journal and note how it lifted their spirits.

Possible Challenge:

You struggle to find positive moments on difficult days.

Solution:

Focus on the smallest positive moments, even if they seem insignificant, such as a delicious cup of coffee or a moment of peace. Gradually, you'll learn to find more positivity in each day.

Reflection:

Think about the positive moments you recorded. How do these small joys affect your overall well-being? Do they help maintain a positive outlook on life?

Day 5: Analyzing Your Entries

Task:

Analyze your entries from the previous days to identify patterns and emotional triggers.

Example:

A person notices that they feel anxious on certain days of the week when the workload is particularly high. They decide to change their approach to planning their work time to avoid such stressful situations.

Possible Challenge:

You don't see clear patterns or find it difficult to analyze your entries.

Solution:

Try asking yourself specific questions during the analysis, such as "What triggered this feeling?" or "How can I avoid this in the future?" This will help you focus on key moments.

Reflection:

What did you discover when analyzing your entries? Are there any recurring emotions or events? What conclusions can you draw to improve your life?

Day 6: Goal Journaling

Task:

Start a separate journal for recording your goals and tracking progress toward achieving them.

Example:

A person sets a goal to improve their professional qualifications over the next six months. They write down specific steps to achieve this goal and track progress weekly.

Possible Challenge:

You find it difficult to define specific goals or steps to achieve them.

Solution:

Start with small goals and gradually move on to larger ones. Use the SMART methodology to formulate goals that are Specific, Measurable, Achievable, Relevant, and Time-bound.

Reflection:

How has keeping a goal journal affected your motivation? Does it help you stay focused on achieving desired outcomes?

Day 7: Visualizing Entries

Task:

Create graphical elements to track progress and visualize your goals.

Example:

A person creates a chart showing their progress in increasing physical activity over a month. They mark each day they completed their planned exercises, which helps them stay motivated.

Possible Challenge:

Visualization seems too complicated or time-consuming.

Solution:

Use simple tools like tables or charts that are easy to create in a digital format. The key is that the visualization is clear and useful to you.

Reflection:

How does visualization help you track progress? Does It bring more clarity and motivation to your plans?

Day 8: Collaborating with Others

Task:

Share your journaling experience with friends or family to get feedback.

Example:

A person tells their friend how journaling helped them organize their thoughts and reduce stress. The friend becomes interested in the practice and decides to try journaling as well.

Chapter 5: Journaling

Possible Challenge:

You fear that others won't understand or support your practice.

Solution:

Choose people you trust who will understand your goal. If you're still unsure, start by sharing only the general aspects of your practice without personal details.

Reflection:

How did discussing your journaling experience with others impact your approach? Did you receive useful advice or inspiration to continue this practice?

Day 9: Using Journaling for Event Preparation

Task:

Use your journal to plan and prepare for important events or tasks.

Example:

A person uses their journal to plan an important work presentation. They write down key ideas, the structure of the presentation, and anticipated questions from the audience. This helps them prepare and reduces anxiety before the event.

Possible Challenge:

You feel that journaling isn't helping you prepare for important events.

Solution:

Break the task into smaller steps and record them in your journal. This will help you focus on each stage of preparation and reduce feelings of overwhelm.

Reflection:

How did journaling help you prepare for an important event? Do you feel more confident and ready?

Day 10: Assessing Progress and Planning for the Future

Task:

Review your entries from the past 10 days and note positive changes in your life.

Example:

A person notes that journaling has made them more aware of their emotions, improved planning skills, and brought more inner peace. They decide to continue journaling and set new goals for the future.

Possible Challenge:

You don't see significant changes after 10 days of journaling.

Solution:

Remember that changes can be gradual. Continue journaling, and over time, you'll notice positive results. You may need more time to establish this habit and see tangible outcomes.

Reflection:

What changes have you noticed in your life after 10 days of journaling? What new habits or practices do you want to continue and develop?

This 10-day plan will help you incorporate journaling into your life, making it a valuable and effective practice for personal development. By following this plan and addressing possible challenges, you'll build a strong habit of journaling and gain the most benefit from it.

Reflection and Conclusions

Reflection is a crucial part of the development process that allows you to pause, analyze your experience, assess achievements, identify successes and mistakes, and draw conclusions. This process enables you to create new strategies for further improvement. In this section, we'll explore how to reflect on your journaling experience effectively and discuss how to make conclusions that will help you enhance this practice in the future.

The Importance of Reflection

Reflection allows you to delve into an analysis of your inner world, understand what drives your growth, and recognize what might be hindering it. It helps you identify the underlying causes of your actions and reactions, which is a significant step toward self-awareness and self-improvement.

Why Reflection is Important:

1. Identifying Successes and Mistakes: Reflection helps you understand which methods work best and which need adjustment. By analyzing your entries, you can see what helped you achieve specific goals or overcome difficulties.

2. Deepening Self-Understanding: Reflection allows you to better understand your emotions, motivations, fears, and dreams. This is an important aspect of self-awareness, helping you become more conscious and confident in your decisions.

3. Developing Strategies: Reflection aids in developing new strategies for overcoming challenges and achieving goals. It helps formulate new approaches to problem-solving based on past experiences.

Example:

A person who regularly journals notices that during stressful periods, analyzing the causes of their emotions helps them manage those emotions better. They realize they can better control their emotions by learning to recognize triggers early and addressing them in their initial stages.

How to Reflect Effectively

Reflection requires discipline and regularity. To gain maximum benefit from this practice, it's important to follow a few basic principles.

1. Regularity: It's essential to regularly set aside time for reflection to analyze changes and progress. This can be done daily or weekly, depending on your schedule.

2. Openness: Be honest with yourself. Reflection will not be effective if you avoid difficult questions or hide your true emotions. Honest analysis of your actions and feelings is key to deep self-awareness.

3. Structured Approach: Use a structured approach to reflection. You can apply specific questions or templates to guide your thoughts. For example, ask yourself: "What did I do well?", "What can I improve?", "What new strategies can I try?".

Example:

A person who journals decides to dedicate time every Sunday to analyzing their week. They ask themselves what helped them stay motivated and which moments required more attention. This helps them plan the following week consciously and avoid repeating mistakes.

Feedback

Receiving feedback from others can be a valuable addition to the reflection process. Communicating with friends, colleagues, or mentors allows you to see your actions from a different perspective, gain new ideas, or receive useful advice.

How to Use Feedback:

1. Choosing the Right People: Choose people you trust and who can provide constructive criticism. These might be close friends, family members, or colleagues familiar with your goals and aspirations.

2. Being Specific: When receiving feedback, be specific in your questions. Instead of asking, "What do you think?", ask, "How do you think I can improve my journaling skills?"

3. Openness to Criticism: Be prepared to accept criticism and use it for growth. Even if you feel the feedback is unfair, try to analyze it and understand if it can be useful to you.

Example:

A person discusses their journaling results with a friend over the past month. The friend points out that they often focus on negative moments and suggests adding more positive reflections. This advice helps the person change their approach to journaling and focus more on the positive aspects of their life.

Reviewing and Adjusting Plans

Reflection also involves regularly reviewing and adjusting your plans and goals. Life constantly changes, and what was relevant a month ago may no longer be significant today. Therefore, it's important to adapt your plans to match new realities.

1. Flexibility: Be ready to change your goals or approaches if necessary. Flexibility in planning helps you quickly adapt to changes and seize new opportunities.

2. Analyzing Changes: When reviewing your plans, analyze what has changed in your life and how it has impacted your goals. Determine if you need to adjust your plans or strategies.

3. Setting New Priorities: If your circumstances or priorities have changed, adjust your plans accordingly. This will help you stay focused on what's important and maintain motivation.

Example:

A person who journals notices that their professional goals have changed after receiving a new position. They decide to adjust their plans and focus on new tasks that align with their new role. This helps them remain productive and motivated.

Final Recommendations

After analyzing your experience and receiving feedback, it's important to draw conclusions that will help you improve your journaling practice.

1. Continue Developing Your Skills: Journaling is an ongoing process of development. Continue exploring new methods and approaches that will help you get more out of this practice.

2. Find New Ways to Improve: Constantly experiment with new formats, questions, or tools for journaling. This will help you avoid routine and maintain interest in journaling.

3. Be Flexible and Open to Change: Remember that your journal is your personal space that should reflect your needs and aspirations. Don't be afraid to change your approach if you feel it's necessary.

4. Use the Experience Gained: Apply the lessons learned from journaling in other areas of your life. Journaling can become a powerful tool for achieving your goals and growing in various aspects of life.

Example:

A person who has been journaling for a year decides to incorporate some journaling principles into their work. They start keeping a work journal where they record their professional goals, tasks, and reflections on completed work. This helps them increase productivity and better organize their time.

Conclusion

Reflection and conclusions are essential elements of journaling. They help you understand yourself better, grow, and achieve your goals. Regularly set aside time for reflection, receive feedback from others, and adjust your plans according to new circumstances. By doing so, you'll be able to fully harness the potential of journaling for personal development and self-improvement.

Recommended Resources for Further Exploration of Journaling

If you want to deepen your knowledge and learn more about journaling, here are some useful resources and books that can help:

1. "The Bullet Journal Method" by Ryder Carroll: This book describes the "Bullet Journal" method, one of the most popular journaling systems. It includes goal structuring, progress tracking, and reflection.

2. "The Artist's Way" by Julia Cameron: This book includes exercises and practices for developing creativity through journaling. Julia Cameron recommends the "Morning Pages" technique, which helps unlock creative potential.

3. "Journaling for Joy" by Joyce Chapman: This book offers various journaling techniques aimed at increasing joy and satisfaction in life. The author provides many tips on how to keep a journal and make the process enjoyable and effective.

4. "Writing Down Your Soul" by Janet Conner: This book focuses on the spiritual aspect of journaling, exploring how journaling can help you connect with your inner self and find answers to important questions.

5. "The 5 Minute Journal" by Intelligent Change: A practical guide that helps you start your day with positivity and gratitude through a simple yet effective journaling system.

6. Courses and Workshops: Many online platforms offer journaling courses where you can get more tips and practical tools to improve your technique. Check out platforms like Udemy, Coursera, or Skillshare.

Chapter 6: Meditation and Mindfulness

Introduction and Context

In today's world, where every day is filled with stress, constant tasks, and an unrelenting flow of information, the ability to pause and find inner peace has become a true necessity. We live in an era where multitasking is considered normal, and the speed of decision-making often determines success in business and personal life. But what price do we pay for this constant acceleration? Chronic stress, emotional burnout, and the inability to enjoy the moment are just some of the consequences that modern people face.

At this juncture, meditation and mindfulness emerge as powerful tools that help us find harmony and inner balance amidst the chaos. These practices have roots in ancient spiritual traditions but have now become an integral part of modern life for millions of people worldwide. Meditation and mindfulness are not just methods of relaxation; they represent a holistic philosophy of life that allows us to be present in the moment, accept ourselves as we are, and achieve harmony with the world around us.

What is Meditation?

Meditation is a practice that allows you to focus your attention on a single object, whether it's your breath, a mantra, an image, or even your thoughts, with the aim of achieving a state of inner calm and clarity. It is a way to relax the mind, allowing it to break free from the cycle of constant thoughts and worries. Meditation helps us pause, focus on the present moment, and experience deep inner peace.

What is Mindfulness?

Mindfulness is the ability to be fully present in each moment of life, perceiving all events, thoughts, and feelings without judgment or attempts to change them. It is the skill of living in the present moment, not getting distracted by past mistakes or anxieties about the future. Mindfulness helps us learn to accept everything that happens to us and around us as it is, and to respond to these events with clarity and calmness.

The Importance of Meditation and Mindfulness in Modern Life

The world we live in places immense pressure on our psyche. The constant flow of information, workplace pressures, and family obligations all contribute to stress and anxiety. In this context, meditation and mindfulness become vital practices that help us maintain mental health, increase emotional resilience, and find inner balance.

These techniques are especially useful for entrepreneurs and leaders who must constantly make important decisions under time pressure and challenging circumstances. For example, in my life as an entrepreneur successfully developing a business selling decorative items worldwide, meditation has become a tool that allows me to maintain concentration and emotional stability even in the most difficult situations.

At 42 years old, when my career has reached its peak, I have personally experienced how important it is to be able to stop and pay attention to my inner state. While growing my business, I faced numerous challenges—from the need to make quick decisions in stressful situations to managing large teams and finding new markets. Incorporating meditation and mindfulness into my daily routine not only helped me overcome these challenges but also enhanced my work efficiency.

By practicing meditation daily, I noticed a significant reduction in stress levels, improved sleep quality, increased concentration, and overall life satisfaction. These results led me to a deeper study of psychology and self-development, which, in turn, further intensified my interest in these practices. Thanks to meditation, I was able to better understand myself, my true desires and motivations, which helped me make more conscious decisions both in business and in my personal life.

The Purpose of This Chapter

The purpose of this chapter is to teach you how to use meditation and mindfulness as tools to improve your quality of life. We will explore the fundamental principles of these practices, provide practical recommendations for incorporating them into your daily life, and help you create an effective plan to achieve inner balance.

You will learn how meditation and mindfulness can help you reduce stress levels, increase concentration, and enhance emotional resilience. We will also look at real-life examples where these practices have helped people overcome challenges and achieve significant success.

This chapter will be your guide to the world of meditation and mindfulness, helping you find peace amid daily challenges and learn to live in the present moment. You will discover how to accept life as it is and find inner balance regardless of external circumstances.

Main Theory

Meditation and mindfulness are powerful practices that help you focus on the present moment, find inner peace, and achieve harmony. They have a strong scientific foundation and are widely used to improve quality of life, reduce stress, and develop emotional resilience. Let's explore the basic principles of these practices, as well as the theoretical aspects that explain their effectiveness.

Key Principles of Meditation

1. Focus on Breathing

Breathing is one of the most important aspects of meditation. It serves as an "anchor" that helps you focus and distract from external stimuli. Calm and rhythmic breathing promotes relaxation of both body and mind. When you focus on your breath, you shift your attention from scattered thoughts to the process of inhaling and exhaling, allowing you to become more present in the moment.

Practical Tip: Find a quiet place where you won't be disturbed. Sit comfortably, close your eyes, and focus on your breath. Feel the air entering and leaving your lungs. Don't try to control your breath; simply observe it. If your mind starts to wander, gently bring your attention back to your breath. Practice this daily for 5-10 minutes and gradually increase the meditation time.

2. Acceptance of Thoughts

During meditation, it is important not to fight your thoughts but to accept them as they are, without judgment. This helps develop the ability not to attach to negative emotions and thoughts that arise during meditation. Instead of trying to get rid of them, try to perceive them as simple observations.

Practical Tip: When you notice thoughts arising during meditation, don't try to ignore or change them. Accept them as part of your experience. You can imagine that your thoughts are clouds in the sky, slowly drifting by. Don't try to stop them; just observe, and they will gradually disperse.

3. Regularity

One of the key aspects of meditation is its regularity. To gain the maximum benefit from this practice, it's important to make it a part of your daily life. Even a few minutes of meditation each day can have a significant positive impact on your well-being.

Practical Tip: Set a specific time of day for meditation. This could be in the morning, before starting your workday, or in the evening before bed. Create a ritual for yourself: choose a comfortable place and prepare it for meditation.

Practice regularly, even if you only have a few minutes. Regular practice will help you develop the habit, and over time, you'll notice positive changes in your life.

4. Patience

Meditation is a process that requires patience. It's not always possible to achieve complete calm immediately, but with time and practice, you will develop this skill. It's important to be patient with yourself and not get discouraged if meditation doesn't go perfectly the first time.

Practical Tip: Remember that meditation is a journey, not a destination. If you feel that meditation doesn't bring immediate peace, that's okay. Continue practicing, focusing on the process rather than the result. Over time, you will see progress and be able to achieve a deeper level of relaxation.

Key Principles of Mindfulness

1. Living in the Present Moment

Mindfulness helps you focus on the present moment without dwelling on the past or future. This allows you to enjoy each moment and reduces anxiety. Instead of constantly worrying about past mistakes or future problems, mindfulness teaches us to appreciate what is happening right now.

Practical Tip: While performing daily tasks, try to be fully present in what you are doing. For example, during a meal, pay attention to the taste, texture, and smell of the food, instead of thinking about work tasks. This will help you develop the ability to live in the present moment.

2. Non-Attachment

Mindfulness involves accepting everything that happens without judgment and without attachment to the outcome. This helps maintain inner peace, even in difficult situations. It's important to learn to accept reality as it is, without trying to change or control everything around you.

Practical Tip: When facing challenges, try to accept the situation as it is, without the immediate desire to change it. Ask yourself: "Can I change anything in this situation right now?" If the answer is no, try to let go of the desire to control the situation and focus on what you can do.

3. Observation Without Judgment

Mindfulness helps you learn to observe your thoughts and emotions without judgment, which allows for better self-understanding and reactions. Instead of judging yourself for negative thoughts or feelings, mindfulness teaches us to accept them as part of our experience.

Practical Tip: When you experience negative emotions or think about something unpleasant, try simply observing these thoughts and feelings without trying to change them. For example, if you feel anxious, pay attention to how it manifests in your body: where exactly do you feel tension? This will help you better understand your emotions and more effectively control them in the future.

Scientific Basis of Meditation and Mindfulness

Research shows that regular practice of meditation and mindfulness has a significant positive impact on our brain and body. Scientists have proven that these practices can change the brain's structure, improving functions related to emotional regulation, attention, and self-awareness.

One of the most impressive studies was conducted at Harvard University, where scientists found that meditation can increase the thickness of the brain's cortex in areas responsible for attention and emotional regulation. This study showed that people who regularly practice meditation are better able to cope with stress and have higher levels of self-control.

Moreover, other studies have found that meditation can reduce levels of cortisol-a stress hormone that contributes to improved overall health. Regular meditation practice is also associated with reduced symptoms of depression and anxiety, improved sleep quality, and even lower blood pressure.

Mindfulness also has a significant impact on the brain. Research shows that mindfulness practice can increase activity in the prefrontal cortex-the area of the brain responsible for self-control and decision-making. This allows people to better control their emotions, cope with stressful situations, and make more conscious decisions.

Overall, scientific research confirms that meditation and mindfulness are effective tools for improving quality of life. They contribute to reducing stress levels, improving mood, enhancing attention levels, and even improving physical health. Through these practices, we can develop emotional resilience, increase productivity, and find inner peace in our fast-paced world.

Challenging Situations and Examples

Meditation and mindfulness might seem like simple practices, but their impact on people's lives is profound and multifaceted. They have the power to change how we perceive ourselves and the world around us, helping us effectively deal with the various challenges of modern life.

In previous sections, we explored the fundamental principles of these practices, their scientific basis, and their positive effects on our mental and physical health. However, the true power of meditation and mindfulness is revealed in real-life situations where these techniques help people overcome difficulties, find inner peace, and improve their quality of life.

Chapter 6: Meditation and Mindfulness

This section focuses on specific examples from the lives of individuals who have faced different challenges-ranging from stress and anxiety to emotional burnout and loss of motivation. These stories will demonstrate how meditation and mindfulness can become powerful tools for resolving these problems. We will also review examples of the successful application of these practices by well-known figures from various fields.

Our goal is not only to discuss these practices but also to show how they can be integrated into your daily life, helping you better handle challenges and achieve inner balance. Regardless of the issues you face, these examples will provide you with inspiration and practical advice for using meditation and mindfulness in your own life.

Situation 1: Work Stress and Anxiety

John, 35 years old, Project Manager

John works as a project manager in a large tech company. His job requires constant attention to detail, coordination between teams, and meeting tight deadlines. Recently, John has been experiencing increased stress levels due to additional responsibilities placed on him after a company restructuring. This pressure started affecting his sleep, making him irritable, and he began experiencing panic attacks. John consulted a doctor, who recommended trying meditation as a way to reduce stress and anxiety.

Starting with simple breathing exercises for a few minutes a day, John gradually progressed to 20-minute meditation sessions. He noticed that these practices helped him reduce anxiety and regain his inner peace. Thanks to meditation, John was able to regain control over his emotions, better handle work pressures, and improve his sleep quality. He now practices meditation every day before work, which allows him to stay focused and calm throughout the day.

Situation 2: Emotional Burnout from Multitasking

Sarah, 42 years old, Chief Editor of a Magazine

Sarah has always been passionate about her job as the chief editor of a popular women's magazine. She constantly juggled multiple projects simultaneously, managed a team of journalists, and ensured editorial deadlines were met. However, over time, she began to feel emotionally burned out. Sarah no longer found joy in her work; instead, she felt drained and irritated.

Sarah decided to try mindfulness as a way to restore balance in her life. She started with small breaks during her workday, focusing on her breathing and releasing tension. These moments helped her return to the present moment and focus on what truly mattered. After a few weeks, Sarah noticed that she had become more resilient to stress, and her feelings of emotional burnout gradually disappeared. She began to enjoy her work again and felt in control of her life.

Situation 3: Difficulty Concentrating

Michael, 28 years old, Software Developer

Michael works as a software developer at a startup, where he is required to solve complex problems quickly and constantly generate new ideas. However, recently he noticed that it was becoming harder for him to focus on his work. Constant distractions such as messages, emails, and tasks from colleagues led to a significant drop in his productivity. Michael began to worry that he wouldn't be able to meet his responsibilities, which further worsened his concentration.

A friend recommended that Michael try meditation and mindfulness to improve his ability to concentrate. Michael began practicing meditation in the morning before work, and he also took short mindfulness breaks during the day. He focused on his breathing exercises and let go of distracting thoughts. After a few weeks, Michael noticed significant improvements: he became more focused, his productivity increased, and his feelings of anxiety disappeared.

Situation 4: Loss of Motivation

Emily, 31 years old, Graphic Designer

Emily always loved her job as a graphic designer, but recently she started feeling fatigued and lost motivation. Creative tasks that used to bring her joy now felt difficult and exhausting. She began doubting her abilities and even considered changing careers.

Emily decided to try mindfulness to regain motivation and find a new approach to her work. She started with short meditations before beginning her workday, focusing on her breathing and letting go of negative thoughts. This helped her clear her mind and feel inspired to be creative again. After a month of regular practice, Emily began to enjoy her work again, and her motivation returned.

Situation 5: Constant Conflicts at Work

Mark, 40 years old, Sales Department Manager

Mark was a successful sales department manager, but his relationships with subordinates and colleagues began to deteriorate. He became too demanding and irritable, leading to frequent conflicts. Mark realized that he needed to change something to keep his team together and restore effective work.

Mark decided to try mindfulness as a way to reduce stress and learn to control his emotions. He started practicing meditation and mindfulness during interactions with colleagues. He focused on his emotions, tried to accept them without judgment, and responded more calmly. Over time, Mark noticed that his relationships with subordinates improved, and conflicts became less frequent. He was able to keep his team together and increase its productivity.

Situation 6: Chronic Insomnia

Lisa, 45 years old, Small Business Owner

Lisa runs a small business selling eco-friendly products. Her work requires a lot of attention and effort, and recently she began suffering from chronic insomnia. Constant thoughts about work kept her from falling asleep, affecting her overall well-being. Lisa felt tired, irritated, and less productive.

A doctor advised Lisa to try meditation before bed to help her relax and let go of her thoughts. She started with short meditations, focusing on her breathing and relaxing her body. After a few weeks, Lisa noticed that her sleep improved, she worried less before bed, and she began waking up refreshed. This allowed her to effectively manage her business again and enjoy life.

Examples of Successful Applications of Meditation and Mindfulness

Business Leaders

Many successful business leaders use meditation and mindfulness to reduce stress and increase concentration. For example, Steve Jobs, the founder of Apple, regularly practiced meditation to stay calm and focused when making important decisions. Jobs believed that meditation helped him expand his creative thinking and better understand user needs. Thanks to this practice, he created innovative products that changed the world of technology.

Athletes

Meditation and mindfulness are widely used by professional athletes to improve focus and manage emotions during competitions. For example, LeBron James, one of the world's most famous basketball players, uses meditation to achieve mental resilience and manage stress during games. Meditation helps him stay focused on the game and cope with the pressure that often accompanies performances on the big stage.

Healthcare Professionals

Meditation and mindfulness help doctors and nurses maintain emotional balance in high-pressure environments. Renowned surgeon and author Atul Gawande, who works in the intensive care unit, began practicing meditation to reduce stress and improve his ability to make complex decisions. This practice allowed him to maintain clear thinking and be effective even in the most critical situations.

Musicians

Musicians also turn to meditation to improve their creative productivity and manage stress. For example, Paul McCartney, the legendary musician and former member of The Beatles, has been practicing meditation for a long time. He claims that this practice helps him find inner peace and inspire himself for new musical projects. McCartney believes that meditation has been one of the key components of his long-term success in the music industry.

Actors

Meditation and mindfulness help actors cope with a demanding schedule and the emotional demands of their profession. For example, Oprah Winfrey, a famous television host and actress, regularly practices meditation. She claims that meditation helps her maintain inner balance and sustain a high energy level in her busy work schedule. Thanks to this practice, Oprah stays productive and positive even during challenging life situations.

Politicians

In the political sphere, meditation and mindfulness can also be important tools. For example, Bill Clinton, the former President of the United States, used meditation to maintain calm and resilience during political crises. Clinton believes that meditation helped him maintain clarity of thought and make balanced decisions in stressful situations, significantly contributing to his successful political career.

Practical Tips and Solutions

To successfully incorporate meditation and mindfulness into your life, it's important to have a clear action plan and understand how these practices work. In this section, we will explore the key steps for implementing meditation, the most common methods, potential mistakes to avoid, and additional tips to help you succeed.

Chapter 6: Meditation and Mindfulness

Choosing a Meditation Method

The first step to successfully incorporating meditation is selecting a method that suits you. There are many different types of meditation, each with its unique characteristics and suitable for different purposes. Below are some popular methods:

1. Breath Meditation (Beginner Level)

This is one of the simplest and most common methods of meditation, suitable for beginners. It involves focusing on your breath, observing each inhale and exhale. This helps calm the mind, reduce stress levels, and improve concentration.

Instructions: Sit comfortably, close your eyes, and begin observing your breath. Pay attention to the air entering and leaving your lungs. If your mind starts to wander, gently bring your focus back to your breath. Start with 5-10 minutes of daily practice.

2. Mindfulness Meditation (Intermediate Level)

This meditation helps develop mindfulness in everyday life. It involves focusing on the present moment, observing what is happening around and within you without judgment or attempts to change the situation.

Instructions: During daily activities (e.g., eating, walking, or working), try to be fully present in the moment. Pay attention to what you feel, see, hear, and think, but do not judge it. Practice mindfulness throughout the day to gradually integrate it into your life.

3. Object Meditation (Intermediate Level)

This meditation involves focusing on a single object, such as a candle, flower, or mantra. The goal is to develop the ability to concentrate, which helps reduce distracting thoughts.

Instructions: Choose an object to focus on (e.g., the flame of a candle). Sit comfortably, close your eyes, and concentrate on the object. If your mind starts to wander, gently bring your attention back to the chosen object. Practice daily for 10-15 minutes.

4. Body Scan Meditation (Beginner Level)

This method is suitable for those who want to focus on their physical sensations and relax the body. Body scan meditation helps relieve tension and calm the mind.

Instructions: Lie comfortably on your back, close your eyes, and start paying attention to each part of your body, beginning with your toes and moving up to your head. Observe the sensations in each part of the body without trying to change them. This will help you relax and release physical tension.

5. Transcendental Meditation (Advanced Level)

This more complex form of meditation involves repeating a mantra to achieve a deep state of relaxation and self-awareness. This method requires special training and is suitable for those with prior meditation experience.

Instructions: Repeat a mantra (a word or phrase) quietly or aloud for 20 minutes twice a day. This will help you achieve a deep state of calm and focus. It is recommended to receive training from a certified instructor to master this technique.

6. Metta Meditation (Loving-Kindness Meditation) (Beginner Level)

This method is aimed at developing compassion and kindness toward yourself and others. It involves sending kind intentions first to yourself and then to other people.

Instructions: Sit comfortably, close your eyes, and start repeating phrases like, "May I be happy," "May I be healthy." Then move on to others, starting with loved ones and ending with those with whom you may have difficult relationships. This will help you develop compassion and kindness.

Creating a Favorable Environment

One of the key aspects of successful meditation is creating a conducive environment for practice. This will allow you to focus as much as possible and experience all the benefits of meditation.

1. Choosing a Place for Meditation

Find a quiet and cozy place where you won't be disturbed. This could be a corner in your home, a garden, a park, or even a room where you can be alone. It's important that the place is comfortable and conducive to relaxation.

2. Setting Up the Space

Create a space that will promote meditation. You can use candles, essential oils, meditation cushions, or other items that help you focus. It's important that everything in this space helps you feel comfortable and calm.

3. Ensuring Silence

If possible, turn off all sources of noise (phone, TV) and ask loved ones not to disturb you during meditation. If complete silence is unattainable, you can use noise-canceling headphones or calm music to create the right atmosphere.

Regular Practice

Regularity is one of the main factors of success in meditation. Even if you start with just a few minutes a day, it's important to stick to this schedule.

1. Setting a Time for Meditation

Choose a time when it is most convenient for you to meditate. This could be in the morning to set the tone for the day or in the evening to relax before bed. It's important that this time remains consistent to develop a habit.

2. Increasing the Duration of Meditation

Start with short sessions of 5-10 minutes and gradually increase the duration as you become more comfortable. This will help you avoid feeling overwhelmed and allow you to smoothly integrate meditation into your life.

3. Keeping a Meditation Journal

Keeping a journal can be a useful tool for tracking your progress. Record your feelings after each session, noting what worked and what was challenging. This will help you better understand your emotions and see progress in your practice.

Observing Thoughts

Observing your thoughts during meditation is an important skill that helps you develop mindfulness and learn to accept your thoughts without judgment.

1. Accepting Thoughts

Don't try to force your thoughts to disappear during meditation. Instead, accept them as part of your experience. This will help you reduce tension and focus on your breath.

2. Gently Returning to the Breath

When you notice that your mind is wandering, gently bring your focus back to your breath. Don't judge yourself for getting distracted; simply acknowledge it as a natural process and continue meditating.

3. Observing Without Judgment

Observe your thoughts like clouds floating in the sky. Don't label them as good or bad; just let them pass. This will help you maintain inner calm and avoid attachment to negative emotions.

Developing Mindfulness

Mindfulness is the ability to be fully present in the moment and focused on what you are doing.

1. Integrating Mindfulness into Daily Life

Mindfulness can be practiced not only during meditation but also in daily activities. Try to be present in the moment while eating, walking, or talking with loved ones. This will help you develop a deeper understanding of yourself and your surroundings.

2. Mindful Breathing Throughout the Day

During stressful moments, pause for a few seconds and focus on your breathing. This will help you return to the present moment and reduce stress levels.

3. Practicing Mindful Listening

When communicating with others, try to listen mindfully without interrupting or immediately expressing your opinion. This will improve your relationships and help develop empathy.

Common Mistakes When Implementing Meditation and Mindfulness

Implementing meditation and mindfulness can be accompanied by certain challenges. Below are six common mistakes to avoid:

1. Impatience

Situation: Sarah, a beginner in meditation, expected quick results after the first few sessions. She hoped that meditation would immediately calm her mind and relieve stress. When this didn't happen, Sarah began to doubt the practice's benefits and lost motivation.

Conclusion: Meditation is a process that develops gradually. It's important to be patient and not expect immediate results. Focus on regular practice, and over time, you will see positive changes.

2. Excessive Control

Situation: Michael tried to control his thoughts during meditation, forcing himself to focus only on his breath. This led to additional stress and frustration as his mind kept wandering.

Conclusion: Meditation is not about complete control over thoughts. Learn to accept your thoughts as they are and gently return your attention to your breath. This will help you develop inner calm.

3. Irregularity

Situation: Thomas began meditating but forgot about his practice after a few days, returning to old habits. His irregularity prevented him from experiencing the full benefits of meditation.

Conclusion: Regularity is key to success. Try to make meditation a part of your daily routine. Even a few minutes each day can have a significant positive impact on your life.

4. Overloading

Situation: Lisa decided to start with 30-minute meditations right away, but this caused her to feel overwhelmed and uncomfortable. She quickly lost interest in the practice.

Conclusion: Start with short sessions and gradually increase the duration as you feel more comfortable. This will allow you to adapt to the practice and maintain motivation.

5. Ignoring Physical Comfort

Situation: Amanda often felt discomfort during meditation due to an uncomfortable posture, but she ignored these sensations, thinking it was part of the process. Over time, this led to back pain and reluctance to continue the practice.

Conclusion: Physical comfort is an important aspect of meditation. Choose a comfortable posture and use cushions or other aids to avoid discomfort. This will help you focus on meditation rather than unpleasant sensations.

6. Believing Meditation is Only for Relaxation

Situation: Bob used meditation exclusively for relaxation, not realizing it is also a tool for developing mindfulness and changing thought patterns. As a result, he did not receive all the possible benefits of meditation.

Conclusion: Meditation is not just a way to relax but a powerful tool for developing self-awareness and changing how you perceive the world. Approach the practice with an open mind and use it to deepen your understanding of yourself and the world around you.

Additional Tips for Successfully Implementing Meditation and Mindfulness

1. Create a Ritual

Creating a ritual can help you get into the mindset for meditation. This could be lighting a candle, playing calm music, or using essential oils. A ritual will help you create a conducive atmosphere and focus on the practice.

2. Use Meditation Apps

In today's world, many mobile apps can be great aids in your meditation practice. These apps offer guided sessions, reminders to practice, and even the ability to track your progress.

3. Collaborate with Others

If you find it difficult to maintain motivation, try involving friends or family. Group meditations can be more engaging and help you stay consistent. You can also discuss your feelings and share experiences.

4. Understand Your Expectations

It's important to understand that meditation is a process, not a quick fix for all problems. Approach the practice with realistic expectations and a willingness to gradually develop new skills.

5. Seek Support from a Specialist

If you're struggling or unsure of your abilities, seek help from a specialist. This could be a certified meditation instructor who can help you master the practice and adapt it to your needs.

6. Integrate Meditation into Your Lifestyle

Find a way to integrate meditation into your daily life. This could be a short meditation before bed or mindfulness during routine tasks. Gradually, these practices will become an integral part of your life and help you achieve inner balance.

10-Day Meditation and Mindfulness Implementation Plan

This 10-day plan is designed to help you gradually integrate meditation and mindfulness into your life. Each day includes specific tasks, situational examples, potential challenges, and recommendations for overcoming them.

Day 1: Choosing a Meditation Method

Task: Familiarize yourself with different types of meditation and choose the one that suits you best.

- **Example:** You might start with breath meditation if you need to reduce stress and learn to focus. If you're interested in developing compassion, try Metta meditation (loving-kindness meditation).

- **Possible Challenge:** You may feel overwhelmed by the variety of options available.

- **Solution:** Read a brief description of each method and start with the one that seems most accessible. Remember, you can always change methods later if you find it doesn't suit you.

Day 2: Creating a Favorable Environment

Task: Find a quiet place where you won't be disturbed.

- **Example:** This could be a corner in your bedroom or a quiet room where you can be alone.

- **Possible Challenge:** Noise or the presence of others may interfere with your concentration.

- **Solution:** Try meditating early in the morning or late at night when the house is quieter. You can also use headphones with calm music or white noise to isolate yourself from external distractions.

Day 3: Allocating Time for Meditation

Task: Start with 5-10 minutes of meditation daily, gradually increasing the duration.

- **Example:** In the morning, before starting your workday, sit for 5 minutes and focus on your breathing. If you have a busy day, use this time to prepare your mind for work.
- **Possible Challenge:** You might feel that you don't have enough time for meditation.
- **Solution:** Schedule a specific time for meditation in your daily routine. Remember that even a few minutes can significantly impact your well-being.

Day 4: Observing Thoughts

Task: During meditation, observe your thoughts without trying to control or change them. Simply notice them and return to your breath.

- **Example:** During meditation, you might notice thoughts about work or personal issues. Instead of fighting these thoughts, simply acknowledge their presence and gently return your focus to your breath.
- **Possible Challenge:** You may feel frustrated by constant distractions from your thoughts.
- **Solution:** Accept that this is a natural part of the process. Don't judge yourself for getting distracted, and remember that these distractions will decrease with practice.

Day 5: Practicing Mindfulness in Daily Life

Task: Focus on the present moment while eating, working, interacting with others, or engaging in other activities.

- **Example:** When you eat, focus on the taste, texture, and smell of the food. Enjoy each bite instead of rushing or getting distracted by other thoughts.
- **Possible Challenge:** You might forget to practice mindfulness during daily tasks.
- **Solution:** Use reminders on your phone or notes at your workplace to remember to practice mindfulness throughout the day.

Day 6: Creating a Meditation Ritual

Task: Create a meditation ritual that helps you focus on the practice. Light a candle, play calming music, or perform other actions that help you concentrate.

- **Example:** Before starting your meditation, light a candle and inhale its aroma to prepare your mind for the practice. This can become a symbol of transitioning from everyday tasks to time for yourself.

- **Possible Challenge:** You might feel that the ritual takes too much time or becomes an additional burden.

- **Solution:** Keep the ritual simple and enjoyable. Choose actions that calm you and don't overwhelm you with additional tasks. Remember, the ritual should enhance meditation, not complicate it.

Day 7: Using Meditation Apps

Task: Use meditation apps that offer guided sessions and practice reminders.

- **Example:** Try apps like Headspace or Calm, which provide guided meditations and help structure your practice.

- **Possible Challenge:** You might find that some apps don't meet your expectations or suit your meditation style.

- **Solution:** Experiment with different apps to find the one that best suits you. If you don't like guided sessions, use the app only for reminders or progress tracking.

Day 8: Involving Friends or Family

Task: Involve friends or family for support and motivation. Meditating together can be easier and more enjoyable.

- **Example:** Invite a friend or family member to join you for morning meditation or mindfulness practice.

- **Possible Challenge:** Others may not share your interest in meditation or may not want to participate.

- **Solution:** Respect their decision but keep the invitation open. You can continue practicing alone but still share your experiences and achievements to encourage them in the future.

Day 9: Evaluating Achievements

Task: Evaluate your achievements in meditation and mindfulness. Note any changes in your well-being and concentration.

- **Example:** You may notice that you've become calmer in stressful situations or that your overall well-being has improved since you started practicing.

- **Possible Challenge:** You might not see immediate or significant changes, leading to frustration.

- **Solution:** Remember that changes can be gradual. Record even small improvements, such as waking up more easily in the morning or feeling less stressed. These small changes are signs that meditation is beginning to work.

Day 10: Summarizing and Reviewing Results

Task: Review the results of your meditation and mindfulness practice and note the positive changes in your life.

- **Example:** You may notice that your overall well-being has improved, you've become more productive at work, or your relationships with loved ones have become more harmonious.

- **Possible Challenge:** The absence of noticeable changes may cause doubts about the benefits of meditation.

- **Solution:** If you don't see significant changes, continue the practice for a few more weeks and review your expectations. You might try a different meditation method or change your approach. Continue to be open to new experiences and focus on the long-term process.

This 10-day plan will help you gradually incorporate meditation and mindfulness into your life. Each day, you will develop new skills, overcome challenges, and observe positive changes in your well-being.

Reflection and Conclusions

Evaluating the success of implementing meditation and mindfulness is a crucial step in personal development. Reflection, feedback from others, and regular review of your practices deepen your understanding of your experiences and help refine processes to keep them relevant and aligned with your life priorities. This section focuses on the importance of reflection, ways to receive feedback, and the necessity of adjusting practices to ensure their long-term effectiveness.

The Importance of Reflection

Reflection is a key element in developing mindfulness and meditation. It allows you to pause, assess your experience, and understand what has been successful and what needs improvement. Reflection helps you not only recognize achievements but also identify possible mistakes or shortcomings in your practice, paving the way for their correction.

Why is Reflection Necessary? Reflection enables you to approach your development consciously by analyzing each stage and drawing conclusions that can be applied in the future. It helps you identify which aspects of meditation and mindfulness work best for you and which require adjustment. It also provides an opportunity to acknowledge your progress, which is an important motivating factor for further improvement.

How to Reflect? Reflection can be formal or informal. Formal reflection might involve keeping a journal where you record your thoughts and impressions after each meditation session, helping structure your experience and better understand your progress. Informal reflection could simply be taking a moment to think after meditation, where you analyze your feelings and achievements.

Feedback

Receiving feedback from others can be a valuable addition to your own reflection. Talking with friends, colleagues, or mentors can provide an objective view of how your meditation and mindfulness practices are affecting your life and relationships.

Why is Feedback Important? Sometimes we may not notice our own successes or mistakes because we are too immersed in our experiences. Objective feedback can help you see the situation from another perspective and find new ways to improve. Friends or mentors might notice changes in your behavior, emotional state, or productivity that you might not be aware of.

How to Get Feedback? To receive feedback, it's important to open a dialogue with people you trust. You can ask them what changes they've noticed in your behavior or well-being since you started meditating. You can also ask for advice on how to improve your practice or better adapt it to your current life circumstances.

Reviewing and Adjusting Practices

Regularly reviewing and adjusting meditation and mindfulness practices is essential for their long-term effectiveness. Life circumstances can change, and what worked before may not be as effective in new conditions. Therefore, it's important to be ready to adapt your plans according to new challenges and opportunities.

Why is it Important to Review Practices? Constantly reviewing practices helps ensure their relevance and alignment with your needs. For example, if your stress levels have decreased, you might focus on deeper aspects of meditation, such as developing compassion or increasing concentration. Conversely, if new stress factors have emerged, you might want to devote more time to relaxation techniques.

How to Review and Adjust Practices? Regularly analyze your practices, paying attention to their effectiveness and how they affect your well-being. If you notice that a particular technique no longer delivers the expected results, don't hesitate to experiment with other methods or adapt the existing ones. For instance, if you usually practice breath meditation but feel the need for deeper calmness, you might try body scan meditation or Metta meditation.

Final Recommendations

After completing the initial stage of implementing meditation and mindfulness, it's important to continue developing these skills and finding new ways to improve them. Below are some recommendations to help maintain and enhance these practices in the long term:

1. Continue Developing Your Meditation and Mindfulness Skills: Don't stop at what you've achieved. Continue to develop your practices, explore new methods and techniques. Regularly read literature on the subject, watch videos, or take courses to learn more about the possibilities of meditation.

2. Use Your Experience to Develop Effective Strategies for the Future: Apply what you've learned during your practice to address new life challenges. Meditation and mindfulness can form the foundation for developing strategies to manage stress, increase productivity, or improve relationships with others.

3. Be Flexible and Open to Change: Don't be afraid to adapt your practices according to new circumstances. If you feel that a certain method is no longer working for you, try something new. It's important to be open to experimentation and ready to change your approach to ensure maximum effectiveness of your practices.

4. Incorporate Meditation and Mindfulness into Various Aspects of Life: Try to integrate these practices not only into your daily rituals but also into your professional life, interactions with others, and even decision-making processes. This will help you achieve a deeper level of mindfulness and use meditation as a tool to improve your quality of life.

5. Remember the Importance of Balance: Meditation and mindfulness should be part of an overall strategy to maintain inner balance. Combine these practices with other healthy habits such as physical activity, proper nutrition, and adequate rest to ensure harmony between body and mind.

6. Share Your Experience with Others: If you've succeeded in meditation and mindfulness, share your experience with others. This can be helpful for people who are just beginning their journey and will also help reinforce your knowledge and skills.

Conclusion

Meditation and mindfulness are powerful tools that can significantly improve the quality of your life. Having completed the initial stage of implementing these practices, you've already made a significant step towards developing inner peace and harmony. Remember that this is a long-term process that requires continuous work on yourself, but the results are worth the effort.

Always remain open to new experiences and ready for change. Use your knowledge and skills to continue growing and developing, and you will see how meditation and mindfulness become an integral part of your life, helping you reach new heights in all areas.

Recommended Additional Reading and Resources

To deepen your understanding of meditation and mindfulness, I recommend the following books and resources:

1. "Mindfulness for Beginners" by Jon Kabat-Zinn

♦ Jon Kabat-Zinn is one of the pioneers of modern mindfulness practice. His book provides a great introduction to the basic principles of mindfulness and offers practical advice on how to implement this method into daily life.

2. "The Power of Now" by Eckhart Tolle

♦ Eckhart Tolle's book has become a bestseller and inspired millions of people to find inner peace by living in the present moment. It explores the concept of the present and helps understand how mindfulness can change your perception of the world.

3. "How to Meditate: A Practical Guide to Making Friends with Your Mind" by Pema Chödrön

♦ Pema Chödrön is a renowned Buddhist teacher who explains how meditation can help reduce stress, calm the mind, and find inner balance. The book contains practical advice and guided meditations.

4. Meditation Apps

♦ **Headspace:** One of the most popular meditation apps that offers guided sessions for beginners and experienced practitioners. It also includes programs for stress reduction, better sleep, and increased concentration.

♦ **Calm:** An app offering a wide selection of meditations on various topics, from anxiety reduction to productivity enhancement. Calm also includes sleep programs and breathing exercises.

5. Online Meditation and Mindfulness Courses

♦ **Coursera:** Coursera offers meditation and mindfulness courses from leading universities, such as Yale University and the University of California.

The courses provide both theoretical and practical knowledge that will help you better understand these practices.

♦ **Udemy:** Udemy offers numerous meditation and mindfulness courses, from basic to advanced levels. They cover various meditation techniques and help integrate them into daily life.

By using these resources, you will be able to deepen your understanding of meditation and mindfulness, discover new approaches and techniques, and continue your journey towards inner balance and harmony. Continuous development and openness to new experiences are key elements of successful practice, helping you achieve lasting positive changes in your life.

Chapter 7: Energy Management

Introduction and Context

Energy management is a critically important aspect of effectiveness and productivity in any area of life. Often, people focus on time management, creating detailed schedules and timelines, but this is only part of the success equation. It's crucial to understand that while time is a limited resource that we cannot change, energy is what truly determines our ability to accomplish tasks, make decisions, and stay motivated throughout the day.

Energy impacts all aspects of our lives: physical condition, emotional well-being, mental productivity, and spiritual growth. When our energy levels are high, we can perform tasks more efficiently, with greater enthusiasm and confidence. Conversely, low energy levels lead to burnout, stress, and decreased productivity.

A person's energy consists of four main components: physical, emotional, mental, and spiritual. Each plays a vital role in maintaining overall energy levels, and they are all interconnected. For example, physical exhaustion can lead to emotional burnout, and losing a sense of purpose can decrease mental productivity. Therefore, the ability to effectively manage your energy helps maintain high productivity levels, reduce stress, and achieve goals without burning out.

In a world where multitasking and a fast pace of life have become the norm, energy management is the key to long-term success. It allows us to maintain balance between work and personal life, sustain high levels of motivation and emotional resilience. Energy management is not just a set of rules or tips; it's a holistic approach to life that takes into account all aspects of our existence.

The Importance of Energy Management

Proper energy management not only enables us to work more efficiently but also helps maintain the quality of life. For example, by focusing on maintaining physical energy through proper nutrition, regular exercise, and sufficient sleep, we create a foundation for all other types of energy. Emotional energy, which depends on our mood and relationships with others, affects how we feel throughout the day. Mental energy helps us focus and make decisions, while spiritual energy gives us meaning and motivation to achieve our goals.

Successful people, whether they are entrepreneurs, athletes, or executives, understand that their success depends not only on the number of hours they spend working but also on how effectively they manage their energy. By recognizing the importance of energy management, they can achieve more in less time while maintaining a high quality of work. This approach helps them avoid burnout, stay motivated, and remain focused on important tasks, all while maintaining a balance between professional and personal life.

How Energy Management Affects Productivity

When we learn to manage our energy effectively, it positively impacts all aspects of our activities. Proper energy distribution helps avoid overload, reduce stress levels, and ensure stable productivity even in challenging conditions. For example, if you maintain a high level of physical energy through regular exercise and healthy eating, you can work more efficiently throughout the day.

Emotional management allows you to remain calm and focused even in stressful situations, reducing the risk of burnout. Mental management helps you concentrate on the most important tasks, avoiding multitasking and information overload. Finally, spiritual management gives meaning to our lives, which sustains our motivation even during difficult moments.

Energy management isn't just about achieving high results in the short term. It's about long-term success and well-being, which becomes possible through a balanced approach to life.

Purpose of the Section

This section aims to teach you how to manage your energy to achieve high productivity and emotional balance. We will explore the fundamental principles of energy management, provide advice on how to incorporate them into your life, and help you develop an effective plan to achieve energy balance. You will learn how to improve your physical condition, maintain emotional resilience, enhance mental productivity, and find spiritual meaning in your life.

This will be your roadmap to achieving a stable level of energy, helping you stay motivated, productive, and balanced in all areas of life.

Core Theory

Energy management is a comprehensive approach that involves working with four main aspects of energy: physical, emotional, mental, and spiritual. All these components are closely interconnected, creating an overall level of energy available for completing tasks and achieving goals. To reach optimal energy levels, it's important to understand the nature of each of these aspects and learn to manage them effectively.

1. Physical Energy

Physical energy is the foundation for all other types of energy. It is provided by proper nutrition, regular physical exercise, quality sleep, and the ability to recharge. When our physical condition is at a high level, we have more energy to tackle daily tasks and achieve our goals.

Key Principles of Physical Energy:

- **Proper Nutrition:** A balanced diet that includes adequate proteins, fats, carbohydrates, vitamins, and minerals. It's important to avoid overeating and consuming unhealthy foods that can lower energy levels.

- **Regular Physical Exercise:** Physical activity improves circulation, supplies organs with oxygen and nutrients, and helps relieve stress. Exercise should be regular but not excessive to avoid exhaustion.

- **Quality Sleep:** Sleep is crucial for restoring physical energy. It's important to ensure adequate duration and quality of sleep so the body can recover after an active day.

- **Energy Recovery:** Periodic breaks throughout the day help restore physical energy. These can include short rest periods, stretching, or a walk in the fresh air.

2. Emotional Energy

Emotional energy determines how we feel and react to various situations. Positive emotions such as joy, gratitude, and love increase energy levels, while negative emotions like fear, anger, and anxiety lower them. Managing emotional energy helps maintain calm and confidence even in challenging situations.

Key Principles of Emotional Energy:

- **Positive Emotions:** Actively working on maintaining a positive emotional state, through practices like mindfulness, meditation, and positive thinking, helps keep a high level of emotional energy.

- **Social Connections:** Interaction with supportive and inspiring people significantly boosts emotional energy. It's important to surround yourself with positive individuals and avoid toxic interactions.

- **Stress Management:** Stress management techniques, such as breathing exercises, yoga, or meditation, help reduce stress levels and maintain emotional stability.

- **Emotional Intelligence Development:** The ability to understand and manage your emotions, as well as empathize with others, helps maintain inner balance and avoid emotional burnout.

3. Mental Energy

Mental energy is responsible for the ability to focus, make decisions, and solve problems. It depends on the ability to manage your thoughts, control your attention, and avoid information overload. Mental management includes skills in planning, prioritizing, and developing concentration.

Key Principles of Mental Energy:

• **Concentration:** Learning to focus on one task at a time, using techniques like the Pomodoro method, helps avoid distractions and boosts productivity.

• **Information Management:** It's important to control information flow, avoid overload, and filter what is truly important. This helps maintain clarity of thought and reduce stress.

• **Planning:** Task planning and resource allocation allow you to conserve mental energy by focusing on priority tasks. It's also important to leave room for unforeseen situations.

• **Thinking Development:** Developing critical thinking and problem-solving skills increases mental energy levels, enabling you to handle challenges more effectively.

4. Spiritual Energy

Spiritual energy comes from a sense of purpose and values in life. This type of energy fuels our motivation and gives us the strength to achieve long-term goals. Spiritual management involves developing a deep connection with yourself and understanding your life values.

Key Principles of Spiritual Energy:

• **Values Identification:** Understanding your own values and life priorities helps find inner balance and understand what is truly important in life.

• **Finding Meaning:** Discovering meaning in your activities, whether work, hobbies, or personal life, increases spiritual energy levels and provides motivation to achieve goals.

• **Meditation and Self-Reflection:** Regular meditation and self-reflection practices help delve into yourself, understand your desires and needs, and contribute to spiritual energy development.

• **Connection with Something Greater:** This could be religious faith, a sense of unity with nature, or a community. Such a connection helps you feel supported and maintain spiritual energy even in difficult times.

Chapter 7: Energy Management

Scientific Foundation of Energy Management

Effective energy management is not just a concept based on observation and practice but also has a strong scientific basis. Research in various fields such as psychology, physiology, and neuroscience confirms that energy management significantly impacts overall stress levels, productivity, emotional state, and physical health. Below are several key studies that illustrate the importance of energy management.

1. Research on the Impact of Physical Exercise on Energy Levels and Cognitive Functions

Study: One of the key studies in this area was conducted by a team of scientists from the University of Georgia (O'Connor, P.J., Herring, M.P., & Caravalho, A.). In 2008, they conducted a meta-analysis that included over 70 studies examining the effects of regular physical exercise on energy levels and fatigue.

Study Design: Participants in these studies engaged in various forms of physical activity, from moderate to intense. Over several weeks, participants reported changes in their energy levels, fatigue, and overall well-being. The researchers found that regular physical exercise significantly increased energy levels and reduced feelings of fatigue, even in those who had previously suffered from chronic fatigue.

Results: Even small amounts of physical activity, such as 20 minutes of walking three times a week, were found to significantly increase energy levels and improve cognitive functions like memory and attention. This confirms the importance of physical activity as a component of energy management.

2. Impact of Sleep Quality on Cognitive Functions and Emotional State

Study: In 2013, a study was conducted at the University of California, Berkeley (Walker, M.P., & Stickgold, R.), examining the impact of sleep quality on cognitive functions and emotional state.

Study Design: Participants were divided into two groups. The first group had a full night's sleep, while the second group was deprived of sleep for one night. The next day, participants from both groups were given tasks involving memory, concentration, and problem-solving, as well as assessments of their emotional state.

Results: The study found that participants who had quality sleep performed better on cognitive tests and had a stable emotional state. In contrast, participants in the second group exhibited increased irritability, anxiety, and had significant problems with concentration and memory. This study highlights the importance of quality sleep as an integral part of managing physical and emotional energy.

3. Research on the Impact of Positive Emotions on Physical Health

Study: In 2005, Barbara Fredrickson, a psychologist at the University of North Carolina, conducted a study examining the impact of positive emotions on physical health and the immune system.

Study Design: In this study, participants kept diaries for several weeks, describing their emotional states. Simultaneously, blood tests were conducted to measure antibody levels and overall immune system status. Participants also took part in various group activities aimed at increasing levels of positive emotions.

Results: The study found that participants who experienced more positive emotions had better immune system indicators and overall physical health. This confirms that emotional energy directly affects physical well-being and that positive emotions can boost physical energy, strengthening health.

4. Research on the Impact of Meditation on Mental and Spiritual Energy

Study: One of the important studies in this area is the work of Richard Davidson, a neuroscientist at the University of Wisconsin-Madison. In 2003, he conducted a study examining the impact of meditation on brain activity and emotional state.

Study Design: The study included both experienced meditators and novices. They participated in a meditation program that lasted several weeks. During this time, researchers measured brain activity using electroencephalography (EEG) and conducted surveys on participants' emotional state and stress levels.

Results: The study found that meditation significantly reduces stress levels, improves concentration, and increases overall happiness. Additionally, experienced meditators showed increased activity in the prefrontal cortex, responsible for positive thinking and emotional resilience. This confirms that meditation effectively impacts mental and spiritual energy, helping maintain inner balance.

Conclusion

Effective energy management is a powerful tool for improving quality of life. It allows you to maintain high productivity levels while avoiding burnout, which is crucial for achieving long-term success.

Chapter 7: Energy Management

Problematic Situations and Examples

In today's world, many people face various challenges related to low energy levels, emotional burnout, chronic fatigue, and a lack of motivation. Energy management can be a powerful tool to address these issues, providing a stable level of productivity and emotional balance. Let's look at some common situations where energy management can significantly improve the outcome.

Situation 1: Chronic Fatigue Due to Improper Physical Energy Distribution

Problem Description: You often feel chronic fatigue even after a night's sleep. This may be due to improper distribution of physical energy throughout the day, such as irregular physical exercise, insufficient sleep, or an unbalanced diet. These issues can lead to decreased work productivity, deteriorated overall well-being, and increased stress levels.

Example: You work in an office and typically spend most of your day sitting at a computer. As a result, you feel tired and irritable by the end of the day. In the morning, you drink a lot of coffee to boost your energy, but it only helps temporarily. You also notice that you often skip lunch or settle for quick snacks that don't provide the necessary energy. By the end of the day, you feel exhausted and have no energy left for household chores or hobbies.

Solution: Start paying more attention to physical activity and balanced nutrition. Incorporate regular physical exercise into your schedule, even if it's just a short walk during your lunch break. Also, ensure you eat regularly and include more nutritious foods in your diet. This will help you maintain a stable energy level throughout the day and feel more active and productive.

Situation 2: Emotional Burnout Due to Constant Stress and Negative Emotions at Work

Problem Description: Constant stress and negative emotions at work lead to emotional burnout. You feel like you're losing motivation, not enjoying your work, and are constantly anxious or irritated. This not only worsens the quality of your work but also affects your relationships with colleagues and loved ones.

Example: You work in a high-stress environment where you constantly deal with deadlines and high expectations. As a result, you feel overwhelmed and can't relax even after work. In the evenings, you constantly think about work tasks, which prevents you from sleeping peacefully. Over time, you notice that you become less tolerant of colleagues, feel irritated more often, and lose interest in activities that used to bring you joy.

Solution: Start practicing emotional management techniques such as mindfulness and meditation. Set aside time during the day for short breaks to calm your mind and restore emotional energy. Try focusing on the positive aspects of your job and learning to let go of stressful situations. This will help you reduce stress levels, maintain emotional resilience, and avoid burnout.

Situation 3: Difficulty Concentrating Due to Information Overload and Multitasking

Problem Description: You constantly struggle to concentrate due to the large flow of information and the need to perform multiple tasks simultaneously. This leads to scattered attention, reduced productivity, and increased work errors. Constant multitasking and information overload can also cause anxiety and fatigue.

Example: You work in a position that requires you to perform several tasks simultaneously, such as responding to emails, attending meetings, and preparing reports. Constantly switching between tasks makes you feel like you can't complete any of them at a high level. As a result, you feel frustrated and anxious, and the quality of your work begins to decline.

Solution: Start using mental energy management techniques such as task planning and breaking work into intervals using the Pomodoro technique. This will help you focus on one task at a time and reduce information overload. Learn to prioritize so you can devote more time to the most important tasks and avoid multitasking.

Situation 4: Loss of Motivation Due to Lack of Meaning in Work or Life

Problem Description: You feel a loss of motivation and interest in your work or life due to a lack of meaning. This can lead to depressive moods, a sense of confusion, and even a desire to change your field of work, but you don't know where to start.

Example: You work in a field that no longer brings you satisfaction. Every day you go to work without much enthusiasm, feeling that your efforts have no significant impact. This leads to decreased productivity, and you spend your free time not finding satisfaction in your usual activities.

Solution: Start by identifying your life values and finding new goals that align with them. This could be a new project, education, or even a career change. Develop your spiritual energy through self-reflection, meditation, or activities that hold deep meaning for you. This will help you regain motivation and find new meaning in your activities.

Situation 5: Physical Exhaustion Due to Lack of Regular Rest

Problem Description: You feel physically exhausted due to a lack of regular rest and breaks throughout the workday. This leads to decreased energy levels, deteriorated overall health, and reduced productivity. Constant overexertion can cause serious long-term health problems.

Example: You constantly work without breaks, trying to complete all tasks on time. Even during lunch breaks, you continue working or thinking about work-related issues. By the end of the day, you feel extremely tired and have no energy left for any other activities. Over time, this exhaustion accumulates, and you start getting sick more often, feeling constant stress, and even losing interest in work.

Solution: Incorporate regular breaks for energy recovery into your schedule. Plan short breaks every 60-90 minutes of work to stretch, take a walk, or simply rest. Ensure you have a full lunch break without working. This will help you maintain energy throughout the day, avoid exhaustion, and sustain high productivity.

Situation 6: Reduced Emotional Resilience Due to Social Isolation

Problem Description: Due to social isolation, you feel reduced emotional resilience and general discomfort. The lack of support from friends or colleagues, as well as insufficient positive social interactions, can lead to feelings of loneliness, stress, and even depression.

Example: You work remotely and spend most of your time at home. Because of this, you have few opportunities to interact with other people. Social gatherings have become rare, and you feel isolated from society. This starts to affect your mood and overall well-being. You often feel lonely, which negatively impacts your emotional energy.

Solution: Work on expanding your social contacts. Include regular meetings with friends, participation in group activities, or joining interest clubs in your schedule. Even short conversations with colleagues or friends can significantly boost your emotional energy and help maintain a positive mood. Don't hesitate to seek support and share your feelings with loved ones.

Examples of Successful Energy Management

Energy management is a key element of success for many well-known individuals in various fields. They use different techniques to maintain high levels of productivity, emotional resilience, and motivation. Let's look at some examples.

1. Jack Ma – Founder of Alibaba

Description: Jack Ma, the founder and former CEO of Alibaba Group, is well-known for his approach to energy management. Despite the immense pressures that accompanied the growth of Alibaba, Jack Ma always paid attention to maintaining a balance between work and personal life.

Methods: Jack Ma actively promotes the concept of 996—working from 9 AM to 9 PM, 6 days a week—while emphasizing the importance of energy management. He regularly practices physical exercises, such as Tai Chi, which help him maintain physical and mental energy. Additionally, he takes time for self-reflection and meditation, which helps him stay focused and make thoughtful decisions.

Result: Jack Ma's approach to energy management helped him build one of the largest companies in the world while maintaining a healthy balance in life. He proves that even with intense work, it's possible to achieve success if you manage your energy properly.

2. Serena Williams – Legendary Tennis Player

Description: Serena Williams, one of the most decorated tennis players in the history of the sport, is known for her meticulous approach to energy management. Her successes on the court are the result not only of her talent but also of how she balances physical, emotional, and mental energy.

Methods: Serena pays great attention to her physical health by engaging in regular training and maintaining a balanced diet. She also works on her mental and emotional state through meditation, visualization, and positive thinking techniques. An important element of her preparation is also working with a psychologist, which helps her maintain emotional resilience during competitions.

Result: Thanks to effective energy management, Serena Williams has remained at the top of world tennis for many years. Her example shows how the right approach to physical, mental, and emotional energy can lead to outstanding achievements in sports.

3. Barack Obama – 44th President of the United States

Description: Barack Obama, who served as President of the United States from 2009 to 2017, is known for his ability to manage energy during an extremely stressful and responsible period in life. His ability to remain focused, positive, and productive is the result of a well-organized approach to managing his energy.

Methods: Obama regularly engaged in physical exercise, such as running and playing basketball, to maintain physical energy. He also paid attention to his spiritual and mental energy through reading, writing, and family traditions that helped him stay connected to his values and maintain a high level of motivation.

Result: Thanks to his ability to manage energy, Obama was able to effectively lead the country through two presidential terms while maintaining emotional resilience and motivation. His example demonstrates how energy management can be critically important for leadership and decision-making.

Description: Arianna Huffington, a well-known media mogul and author, actively promotes the importance of energy management after she experienced burnout from work overload herself. Her experience led to the creation of Thrive Global, a company focused on improving well-being and productivity through energy management.

Methods: After her burnout experience, Arianna revised her approach to work and implemented practices that help preserve energy: healthy sleep, regular breaks, and physical activity became integral parts of her daily routine. She also advocates for the importance of meditation and other mindfulness techniques to support mental and emotional energy.

Result: Thanks to changes in her approach to work and life, Arianna Huffington was able to restore her energy balance and continue successfully managing several large projects. Her example serves as a reminder of the importance of balancing work and rest for achieving long-term success.

Practical Tips and Solutions

Successfully integrating energy management into your life requires an understanding of how to utilize each of the four aspects of energy: physical, emotional, mental, and spiritual. This section provides specific steps to effectively manage these types of energy, avoid common mistakes, and enhance overall productivity and well-being.

1. Physical Energy Distribution

Importance: Physical energy is the foundation for all other types of energy. It depends on how well you take care of your body, including nutrition, physical activity, and sleep.

Implementation Steps:

- **Regular Physical Exercise:** Incorporate physical activities like cardio, strength training, or yoga into your routine to maintain a high level of physical energy. Choose exercises you enjoy to stay motivated.

- **Quality Sleep:** Ensure you get enough quality sleep (7-8 hours per night) to allow your body to recover. Establish a consistent sleep schedule by going to bed and waking up at the same time, even on weekends.

- **Balanced Nutrition:** Eat regularly, prioritizing foods rich in proteins, healthy fats, vitamins, and minerals. Avoid overeating, excessive caffeine intake, and unhealthy foods that can lower energy levels.
- **Hydration:** Drink enough water throughout the day to maintain proper hydration, which is crucial for sustaining physical and mental energy.

Common Mistakes:

- **Ignoring Physical Activity:** A lack of regular physical exercise can lead to decreased energy levels and overall well-being.
- **Irregular Sleep:** Insufficient sleep or a disrupted sleep schedule reduces the body's ability to recover, potentially leading to chronic fatigue.

Example: If you notice constant fatigue despite getting enough sleep, try adding regular physical exercises like morning jogging or yoga to your routine. This can improve circulation, increase energy levels, and enhance overall well-being.

2. Managing Emotional Energy

Importance: Emotional energy determines how you feel throughout the day and how you react to various situations. Positive emotions increase energy levels, while negative ones can deplete them.

Implementation Steps:

- **Mindfulness Practices:** Regularly practice mindfulness and meditation to learn how to manage your emotions and reduce stress. Focus on your breathing, letting go of negative emotions.
- **Emotional Intelligence Development:** Learn to recognize your emotions and respond to them consciously. Practice empathy toward others to improve relationships and reduce emotional strain.
- **Maintaining Social Connections:** Spend more time with friends and family who support and inspire you. Interaction with positive people boosts emotional energy.
- **Gratitude Journaling:** Write down three things you are grateful for each day in a journal. This helps focus on positive aspects and increase emotional energy.

Common Mistakes:

- **Neglecting Emotional State:** Ignoring your emotions can lead to accumulated stress and emotional burnout.

Chapter 7: Energy Management

• **Dwelling on Negative Emotions:** Constantly focusing on negative emotions lowers energy levels and can lead to depression or anxiety.

Example: If work-related stress starts to affect your well-being, try practicing breathing exercises or a short meditation during the workday. This will help restore emotional balance and boost energy levels.

3. Optimizing Mental Energy

Importance: Mental energy is needed for focus, decision-making, and problem-solving. Effective mental energy management helps avoid overload and maintain productivity.

Implementation Steps:

• **Planning and Prioritization:** Organize tasks by priority and plan your day so that you focus on the most important tasks during periods of peak mental energy.

• **Pomodoro Technique:** Use the Pomodoro technique to work in short intervals with breaks. This helps avoid overload and maintain high concentration.

• **Minimizing Distractions:** Create an environment with minimal distractions. Turn off unnecessary notifications on your phone and computer to avoid scattering attention.

• **Reading and Learning:** Regularly devote time to learning and developing new skills. This increases mental energy and helps maintain clarity of thought.

Common Mistakes:

• **Multitasking:** Trying to perform several tasks simultaneously can lead to decreased productivity and mental fatigue.

• **Information Overload:** Constant consumption of large amounts of information can cause stress and lower mental energy.

Example: If you feel overwhelmed by the number of tasks, try planning your day using the prioritization method. Focus on the most important tasks in the first half of the day when your mental energy is at its peak, and leave less important tasks for the afternoon.

4. Restoring Spiritual Energy

Importance: Spiritual energy comes from a sense of purpose and values in life. It fuels our motivation and gives us the strength to achieve long-term goals.

Implementation Steps:

• **Self-Reflection:** Set aside time for self-reflection and meditation to understand your life values and find meaning in your activities.

• **Setting Meaningful Goals:** Establish long-term goals that align with your values and give your life purpose. Develop an action plan to achieve these goals.

• **Seeking Inspiration:** Find sources of inspiration that fuel your spiritual energy, such as books, music, art, or religious practices.

• **Volunteering and Helping Others:** Participating in volunteer programs or helping others can increase spiritual energy by giving you a sense of importance and belonging.

Common Mistakes:

• **Ignoring Spiritual Needs:** Neglecting your spiritual needs can lead to a loss of motivation and a sense of purpose.

• **Lack of Life Goals:** A lack of clear goals can cause feelings of confusion and loss of spiritual energy.

Example: If you feel that your work is no longer fulfilling, set aside time for self-reflection. Think about what is important to you in life and how you can integrate that into your work or find a new activity that aligns with your values.

Final Tips for Implementing Energy Management

Successfully implementing energy management requires not only following certain practices but also a conscious approach to organizing your life. Below are some key tips to help maintain high energy levels and achieve stable productivity in the long term.

1. Recognizing Energy Rhythms

Description: Every person has unique energy rhythms throughout the day. These are times when you feel most energetic and times when your energy decreases. Understanding these rhythms is essential for effectively planning your day.

How to Implement:

• **Monitor Your State:** Over several days, record when you feel most productive and when you experience energy dips. Typically, these are morning hours or the period after lunch.

Chapter 7: Energy Management

- **Plan Tasks:** Schedule the most important and challenging tasks during peak energy periods. Save less critical tasks that don't require high concentration for times when your energy decreases.
- **Use Rhythms for Rest:** Identify times when you feel the need to rest and use them for short breaks or meditation. This will help restore energy and continue working with renewed strength.

Example: If you notice that your highest energy level is in the morning, schedule the most important tasks, such as meetings or complex problem-solving, for this time. After lunch, when energy dips, focus on simpler tasks like checking emails or planning for the next day.

2. Planning Rest

Description: Rest is an integral part of effective energy management. Regular breaks and sufficient rest help prevent burnout, maintain physical and mental health, and ensure stable productivity.

How to Implement:

- **Include Breaks in Your Schedule:** Plan short breaks every 60-90 minutes of work. These can be 5-10 minutes for stretching, walking, or simply relaxing without screens.
- **Ensure Adequate Sleep:** Allocate 7-8 hours for sleep each night. Create a bedtime ritual that helps you relax and prepare for rest, such as reading or meditation.
- **Schedule Longer Periods of Rest:** Include time for full rest in your weekly schedule, such as weekends without work or short vacations. This allows for complete recovery and reduces stress levels.

Example: If you work in an office, you can take short breaks after each task to refresh and restore energy. You can go outside, drink a glass of water, or do a few simple exercises. On weekends, plan time for active rest, such as a walk in the park or a trip out of town.

3. Maintaining a Healthy Work-Life Balance

Description: The balance between work and personal life is a key factor in maintaining high energy levels and overall well-being. It's important to find time for your interests, family, and friends, which helps restore energy and maintain motivation.

How to Implement:

• **Clearly Define Work Hours:** Set clear boundaries between work and personal time. Finish work at a set time and avoid working outside of work hours unless absolutely necessary.

• **Engage in Enjoyable Activities:** Include time in your schedule for hobbies that bring you pleasure and restore energy. This can be sports, reading, creativity, or other activities.

• **Spend Time with Loved Ones:** Allocate time for socializing with family and friends. This helps maintain emotional energy and support a positive mood.

Example: If you often work overtime, try setting a rule to finish work by 6 PM and not check work emails in the evening. Use the evening to spend time with family, engage in sports, or pursue a hobby that helps maintain balance and restore energy.

4. Restoring Energy Through Nature

Description: Nature is a powerful source of energy restoration. Walks in the fresh air, relaxation in a park, or active outdoor recreation help reduce stress levels, improve mood, and increase overall energy levels.

How to Implement:

• **Regular Walks:** Plan regular walks in the fresh air, even if it's just a short outing to the park during your lunch break. A walk helps you relax and restore energy.

• **Outdoor Recreation:** Use weekends or vacations for outdoor recreation. This could be hiking in the mountains, a trip to the beach, or camping in the forest. Such activities not only physically restore but also emotionally recharge.

• **Integrating Nature into Daily Life:** If it's not always possible to get out of the city, create "green corners" at home or in the office. For example, add plants to the interior or set up your workspace near a window with a view of nature.

Example: If you feel overwhelmed by work, try making daily walks in the fresh air a part of your routine. Even a 15-minute walk in the park can significantly reduce stress levels and help restore energy. On weekends, plan active outdoor recreation, such as a hike in the mountains or a bike ride.

Chapter 7: Energy Management

10-Day Energy Management Implementation Plan

Over the next 10 days, follow these steps to successfully incorporate energy management principles into your life. This plan will help you gradually integrate energy management, focusing on each of the four aspects of energy: physical, emotional, mental, and spiritual.

Day 1: Identify Energy Rhythms

Task: Pay attention to your energy levels at different times of the day. Record in a journal when you feel most energetic and productive and when you feel most tired.

• **Challenges:** You may notice that your energy fluctuates depending on the time of day or the type of activity. This is normal as everyone has a unique energy rhythm.

• **Solution:** Use this information to plan the following days. Schedule the most important tasks during peak energy times and less demanding ones during periods of lower activity.

• **Example:** If you notice that your peak productivity hours are in the morning, plan the most challenging tasks, such as strategic planning or solving important issues, during this time.

Day 2: Start Working on Physical Energy

Task: Incorporate regular physical exercises into your routine. Today, choose a physical activity you enjoy, such as running, yoga, or swimming, and find time for it.

• **Challenges:** You might feel a lack of motivation or time to exercise. This is normal, especially if you're not used to regular physical activity.

• **Solution:** Start with small steps. For instance, take a short 20-minute walk or do light stretching in the morning. Gradually increase the duration and intensity of your workouts.

• **Example:** If you usually lead a sedentary lifestyle, start with a 10-minute walk after lunch. This will help improve your mood and boost your energy levels.

Day 3: Focus on Managing Emotional Energy

Task: Begin practicing emotional management techniques. Set aside time for meditation or breathing exercises that will help reduce stress and increase emotional resilience.

- **Challenges:** You might find it difficult to concentrate during meditation or breathing exercises, especially if you have no experience in such practices.
- **Solution:** Start with short 5-minute sessions. Focus on your breathing and try to let go of all thoughts. Gradually increase the duration of the meditation sessions.
- **Example:** Before starting your workday, take 5 minutes to meditate. Sit in a quiet place, close your eyes, and concentrate on your breathing. This will help calm your mind and boost your emotional energy for the day.

Day 4: Optimize Mental Energy

Task: Plan your workday using the Pomodoro technique. Work in 25-minute intervals with short 5-minute breaks. This will help maintain concentration and avoid overload.

- **Challenges:** You might find it difficult to stick to this rhythm due to a habit of working without breaks or frequent distractions.
- **Solution:** Set a timer and strictly follow the intervals. Turn off notifications on your phone and computer to minimize distractions.
- **Example:** If you usually work without a break for several hours, try working in 25-minute intervals with 5-minute breaks today. After several cycles, take a longer 15-20 minute break.

Day 5: Restore Spiritual Energy

Task: Spend time on self-reflection. Identify your life values and think about how they align with your current activities and goals. Write down your thoughts in a journal.

- **Challenges:** You might feel confused or unsure about how to connect your values with everyday activities.
- **Solution:** Ask yourself questions like, "What is truly important to me in life? How does my work or activities align with my values?" This will help you find meaning and motivation.
- **Example:** If you feel a loss of motivation in your work, try thinking about how it might align with your values. For example, if you value helping others, focus on aspects of your work that allow you to make a positive contribution to society.

Day 6: Plan Breaks and Rest

Task: Schedule regular breaks and rest time into your routine. Take short 5-10 minute breaks every 60-90 minutes of work throughout the day.

Chapter 7: Energy Management

• **Challenges:** You might feel that breaks distract you from work or reduce productivity, especially if you're used to working without breaks.

• **Solution:** Try to see breaks as an essential part of the work process that helps maintain high energy and concentration levels. Plan your breaks in advance.

• **Example:** If you usually work for several hours without a break, try taking a 5-minute break after each hour of work today. Use this time to stretch, walk, or simply relax.

Day 7: Restore Energy Through Nature

Task: Spend time outdoors. Arrange a walk in the park or a trip to nature to restore energy and reduce stress.

• **Challenges:** You might feel that you don't have time for walks or outdoor activities due to a busy schedule.

• **Solution:** Find even a short amount of time to spend outdoors. Even a 15-minute walk can significantly improve your mood and restore energy.

• **Example:** If your schedule is very tight, try taking a short walk during your lunch break. Walk through a park or simply step outside for some fresh air. This will help relieve tension and restore your energy.

Day 8: Maintain a Healthy Work-Life Balance

Task: Allocate time for your interests and loved ones. Set clear boundaries between work and personal time today, finish your workday at the set time, and engage in activities that bring you joy.

• **Challenges:** You may feel pressure to continue working outside of work hours or neglect personal time due to work obligations.

• **Solution:** Remember that balance between work and personal life is crucial for long-term success and overall well-being. Set clear boundaries and stick to them.

• **Example:** Finish your workday at 6 PM and spend the evening on activities you enjoy, such as reading a book, meeting friends, or playing sports. This will help maintain emotional energy and improve overall well-being.

Day 9: Evaluate Your Energy Management Achievements

Task: Assess your achievements over the past 8 days. Reflect on what is working well and where improvements are needed. Write down your observations in a journal.

- **Challenges:** You may feel that you haven't achieved everything you planned or that some changes were difficult to implement.

- **Solution:** Be honest with yourself but avoid being too critical. Energy management is a process that takes time. Identify your achievements and continue working on challenging aspects.

- **Example:** If you notice that some habits, like regular breaks or meditation, were difficult to implement, think about ways to make them a part of your daily routine. You might need to find a more convenient time or change your approach.

Day 10: Review and Adjust

Task: Review the results of your energy management implementation over the past 9 days and develop a plan for the future. Make adjustments to the aspects that need improvement.

- **Challenges:** You may find that not all practices are easy to implement in daily life or that some require more time to adapt.

- **Solution:** Make adjustments to your plan, focusing on the aspects that need the most attention. Don't be afraid to experiment and find new approaches that better fit your lifestyle.

- **Example:** If you found that certain practices don't fit your schedule or lifestyle, replace them with others that are more adaptable to your needs. For example, if morning meditation doesn't work, try doing it in the evening before bed.

By following this 10-day plan, you'll gradually integrate effective energy management practices into your life, helping you maintain high energy levels, reduce stress, and achieve greater overall well-being.

Reflection and Conclusions

Assessing the success of energy management implementation is a crucial step toward enhancing personal effectiveness and overall well-being. Reflection allows you to pause, analyze your achievements, identify strengths and weaknesses, and draw conclusions that will help you improve your energy management process in the future.

The Importance of Reflection

Reflection is a process of self-contemplation that helps you better understand your actions, thoughts, and feelings. It allows you to identify successes and mistakes, make conclusions, and develop new strategies for achieving energy balance. Reflection is critically important because it helps you:

Chapter 7: Energy Management

- **Understand Changes:** By understanding how your energy levels and productivity have changed after implementing new practices, you can evaluate the effectiveness of those changes.

- **Identify Barriers:** Analyzing the difficulties and obstacles you encountered helps you identify areas that need further improvement.

- **Develop a Future Plan:** Based on the analysis of your achievements and challenges, you can adjust your energy management plan to achieve even better results in the future.

Feedback

Receiving feedback from others can be a valuable tool for evaluating your progress in energy management. Communicating with friends, colleagues, or mentors can provide an objective view of how your changes have impacted your work and personal life.

Steps for Receiving Feedback:

- **Ask for an Objective Evaluation:** Request that those close to you share whether they have noticed changes in your mood, productivity, or behavior since implementing new energy management practices.

- **Engage in Group Discussions:** Participating in group discussions or meetings with like-minded individuals who are also working on managing their energy can be useful for exchanging experiences and receiving advice.

- **Be Open to Criticism:** Accept feedback with gratitude and view it as an opportunity for improvement. Discuss the feedback and find ways to apply it in practice.

- **Example:** If a colleague notices that you have become more focused and calm at work, this could indicate that your practices for managing emotional and mental energy are working. This may encourage you to continue these practices and perhaps share your experience with others.

Review and Adjustment of Practices

Regularly reviewing your energy management practices is necessary to stay flexible and adapt to life changes. Life circumstances can change, and it's important to be ready to adapt your plans according to new challenges and opportunities.

Steps for Reviewing and Adjusting:

• **Analyze Your Results:** Regularly analyze your achievements and the difficulties you encountered to understand what works well and what needs change.

• **Make Necessary Adjustments:** If certain practices do not yield the expected results or cause difficulties, don't hesitate to make adjustments. You may need to change the time or method of practice to better fit your schedule.

• **Be Open to New Methods:** Don't stop at what you've achieved. Continue to explore new methods and approaches to energy management that can enhance your effectiveness and well-being.

• **Example:** If you find that morning meditations are not suitable for you due to time constraints, try moving them to the evening or choosing another form of meditation that requires less time. It's important to find an approach that is comfortable and effective for you.

Final Recommendations

• **Continue Developing Energy Management Skills:** Energy management is an ongoing process that requires regular improvement. It's important to keep developing your skills and finding new ways to enhance them.

• **Use Gained Experience:** The experience gained during the implementation of energy management will become a valuable resource for developing effective strategies in the future. Use this experience to improve your practices and achieve new goals.

• **Be Flexible and Open to Change:** Life constantly changes, and it's important to be ready to adapt your energy management approaches. Stay open to new ideas and ready to experiment to make the most of growth and development opportunities.

• **Example:** If you notice that a particular practice, such as evening walks, positively affects your energy level and mood, make it a regular part of your routine. At the same time, be ready to make changes if new circumstances require adjustments to your plans.

Additional Literature and Materials

To continue exploring energy management methods and deepen your knowledge in this area, consider the following books and resources:

1. "The Power of Full Engagement" by Jim Loehr and Tony Schwartz

♦ This book examines energy management in the context of work and life, explaining how balancing physical, emotional, mental, and spiritual energy can enhance productivity and life satisfaction.

2. "Atomic Habits" by James Clear

♦ The book focuses on forming beneficial habits that help effectively manage energy and create a system that supports a stable level of productivity.

3. "The Miracle Morning" by Hal Elrod

♦ This book describes how morning rituals can affect energy levels and success in various areas of life. The author offers practical steps for creating the perfect morning routine.

4. Headspace (Meditation App)

♦ This app offers guided meditations and mindfulness practices that can help improve emotional and mental energy management.

5. "Why We Sleep" by Matthew Walker

♦ The book delves into the scientific aspects of sleep and explains how quality sleep impacts physical, mental, and emotional energy.

6. "Resilience: Hard-Won Wisdom for Living a Better Life" by Eric Greitens

♦ This book explores how to develop resilience and the ability to cope with life's challenges. It helps to understand how spiritual energy influences our lives and how to maintain it.

These resources will help you better understand and implement energy management techniques to achieve greater productivity and life satisfaction.

Chapter 8: Planning and Prioritization

Introduction and Context

In today's world, where the number of tasks, obligations, and opportunities is constantly increasing, the ability to effectively plan your time and prioritize tasks becomes essential. Every day, we face numerous challenges that demand immediate attention, but not all of them are equally important. This is why planning and prioritization are key skills that allow you to succeed in all areas of life—whether it's your career, education, personal relationships, or self-development.

The Importance of Planning and Prioritization

Effective planning involves creating a clear, detailed action plan that helps you achieve the desired outcome within set timeframes. It is a process that allows you to define goals, develop paths to achieve them, and monitor task completion at every stage. Prioritization, on the other hand, helps determine which tasks require immediate attention and which can be postponed or delegated to others. It enables you to focus on the most important matters, thereby avoiding overload and reduced productivity.

Every person has a limited amount of resources, with time being the most valuable. Proper planning and prioritization help you optimize this resource, which, in turn, reduces stress, increases productivity, and ensures a balance between work and personal life.

How Planning and Prioritization Impact Productivity

Planning and prioritization are fundamental tools for enhancing personal productivity. When you have a clear plan, you know what to do and when to do it, which helps avoid procrastination and chaotic work. Simultaneously, well-set priorities allow you to focus on the most important tasks without wasting time on secondary matters that can wait.

These skills also help prevent overload and burnout, as they allow you to balance the number of tasks and distribute them over time so that you can work efficiently without losing energy. For example, using methods such as the Eisenhower Matrix allows you to categorize tasks into four categories based on urgency and importance, simplifying decision-making and enabling you to focus on what truly matters.

Purpose of the Chapter

This chapter aims to teach you how to effectively plan your time and prioritize tasks to achieve high productivity and a balanced life. We will explore the basic principles of planning and prioritization that will help you:

1. Set Clear Goals: Learn how to define short-term and long-term goals that will serve as the foundation for your planning.

2. Develop Realistic Plans: Learn how to create detailed action plans that take into account available resources, deadlines, and potential risks.

3. Prioritize: Master task prioritization methods that will help you determine where to focus your efforts first.

4. Manage Time: Learn how to effectively manage your time to complete tasks on time and avoid overload.

5. Adapt to Changes: Understand how to stay flexible and adapt your plans in the face of unforeseen circumstances, allowing you to maintain effectiveness even in challenging situations.

These skills will help you achieve more in less time while maintaining high work quality and balance between personal and professional life. Planning and prioritization are skills that can transform chaos into a structured process of achieving success.

Core Theory

Planning and prioritization are interconnected processes that help structure your day, week, or even month to accomplish important tasks within set deadlines and achieve your goals. These skills are key to achieving both short-term and long-term results.

Key Principles of Planning

1. Goal Setting

♦ **Instructions:** Begin the planning process by clearly defining your goals. It's important that these goals are specific, measurable, achievable, realistic, and time-bound (SMART goals). Divide your goals into short-term (achievements within the next few days or weeks) and long-term (achievements over several months or years).

♦ **Example:** If you aim to enhance your qualifications, a short-term goal might be to complete an online course within four weeks, while a long term goal could be to earn a certification that improves your chances of promotion within the next six months.

2. Plan Development

♦ **Instructions:** Create a detailed action plan that includes specific steps to achieve each goal. Consider the resources you'll need and set clear deadlines for each phase. The plan should be realistic and account for possible obstacles or changes.

♦ **Example:** To complete the online course, set deadlines for each module. For instance, "Finish Module 1 by Friday, Module 2 by the next Monday." This helps you stay focused on specific tasks and steadily progress toward your goal.

3. Adaptability

♦ **Instructions:** Always be ready to make changes to your plan in response to changing circumstances. Regularly review your plan and adjust it according to new challenges or opportunities. Do not view the plan as a fixed set of actions-it should be a flexible tool.

♦ **Example:** If you planned to finish a course module by Friday but received new work assignments requiring immediate attention, reschedule the module for Saturday or Sunday. This allows you to maintain a balance between work and learning.

4. Time Management

♦ **Instructions:** Set clear time frames for each task and use timers or other time-management tools to monitor your time usage. It's important to stick to the set deadlines and avoid distractions while working on a task.

♦ **Example:** Use the Pomodoro technique-work on a task for 25 minutes without a break, then take a five-minute break. After four such cycles, take a longer break of 15-30 minutes. This helps maintain high concentration and efficiency.

Key Principles of Prioritization

1. Setting Priorities

♦ **Instructions:** Analyze your tasks daily or weekly and prioritize them. Evaluate each task in terms of its importance for achieving your goals and its urgency. Important tasks should always take precedence.

♦ **Example:** If your goal is to complete a project, the most important tasks might be those that directly impact its completion (writing a report, analyzing data), while less important tasks like checking emails can be done later.

2. Eisenhower Matrix

♦ **Instructions:** Prioritize tasks using the Eisenhower Matrix. Categorize tasks into four categories: urgent and important, important but not urgent, urgent but not important, and neither urgent nor important. This helps you understand what to focus on first and what can be postponed or delegated.

♦ **Example:** An urgent and important task might be preparing a presentation for tomorrow's meeting. An important but not urgent task could be working on a long-term project. An urgent but not important task might be responding to emails that can be delegated. Tasks that are neither urgent nor important can be removed from your schedule.

3. Delegation

♦ **Instructions:** If a task does not require your personal involvement, consider delegating it. Identify who in your team or among your colleagues can complete this task, and provide them with the necessary instructions. Delegation frees up time for you to work on more important tasks.

♦ **Example:** If you're leading a team, assign one of the team members to prepare an initial report or gather data for analysis so that you can focus on strategic planning.

4. Resource Allocation

♦ **Instructions:** Consider the limited resources (time, energy, finances) and allocate them in a way that maximizes task efficiency. Focus more resources on the most important tasks and minimize spending on secondary ones.

♦ **Example:** If you have limited time to prepare for an important project, focus on the key aspects of the work and avoid spending too much time on minor details that do not affect the overall result.

Scientific Justification for Planning and Prioritization

The effectiveness of planning and prioritization is supported by numerous studies in psychology, neuroscience, and time management. These studies show that people who regularly use these skills achieve higher results, experience less stress, and maintain a balance between work and personal life.

Stanford University Study: A study conducted at Stanford University found that people who use time management and planning techniques achieve their goals 20-30% more often than those who do not. They also reported reduced stress levels and improved overall well-being.

Harvard University Study: Another study conducted at Harvard showed that effective planning increases productivity by 25%. The study also found that using prioritization, particularly the Eisenhower Matrix, reduces distractions by 40%, significantly improving work efficiency.

Neuroscience Research: Brain activity studies have shown that people who use structured planning have better cognitive function and problem-solving abilities. This is because planning helps reduce cognitive load, allowing the brain to focus on completing specific tasks. Specifically, research has shown that effective planning activates the prefrontal cortex of the brain, which is responsible for decision-making and impulse control.

Project Management Research: Research in project management has shown that effective task prioritization reduces the risk of project deadline overruns by 30%. This study emphasizes the importance of prioritizing tasks and ensuring appropriate resource allocation.

These studies confirm that planning and prioritization not only help increase productivity but also contribute to improved overall well-being, reduced stress levels, and achieving work-life balance. They also demonstrate that these skills are key to effective resource management and achieving long-term goals.

Problematic Situations and Examples

In life, there are often situations where the lack of a clear plan or the inability to prioritize leads to chaos, overload, and decreased productivity. Planning and prioritization can help solve these problems and ensure a stable level of efficiency. Let's examine some common situations where these skills can significantly improve the outcome:

Situation 1: Feeling Overwhelmed by Too Many Tasks

Problem Description: You constantly feel stressed by the enormous number of tasks that need to be completed. Despite being constantly busy, it seems like you're not making any progress. You spend your time working on many tasks simultaneously, but none of them are completed.

- **Example:** One of your days looks like this: you start by responding to emails, then switch to working on a presentation, and after a while, you're distracted by a colleague's call. In the end, neither the presentation, the emails, nor the colleague's issue are fully addressed, leaving you frustrated by the lack of results.

- **Solution:** Use the principle of prioritization. Start your day by analyzing tasks and determining which ones are the most important and urgent. Use the Eisenhower Matrix to categorize tasks by priority and focus on completing one important task at a time. This will help reduce the feeling of being overwhelmed and allow you to achieve specific results.

Situation 2: Procrastination Due to Lack of a Clear Plan

Problem Description: You often postpone important tasks, leading to a buildup of work and increased stress. Procrastination prevents you from completing tasks on time and affects the quality of your work.

• **Example:** You know you need to prepare a report by the end of the week, but due to a lack of a clear plan, you keep putting it off, spending time on less important tasks like checking social media or working on other, less critical tasks.

• **Solution:** Create a detailed plan for completing the task. Break the work into several stages and set clear deadlines for each. Use the Pomodoro technique to maintain concentration while working. This will help you avoid procrastination and complete tasks on time.

Situation 3: Inability to Prioritize

Problem Description: You have many tasks, but you don't know where to start. All tasks seem important, and you spend time on less priority tasks, leaving the important ones for later.

• **Example:** You have several projects on your desk, all of which seem important, but you can't decide where to focus first. As a result, you spend the day working on less important tasks, leaving the most crucial ones for later.

• **Solution:** Use the Eisenhower Matrix to prioritize tasks based on urgency and importance. This will help you clearly understand which tasks require immediate attention and which can be postponed or delegated. Focus on completing the most important tasks first.

Situation 4: Burnout Due to Lack of Work-Life Balance

Problem Description: You feel that work occupies all your time, leaving no room for personal life. This leads to burnout, decreased productivity, and negatively affects your overall well-being.

• **Example:** You constantly stay late at work to complete all tasks, but this affects your relationships with family and friends, as well as your physical and emotional health. You start feeling constantly tired and lose motivation for work.

• **Solution:** Set clear boundaries between work and personal life. Plan your day to leave time for rest and activities that bring you joy. Use planning and prioritization techniques to focus on the most important tasks and complete your work on time.

Situation 5: Inability to Complete Projects

Problem Description: You often start new projects but rarely finish them. This leads to scattered efforts and a sense of dissatisfaction due to unfinished business.

- **Example:** You take on a new project with great enthusiasm, but after a while, you lose interest or face obstacles that cause you to put the work aside. As a result, you have several unfinished projects and a constant feeling of dissatisfaction.

- **Solution:** Focus on one project at a time and develop a clear action plan for completing it. Use the "eating the elephant one bite at a time" technique-break a large project into smaller stages and gradually complete them. This will help maintain motivation and achieve results.

Situation 6: Constant Distraction by Less Important Tasks

Problem Description: You are constantly distracted by unimportant tasks or minor issues, which prevent you from focusing on important projects. This reduces your productivity and leads to delays in completing important tasks.

- **Example:** You start the day by working on an important report, but constantly interrupt to answer emails, take calls, or deal with other unimportant matters. As a result, you don't finish the report on time.

- **Solution:** Set clear time frames for working on important tasks and minimize distractions. Turn off notifications on your phone and computer while working, and focus on completing one task at a time. This will help you increase productivity and complete important projects on time.

Examples of Successful Application of Planning and Prioritization

Example 1: Indra Nooyi (Former CEO of PepsiCo)

- **Description:** Indra Nooyi, who led PepsiCo for 12 years, is known for her strategic approach to planning and prioritization. She always developed clear long-term plans for the company, allowing her to achieve significant results and remain competitive in the market.

- **Result:** Thanks to her strategic planning, Nooyi transformed PepsiCo into one of the most successful companies in the world. She also managed to balance her professional and personal life while remaining one of the most influential women in business.

Chapter 8: Planning and Prioritization

Example 2: Richard Branson (Founder of Virgin Group)

• **Description:** Richard Branson, the founder of Virgin Group, manages a large number of businesses in various industries. He is known for his creative approach to planning and prioritization, which allows him to effectively manage companies while also finding time for personal interests.

• **Result:** Branson successfully manages various businesses, including airlines, media, financial services, and space travel, thanks to his ability to effectively plan and prioritize. His approach to time management allows him to stay at the forefront of innovation.

Example 3: Michelle Obama (Former First Lady of the United States)

• **Description:** Michelle Obama, the former First Lady of the United States, is known for her ability to juggle multiple responsibilities through clear planning and prioritization. She successfully balanced her role as First Lady, mother, and public figure while remaining active in social initiatives.

• **Result:** Thanks to her approach to planning, Michelle Obama implemented several national programs, including the "Let's Move!" initiative to combat childhood obesity. She also found time to write her memoirs, which became a bestseller.

Example 4: Serena Williams (Professional Tennis Player)

• **Description:** Serena Williams, one of the most successful tennis players in history, is known for her approach to planning training and prioritizing goals. She meticulously plans every aspect of her career, including training, rest, and recovery, allowing her to stay at the top of the sports world for many years.

• **Result:** Williams achieved success on the international stage, winning numerous Grand Slam tournaments thanks to her discipline and ability to prioritize the most important aspects of her career.

Example 5: Andrew Carnegie (Industrialist and Philanthropist)

• **Description:** Andrew Carnegie, one of the most famous industrialists and philanthropists of the 19th century, used planning and prioritization to develop his steel empire. He always clearly defined his goals and developed strategies to achieve them, which allowed him to become one of the wealthiest people of his time.

- **Result:** Carnegie was able to build a steel empire thanks to his approach to planning and prioritization. After achieving his business goals, Carnegie focused on philanthropy, donating a significant portion of his wealth to the development of education and culture.

Example 6: J.K. Rowling (Author of the Harry Potter Series)

- **Description:** J.K. Rowling, the author of the Harry Potter series, used planning and prioritization to balance writing books with raising children and overcoming financial difficulties.
- **Result:** Thanks to clear planning and prioritization, Rowling was able to complete the series, which became a global bestseller and changed her life.

These examples demonstrate how effective planning and prioritization can lead to success in various fields, whether it's business, sports, or personal endeavors.

Practical Tips and Solutions for Implementing Planning and Prioritization

To successfully incorporate planning and prioritization into your life, it is essential to follow certain principles and apply proven techniques. Below are practical tips and solutions that will help make planning and prioritization an integral part of your daily routine.

1. Goal Setting

Description: Start by setting clear goals. Goal setting is the foundation of the entire planning process. It's important that your goals are SMART: Specific, Measurable, Achievable, Relevant, and Time-bound.

Instructions: After setting your goals, write them down. Divide your goals into short-term and long-term. Short-term goals can be achieved within a few days or weeks, while long-term goals may take months or even years.

Example: Imagine you work in the sales department, and your company has tasked you with increasing sales by 20% over the year. To achieve this goal, you need to set several short-term and long-term goals. Short-term goals could include increasing the number of client calls by 15% over the next month or completing a sales techniques training course within six weeks. A long-term goal could be increasing sales in your region by 20% by the end of the year. To make these goals SMART, you should specify them, such as increasing the number of client calls from 50 to 58 per week, completing the training and passing the final test by October 31, and achieving sales of $1.2 million by the end of December.

Solution: Regularly review your goals and adjust them as needed. This will help you stay on track and maintain motivation.

2. Creating a Plan

Description: After setting goals, create a detailed action plan. The plan should consider all the necessary steps to achieve your goals and the resources needed.

Instructions: Distribute tasks over time. For each goal, identify the key stages to achieve it. Set deadlines for each stage to ensure timely completion.

Example: Imagine you are planning to organize a large conference for your company in six months. To successfully manage this task, you need to create a detailed action plan. You first identify key stages: selecting a venue, finding speakers, marketing the event, registering participants, organizing technical support, and finally, the day of the conference. Each of these stages is broken down into smaller tasks. For example, selecting a venue involves finding available locations, signing contracts, and planning logistics. Finding speakers includes creating a list of potential speakers, contacting them, discussing topics, and signing contracts. You set deadlines for each task: the venue should be chosen four months before the event, speakers confirmed three months before, the marketing campaign started two months before, and so on.

Solution: Use project management apps or simple task lists to track progress. This will help you stay organized and not miss important details.

3. Using the Eisenhower Matrix

Description: The Eisenhower Matrix is an effective tool for prioritizing tasks. It helps determine which tasks are important and urgent and which can be postponed or delegated.

Instructions: Divide your tasks into four categories: urgent and important, important but not urgent, urgent but not important, and neither urgent nor important. Start with the most important tasks.

Example: Imagine you are a project manager with several tasks for the week. You need to complete a report for a client, prepare a presentation for an internal meeting, respond to dozens of emails, and meet with a supplier to discuss the terms of a new contract. All these tasks seem important, but they vary in urgency.

Using the Eisenhower Matrix, you can categorize these tasks:

Urgent and Important: Completing the client report (deadline tomorrow).

Important but Not Urgent: Preparing the presentation for the internal meeting (meeting in three days).

Urgent but Not Important: Responding to emails (must be done today but does not impact strategic goals).

Neither Urgent nor Important: Preparing for the meeting with the supplier, which can be postponed.

Solution: Review your tasks weekly using the Eisenhower Matrix to ensure you focus on the most important tasks.

4. Time Management

Description: Effective time management is a key factor for successful planning. Time control helps avoid overload and ensure timely task completion.

Instructions: Use timers or other tools to track the time you spend on each task. The Pomodoro Technique is one of the most effective time management methods.

Example: You are working on a complex analytical report that requires high concentration and attention to detail. However, you often get distracted by checking emails, messages, or colleagues coming in with questions. As a result, working on the report takes all day, and you don't finish it on time. To avoid this, you decide to apply the Pomodoro Technique. You set a timer for 25 minutes and focus exclusively on the report, not allowing yourself to get distracted. After 25 minutes of work, you take a 5-minute break, during which you can check your mail or do other small tasks. After four such cycles, you take a longer break of 15-30 minutes. Using this approach, you notice that your productivity increases, and you finish the report faster than before. Additionally, regular short breaks help avoid fatigue and maintain high concentration throughout the day. This approach allows you to use your time efficiently and avoid distractions.

Solution: Use digital tools like Trello or Todoist to track time and plan tasks. This will help you maintain high productivity and avoid distractions.

5. Adaptability

Description: Life often brings surprises, so it's important to stay flexible and ready to adjust your plans. Adaptability allows you to respond effectively to new challenges and adjust your actions to new conditions.

Instructions: Regularly review your plans and be ready to make changes if necessary. If a new situation arises that requires your attention, adjust your priorities and plans.

Example: Imagine you are managing a marketing campaign for a new product. Initially, you developed a detailed plan that included preparing promotional materials, launching the campaign on social media, and collaborating with influencers. However, during the preparation for the campaign launch, new data emerges about changes in consumer behavior, and you realize that the initial plan needs adjustment. Instead of following the old plan, you decide to revise the strategy. You conduct additional analysis and decide to shift the campaign's focus from social media to platforms where the new target audience spends more time. You also change the content of the promotional materials to align with new trends. By taking this approach, you maintain flexibility and adapt to new conditions, allowing the campaign to remain effective. Adaptability helps you avoid failure and achieve your goals despite changing circumstances.

Solution: Create "buffer time" in your schedule for unforeseen situations. This will help you stay flexible and ready for changes.

6. Delegation

Description: Delegation is an essential part of prioritization. It allows you to free up time for important tasks by assigning less critical tasks to others.

Instructions: Identify tasks that can be done by others and delegate them to the appropriate people. Provide clear instructions and monitor the progress of the delegated tasks.

Example: You work as a department manager in a company and are tasked with developing a new sales strategy. However, in addition to this task, you have many other responsibilities, including routine administrative tasks like preparing reports, checking documents, and coordinating meetings. To effectively allocate your time and focus on developing the strategy, you decide to delegate some of your responsibilities to your team. You assign one of your employees to prepare reports and coordinate meetings, and another to check documents. You provide them with clear instructions and define the expected results. By delegating, you free up time to work on the strategy and can focus on the task that is most important to the company. Meanwhile, your employees have the opportunity to develop their skills and take on more responsibility. This creates a positive atmosphere in the team and increases overall productivity.

Solution: Learn to trust your team and avoid micromanaging. This will help you use your time more effectively and focus on more important tasks.

7. Resource Allocation

Description: Resources like time, energy, and finances are limited, so it's important to learn how to allocate them properly among tasks. This will allow you to achieve maximum results with minimal costs.

Instructions: Analyze your resources and determine which tasks require the most time and energy investments. Focus on tasks that have the greatest impact on achieving your goals.

Example: You are working on several projects simultaneously and feel that you cannot complete everything on time. Some tasks require more time and attention than others, and you begin to notice that you are spending a lot of time on less important matters, leaving important projects for later. To solve this problem, you decide to analyze how you use your resources-time and energy. You identify that the most important tasks, which have the greatest impact on achieving your goals, are completing a project with a major client and preparing for a strategic meeting. You decide to allocate more time to these tasks, working on them in the first half of the day when your productivity is highest. Less important tasks, like routine correspondence and meetings, you plan for the second half of the day when your energy level may be lower. This allows you to use your resources effectively and achieve maximum results without overloading.

Solution: Identify your peak productivity periods (times of day when you work best) and use them to complete the most important tasks. This will help you use your energy efficiently.

8. Creating Habits for Successful Planning

Description: Planning should become part of your daily routine. Creating useful habits will help you automate the planning process and make it more effective.

Instructions: Set a specific time each day or week for planning. For example, you can dedicate 10-15 minutes at the beginning or end of the day to reviewing tasks and creating a plan for the next day.

Example: Imagine you often start your workday without a clear plan and spend a lot of time solving urgent but unimportant tasks. This leads to important matters being left unfinished, and you feel stressed due to inefficiency. To change this situation, you decide to create a habit of daily planning. Every evening before bed, you dedicate 15 minutes to analyzing tasks for the next day and creating an action plan. You write down the main goals for the day, identify priority tasks, and allocate time for their completion. Thanks to this habit, you start each day with a clear plan and focus on important tasks. This helps you increase productivity and reduce stress levels. Additionally, the habit of planning allows you to better control your time and achieve your goals.

Solution: Use planning apps or paper planners to write down your tasks and monitor their completion. This will help you stay organized and not forget important matters.

9. Reflection and Plan Adjustment

Description: Reflection is an important part of the planning process. It allows you to assess successes and failures and adjust plans accordingly.

Instructions: Regularly review your plans and analyze their effectiveness. Ask yourself what was done well and what could be improved. Use this analysis to adjust your future plans.

Example: You complete a major project and want to understand what went well and what can be improved in the future. To do this, you decide to reflect and analyze your experience. You set aside time to review all project stages and ask yourself a few questions: What worked best? What challenges arose during task execution? How could I improve project management? You also ask for feedback from team members to get their opinions on what could have

Chapter 8: Planning and Prioritization

been done better. Thanks to this reflection, you draw conclusions that will help you improve your planning and project management skills in the future. You also adjust your approaches to work, considering the experience gained. This allows you to constantly improve and achieve better results in future projects.

Solution: Keep a reflection journal where you write down your observations and conclusions. This will help you better understand your successes and challenges and draw conclusions for the future.

10. Maintaining Work-Life Balance

Description: Work-life balance is a key factor for long-term productivity and well-being. Proper planning helps maintain this balance by ensuring time for work, rest, and personal activities.

Instructions: Plan your time to leave room for rest and personal matters. Set clear boundaries between work time and personal life to avoid burnout.

Example: You work in a managerial position, and your job takes up most of your time. Often, you stay late at work to finish all the tasks, but this begins to affect your personal life. You feel tired and burnt out, and your relationships with family and friends start to suffer. To solve this problem, you decide to create clear boundaries between work and personal life. You start planning your workday to finish all major tasks by 6 PM and not take work home. You also allocate time for rest and activities that bring you joy and help restore energy. Thanks to this approach, you begin to feel better, productivity at work increases, and you find more time to spend with family and friends. This helps you maintain a work-life balance and avoid burnout.

Solution: Use time management techniques like time blocking to create clear boundaries between work and personal life. This will help you maintain a healthy balance and stay productive in the long term.

10-Day Implementation Plan for Effective Planning and Prioritization

Day 1: Goal Setting

- **Task:** Define short-term and long-term goals.

- **Details:** Dedicate the first day to analyzing your priorities and setting clear goals. Write them down in your planning journal and prioritize them. Ensure each goal meets SMART criteria. Setting specific goals gives you a clear direction and establishes a foundation for the upcoming steps.

- **Example:** A marketing professional might set a short-term goal to increase the company's social media followers by 15% over the next three months. A long-term goal could be to achieve a managerial position within two years.

- **Potential Challenges:** You might find it difficult to pinpoint specific goals. Start by analyzing your current responsibilities and tasks, focusing on those with the most significant impact on your growth and career.

Day 2: Detailed Action Plan Creation

- **Task:** Develop a detailed action plan to achieve your goals.
- **Details:** Break down each goal into specific tasks and set deadlines for their completion. The plan should be realistic, considering available resources. Record the plan in your journal to track progress.
- **Example:** Someone aiming to increase social media followers might create a plan involving ad campaigns, influencer partnerships, and regular content analysis. Set deadlines for each step, such as "launch the ad campaign within the next week."
- **Potential Challenges:** There may be a temptation to overload yourself with tasks. Remember, the plan should be achievable, so avoid excessive task load.

Day 3: Task Prioritization

- **Task:** Prioritize tasks using the Eisenhower Matrix.
- **Details:** Categorize your tasks into four quadrants: urgent and important, important but not urgent, urgent but not important, and neither urgent nor important. This will help you focus on the most critical tasks and avoid overload.
- **Example:** A project manager might prioritize tasks like preparing a client presentation (urgent and important), planning a strategy for a new product (important but not urgent), and responding to emails (urgent but not important).
- **Potential Challenges:** It may be challenging to determine which tasks are truly important. Focus on those that significantly impact your goals.

Day 4: Time Management

- **Task:** Set clear deadlines for each task and monitor your time.
- **Details:** Use timers or apps to track the time spent on each task. Setting deadlines will help you stick to your plan and avoid delays.
- **Example:** Someone preparing a report might use the Pomodoro Technique: work for 25 minutes without interruption, followed by a 5-minute break. This maintains concentration and efficient use of time.
- **Potential Challenges:** It might be difficult to stick to deadlines due to unforeseen circumstances. If issues arise, review and adjust your plans.

Day 5: Start a Planning Journal

- **Task:** Begin keeping a planning journal.
- **Details:** Record your plans, tasks, and priorities in a dedicated journal or app. This will help you better structure your time and track your progress.
- **Example:** A person managing multiple projects simultaneously can use a planning journal to track deadlines, record ideas, and analyze completed tasks. This helps manage time more effectively and avoid overload.
- **Potential Challenges:** There might be a temptation to ignore the journal or only record some tasks. Try to be consistent and write down all important tasks and plans.

Day 6: Pre-Planning Your Day

- **Task:** Plan your day in advance.
- **Details:** In the evening before bed, create a plan for the next day. Write down the main tasks, prioritize them, and estimate how much time you plan to spend on each task.
- **Example:** Someone planning an important meeting the next day can prepare by writing down all necessary tasks and preparing materials. This allows for a clear start to the day and avoids morning chaos.
- **Potential Challenges:** It might be difficult to find time for planning in the evening. Try to set aside specific time, such as before bed.

Day 7: Review Plans and Priorities

- **Task:** Review your plans and priorities.
- **Details:** Weekly, analyze your tasks and priorities to ensure you are focused on the most important goals. Make necessary adjustments.
- **Example:** A project manager can review progress weekly and adjust the plan according to new challenges and opportunities. This helps maintain flexibility and respond to changes.
- **Potential Challenges:** Finding time for regular plan reviews might be challenging. Try to make it part of your weekly routine, such as Friday evening or Monday morning.

Day 8: Practice Adaptability

• **Task:** Practice adaptability.

• **Details:** If unforeseen situations arise, be ready to make changes to your plan. This will help you stay effective even in changing conditions.

• **Example:** A person working on a long-term project might face unexpected changes in client requirements. Instead of panicking, review your plan and adapt it to the new conditions.

• **Potential Challenges:** It can be difficult to change plans if you're used to a clear structure. Remember that flexibility is key to success in a dynamic environment.

Day 9: Time Tracking Focus

• **Task:** Focus on time tracking.

• **Details:** Use timers or specific apps to track task completion within set deadlines. This helps increase productivity and avoid delays.

• **Example:** A person preparing for an important project might use a timer to track the time spent on different work stages. This helps avoid delays and finish the project on time.

• **Potential Challenges:** Sticking to deadlines might be difficult due to external factors. If this happens, review your plans and make necessary adjustments.

Day 10: Achievement Assessment

• **Task:** Assess your achievements in planning and prioritization.

• **Details:** Note any changes in your productivity and overall stress levels. Record what worked best and what needs improvement.

• **Example:** Someone implementing planning and prioritization can evaluate their progress after 10 days and identify the most effective methods. For instance, you might find that evening planning significantly reduced stress and increased productivity.

• **Potential Challenges:** Not all methods may work as expected. This is normal-experiment and adjust your approach to find what works best for you.

Reflection and Conclusions

Reflection is a critical component in the process of implementing any new practice, and planning and prioritization are no exception. Evaluating success, identifying challenges, and developing ways to improve help to refine skills and achieve greater results in the future.

The Importance of Reflection

Reflection allows you to pause and assess how successfully you have incorporated new approaches to planning and prioritization. This is the time to analyze which methods worked best, what can be improved, and what changes should be made to your daily routine.

Example: Someone who has been actively working on improving their planning skills over the past two weeks might reflect to evaluate the effectiveness of the methods used. For instance, they may discover that using the Eisenhower Matrix significantly boosted productivity, but time management with the Pomodoro Technique needs improvement.

Reflection helps identify mistakes or gaps and develop strategies to address them in the future. This not only enhances skills but also maintains high motivation on the path to achieving goals.

Feedback

Feedback from others can also be a valuable tool for improving your planning and prioritization process. Engaging with colleagues, friends, or mentors provides another perspective on your successes and areas for improvement.

Example: A person working on enhancing their time management system might ask their supervisor or a colleague to evaluate their productivity over the past month. If colleagues notice that you have become more organized and timely in completing tasks, it confirms that your new approaches are working. If shortcomings are pointed out, it gives you the opportunity to review your methods and make necessary adjustments.

Feedback provides an objective view of your achievements and identifies areas for further growth. It helps reinforce successful practices while uncovering areas that need additional effort.

Reviewing and Adjusting Practices

After analyzing your achievements and receiving feedback, it's crucial to regularly review your planning and prioritization practices. Life circumstances can change, so it's essential to be ready to adapt your plans and methods to new conditions.

Example: Someone working in the IT field who is implementing prioritization methods might find that a new major project requires revisiting their daily plans and allocating more time to new tasks. They might decide to reduce time on less important tasks or delegate some responsibilities to ensure effective execution of new duties.

Regularly reviewing practices helps you stay flexible and adapt to changes. It ensures continuous development and prevents stagnation in your achievements.

Final Recommendations

1. Continue Developing Planning and Prioritization Skills: This is an ongoing process that requires continuous practice and improvement. Learn new methods, experiment with different approaches, and find what works best for you.

2. Use Gained Experience to Develop Effective Strategies for the Future: Analyze your successes and failures to apply more effective strategies in the future. Develop new plans based on your experience and constantly refine them.

3. Be Flexible and Open to Change: Life constantly changes, and your plans should be ready to adapt. Don't hesitate to change your approaches if they cease to be effective, and remain open to new opportunities.

4. Allow Time for Reflection: Regularly analyze your achievements and adjust your plans according to new circumstances. This will help you stay on track and achieve your goals.

5. Seek Inspiration and Learn from Others: Explore how other successful people use planning and prioritization in their lives. Read books, articles, and blogs on this topic to find new ideas and approaches.

Additional Materials and Literature for Further Study

To further deepen your understanding of planning and prioritization and to continue developing these skills, I recommend exploring the following resources:

1. Books:

♦ "The 7 Habits of Highly Effective People" by Stephen Covey – A classic book covering various aspects of time management and prioritization.

♦ "Eat That Frog!" by Brian Tracy – A practical guide to time management and overcoming procrastination.

♦ **"Essentialism:** The Disciplined Pursuit of Less" by Greg McKeown – A book about focusing on what's most important and avoiding overload.

♦ "Getting Things Done" by David Allen – A detailed approach to task management and planning.

2. Online Courses:

♦ **Coursera:** "Time Management for Personal & Professional Productivity" – A course that helps develop time management and prioritization skills.

Chapter 8: Planning and Prioritization

♦ **Udemy:** "Productivity and Time Management for the Overwhelmed" – A course focused on improving productivity through effective planning.

3. Blogs and Articles:

♦ **Harvard Business Review:** Articles on time management and productivity improvement.

♦ **Zen Habits:** A blog dedicated to simplicity, efficiency, and time management.

♦ **Lifehacker:** Tips and strategies for boosting productivity and organizing life.

These resources will help you delve deeper into the subject and find additional strategies for successful planning and prioritization in your life.

Chapter 9: Building a Supportive Environment

Introduction and Context

Success and personal development are inextricably linked to the environment we find ourselves in. The people around us can significantly influence our beliefs, decisions, and motivation. This is why building a supportive environment is one of the key factors in achieving life and professional goals.

A supportive environment is a group of people who contribute to your personal and professional growth, provide emotional support during difficult times, and motivate you to achieve your goals. Such an environment may include friends, family, colleagues, mentors, and other people with whom you regularly interact. They can not only support you in challenging times but also help broaden your horizons, overcome obstacles, and develop new skills.

On the other hand, a negative environment can act as a brake on your development. People who devalue your achievements, criticize your ideas, or constantly remind you of risks and failures can lead to a loss of motivation, increased stress, and even emotional burnout. In such an environment, it is challenging to achieve your goals and maintain self-belief.

The Importance of a Supportive Environment

A supportive environment is crucial for personal development. When you are surrounded by people who believe in you and support your aspirations, you start to feel more confident in your abilities. This boosts self-esteem and helps you handle difficulties more effectively.

Moreover, a supportive environment helps reduce stress levels. Knowing there are people you can rely on in tough times makes you feel more secure and stable. This helps maintain emotional balance and optimism even in challenging situations.

A supportive environment can also be a source of new ideas and opportunities. The people you interact with can share their experiences, knowledge, and contacts with you, opening up new perspectives for your development. Such an environment stimulates you to reach new heights and supports you on your path to success.

Chapter 9: Building a Supportive Environment

How the Environment Influences Success

Your environment significantly impacts your decisions and behavior. If you are surrounded by people who support your aspirations, motivate you, and help you overcome difficulties, your chances of success increase significantly. They not only inspire you to achieve new goals but also provide valuable advice, help you avoid mistakes, and support you during times of uncertainty.

On the other hand, if your environment consists of people who criticize your ideas, do not believe in your abilities, or constantly remind you of risks, it can hinder your development. A negative environment can lead to self-doubt, loss of motivation, and even burnout. In such an environment, it is challenging to achieve your goals and maintain a high level of productivity.

This is why it is essential to learn how to recognize the influence of your environment on your life and make conscious decisions about who you spend your time with. Building a supportive environment requires effort and time, but the result is worth it-your life becomes more harmonious, and achieving your goals becomes more realistic.

Purpose of the Chapter

This chapter aims to teach you how to build a supportive environment that will help you achieve your goals and grow as a person. We will explore the basic principles of creating such an environment, offer tips for developing healthy relationships, and help you create an effective support network.

You will learn how to choose people who contribute to your development, how to build healthy relationships with those around you, and how to avoid toxic relationships that can negatively impact your life. By applying this knowledge in practice, you will be able to create an environment that not only supports you during difficult times but also stimulates you to reach new heights.

Main Theory

A supportive environment consists of people who provide emotional support, motivate you to achieve your goals, and contribute to your personal development. This environment plays a crucial role in shaping your thinking, behavior, and worldview. Building such an environment requires a conscious approach and time, but the result is consistent support, motivation, and growth.

Key Principles of Building a Supportive Environment

1. Choosing Positive People The first step in building a supportive environment is to consciously choose people who positively influence your life. It is important to surround yourself with those who believe in your abilities, support your aspirations, and inspire your development. These people can be friends, colleagues, mentors, or relatives. They help you maintain motivation and confidence in your abilities, even in difficult moments.

Example: A person working on an important project at work constantly feels stressed due to the workload. However, they have several colleagues who support them, help with task distribution, and even offer their ideas. This positive environment not only helps reduce stress levels but also increases productivity as the person feels supported and understood. Additionally, these colleagues inspire them with new ideas, contributing to the overall success of the project.

2. Developing Healthy Relationships Building strong and healthy relationships requires time, effort, and attention. This involves effective communication, mutual respect, and support in difficult situations. Healthy relationships are built on trust and mutual understanding. It is important to be open and sincere in communication, able to listen, and understand others' feelings.

Example: A person leading a team at work can build healthy relationships with colleagues through open communication and mutual support. For instance, during weekly meetings, they encourage the team to discuss not only work-related issues but also how everyone is feeling. This approach creates an atmosphere of trust, where everyone feels valued and supported. This not only strengthens team spirit but also increases work efficiency, as each team member feels appreciated.

3. Mutual Support A supportive environment involves not only receiving support but also providing it. It is important to be ready to help others in difficult moments, offer assistance, and share experiences. Mutual support strengthens relationships and creates a sense of belonging to a community.

Example: A person involved in a volunteer organization actively supports other team members in their endeavors. They not only share their experiences but also offer help in implementing various projects. In turn, other volunteers support them when they initiate a new project. This interaction creates a strong sense of community and contributes to the successful implementation of common goals.

4. Environment that Encourages Development Your environment should stimulate your personal and professional development. This can be a group of people with whom you exchange ideas, knowledge, and experiences. Such an environment helps you broaden your horizons, find new opportunities, and become a better version of yourself.

Example: A person striving for career growth may join a professional community or club where people share their knowledge and experiences. By regularly attending meetings, they meet new people with similar goals and have the opportunity to discuss their ideas with like-minded individuals. This contributes to their professional development and provides new perspectives for career advancement.

5. Recognizing Toxic Relationships It is important to learn to recognize relationships that negatively affect your life. Toxic relationships can lead to lower self-esteem, increased stress, and even depression. It is essential to be able to distance yourself from such people or completely end relationships if they cause more harm than good.

Example: A person notices that one of their colleagues constantly criticizes them and devalues their achievements. Initially, they try to find compromises and improve the relationship, but eventually realize that these interactions cause more harm than good. After this realization, they decide to reduce communication with this person and focus on relationships with those who support and inspire them. This decision helps them regain confidence and reduce stress levels.

Scientific Justification for a Supportive Environment

Scientific studies confirm that social support is an essential factor for improving mental health, reducing stress levels, and increasing overall life satisfaction. Here are three major studies that demonstrate the impact of a supportive environment on our lives:

1. Harvard Study of Adult Development: This is one of the longest-running studies in psychology, which began in 1938 and continues today. It studies the lives of several hundred men, examining the influence of various factors on their health and well-being. One of the key findings of the study is that quality social connections have a greater impact on health and happiness than wealth, fame, or other material factors. People with strong and healthy relationships lived longer, had better health, and were more satisfied with life.

2. University of California, Los Angeles (UCLA) Study: This study examined the impact of social support on stress levels and mental health. It was found that people with strong supportive environments showed lower cortisol levels (the stress hormone) in stressful situations. The study also showed that social support reduces the risk of depression and anxiety disorders and improves the ability to cope with challenges.

3. Organizational Psychology Research: This research showed that employees with supportive environments at work demonstrate higher productivity, less burnout, and greater job satisfaction. A supportive environment contributes to better team interaction, increased trust levels, and reduced conflicts. Employees who feel supported by colleagues and supervisors are more motivated to achieve common goals and have a lower risk of stress-related conditions.

These studies emphasize the importance of building a supportive environment to increase happiness, improve health, and achieve personal and professional goals. They show that the right choice of environment can become a powerful tool for improving the quality of life.

Problem Situations and Examples

In life, there are often situations where the absence of a supportive environment or interactions with toxic people lead to a loss of motivation, increased stress levels, and even depression. Building a supportive environment can help address these issues and provide a stable level of emotional support. Let's consider several typical situations where building a supportive environment can significantly improve the situation:

Situation 1: Loneliness and Feeling of Isolation

Problem Description: A person feels lonely and has no one to share their problems or successes with. They spend most of their time alone, which leads to a feeling of isolation and a gradual decline in emotional well-being. Such a situation can lead to depression and a loss of motivation.

Example: After moving to a new city for work, a person finds it difficult to adapt and make new friends. Work colleagues maintain a professional relationship, but the absence of close friends and family nearby makes them feel lonely. Every evening, returning home, they feel empty as there is no one to share the day's experiences or discuss problems.

Solution: To resolve this situation, it is necessary to actively work on building a new supportive environment. The person can start by joining local clubs, sports teams, or volunteer organizations where there is an opportunity to meet like-minded people. Additionally, they can actively maintain contact with family and friends through video calls to preserve an emotional connection, even being far from them. Creating a supportive environment will help reduce feelings of isolation and increase overall happiness.

Situation 2: Influence of Negative People

Problem Description: A person is surrounded by negative people who constantly criticize and devalue their achievements. This negatively affects their self-esteem and motivation, causing self-doubt and questioning their capabilities. Constant criticism and devaluation from others can lead to emotional burnout and a loss of desire to move forward.

Example: A person works in a team where several colleagues constantly mock their ideas, criticize every step, and do not support new initiatives. Despite putting in a lot of effort to fulfill their duties, the lack of support and constant negative influence from colleagues gradually undermines their confidence. This leads them to start doubting their abilities and even consider leaving the job.

Solution: In such a situation, it is essential to learn to recognize toxic relationships and make decisions to limit contact with negative people. The person can start by finding supportive colleagues or acquaintances who share their values and goals. Additionally, they can consider the possibility of changing jobs or departments where they can work in a more positive environment. A supportive environment will help restore self-confidence and increase motivation.

Situation 3: Lack of Support for Ambitious Goals

Problem Description: A person has ambitions and goals, but their environment does not support their aspirations and even discourages them from achieving them. They face misunderstanding and criticism, which causes doubts about the chosen path and may lead to abandoning their dreams.

Example: A person decides to start their own business, but their family and friends are skeptical about the idea. They constantly remind them of the risks and uncertainties, causing them to feel anxious and doubt their decisions. The lack of support from close people makes them feel lonely in their aspirations, and they begin to wonder if they should even attempt to realize their idea.

Solution: To address this issue, it is crucial to find people who share your ambitions and are ready to support you on the path to achieving your goals. The person can join a business club or entrepreneur community where they can interact with people who have similar experiences and can offer advice and support. Additionally, finding a mentor who can guide them in the business world and provide necessary support would be beneficial. Such an environment will foster development and help confidently move towards their goal.

Situation 4: Need for Professional Mentorship

Problem Description: A person needs mentorship and support in their professional development but doesn't know whom to turn to. They feel lost and lack a clear understanding of how to achieve their career goals. The absence of a mentor or supportive environment can slow down development and cause a loss of motivation.

Example: A young specialist starts working at a large company and wants to build a successful career but doesn't know where to begin. There are no experienced colleagues in their department who could offer advice or help with professional development. This makes them feel lost and unsure about their next steps, negatively affecting their motivation and productivity.

Solution: In this situation, it's important to actively seek opportunities for mentorship. The person can approach more experienced colleagues within the company, join professional communities, or participate in mentoring programs offered in the industry. A mentor can provide valuable advice, share their experience, and help build a clear career development plan. This will help the young specialist feel more confident and motivated, contributing to the achievement of their professional goals.

Situation 5: Team Conflicts Due to Lack of Mutual Support

Problem Description: The team constantly experiences conflicts and misunderstandings due to a lack of mutual support and interaction. This leads to decreased productivity, increased stress levels, and a deteriorating work environment. In such a situation, a supportive environment is absent, making it difficult to achieve common goals.

Example: In a project team consisting of several departments, disputes often arise over the distribution of responsibilities. Colleagues don't support each other, don't share information, and try to avoid extra work. As a result, work progresses slowly, tension builds, and project deadlines are at risk.

Solution: To resolve this issue, it's necessary to create an atmosphere of trust and mutual respect within the team. The leader can organize team-building training sessions where participants learn skills in effective communication, conflict resolution, and mutual support. It's also important to encourage open dialogue among team members and create conditions for the development of healthy relationships. This will help reduce conflicts, increase productivity, and create a more favorable work environment.

Situation 6: Loss of Motivation Due to Toxic Relationships

Problem Description: A person feels a loss of motivation due to prolonged interactions with toxic people. Their ideas and initiatives are constantly criticized or ignored, leading to decreased self-esteem and a loss of desire to act. Toxic relationships can cause burnout and halt personal development.

Example: A person works in a department where their immediate supervisor constantly criticizes their ideas and devalues their contributions to the team. Despite their efforts, they never receive positive feedback or recognition for their achievements. This leads them to start doubting their professional abilities and lose motivation to continue working in the company.

Solution: In such a situation, it is important to assess how much these relationships impact your life and career. If the situation does not change, it may be worth considering changing jobs or transferring to another department where there is a more supportive environment. It's also important to work on building self-confidence, possibly with the help of a coach or psychologist, to overcome the effects of toxic relationships and regain motivation.

Examples of Successful Application of Building a Supportive Environment

A supportive environment plays a crucial role in achieving success in various aspects of life. Here are some examples that illustrate how well-built relationships can foster development and help achieve goals.

Chapter 9: Building a Supportive Environment

Entrepreneurs: An Environment that Supports Business Development

Description: Successful entrepreneurs understand the importance of environment and actively build a network of contacts that includes like-minded people, mentors, and colleagues. They create a supportive environment that helps them overcome difficulties, develop new ideas, and move forward confidently.

Example: Imagine an entrepreneur who decides to launch a new tech startup. Initially, they struggle to find funding, attract customers, and build an effective team. However, they have a mentor who has already succeeded in a similar field. The mentor provides valuable advice on attracting investors, helps develop a business plan, and even introduces them to potential partners. Additionally, the entrepreneur joins a local startup community where they find like-minded individuals to exchange ideas and experiences with. This supportive network helps them overcome initial difficulties and build a successful business that eventually attracts significant investments and becomes one of the leading players in the market.

Successful Person: Sara Blakely, the founder of Spanx, is an example of an entrepreneur who built a strong supportive network around her. At the beginning of her career, Sara had limited business experience but actively sought support from mentors and colleagues who shared her vision. She built a network of contacts that helped her overcome startup challenges and turn Spanx into a multimillion-dollar business. A strong supportive network and belief in her product helped Blakely become one of the most successful female entrepreneurs in the world.

Students: Support on the Path to Academic Success

Description: Students who surround themselves with supportive friends, teachers, and mentors are more likely to succeed in their studies. They can rely on the help of others in preparing for exams, writing papers, and overcoming academic challenges.

Example: A student studying medicine faces high academic demands and constant stress. However, they have a group of friends with whom they study for exams, discuss complex topics, and support each other in times of uncertainty. Additionally, one of their professors becomes their mentor, helping them choose a specialization and providing additional materials for preparation. Thanks to this support, the student not only successfully graduates but also receives a scholarship for further studies abroad.

Successful Person: Bill Gates, even during his time at Harvard, surrounded himself with like-minded individuals with whom he discussed ideas and future projects. His friend Paul Allen became not only a close friend but also a business partner with whom they founded Microsoft. This supportive collaboration was key to their success in the tech world.

Leaders: The Importance of Support in the Workplace

Description: Leaders who have a strong supportive environment find it easier to handle work challenges, as they can rely on the support of their team and colleagues. They create an atmosphere of trust and cooperation, which contributes to the successful achievement of the company's goals.

Example: The leader of a large department in an international company faces the challenge of implementing a complex project within a short timeframe. They understand that they cannot handle all the tasks alone and turn to their colleagues for support. They organize joint meetings where each team member takes on a part of the work, discuss problems, and find solutions together. The supportive environment in the form of colleagues and supervisors helps successfully complete the project within the established deadlines while ensuring high-quality work.

Successful Person: Mary Barra, CEO of General Motors, became the first woman to lead one of the world's largest automotive companies. One of the key factors in her success was creating a strong team she could rely on in the most challenging moments. Barra has always emphasized the importance of a supportive environment and the ability to collaborate with different levels of management to achieve common goals.

Additional Examples of Successful Individuals and Their Cases

1. Warren Buffett: One of the most successful investors of all time, Warren Buffett has always emphasized the importance of the environment in his career. His partnership with Charlie Munger, a renowned financial expert and vice-chairman of Berkshire Hathaway, is an example of a powerful supportive environment that helped Buffett make informed decisions and achieve great business success.

2. Melinda Gates: Melinda, co-founder of the Bill & Melinda Gates Foundation, emphasizes the importance of a supportive environment for the effective work of a charitable organization. She surrounded herself with experts in various fields, helping the foundation achieve significant success in addressing global issues such as fighting infectious diseases and supporting education.

3. Larry Page and Sergey Brin: Google co-founders Larry Page and Sergey Brin always worked in close partnership, which became the foundation for the successful development of the company. They surrounded themselves with talented engineers and managers, helping Google become one of the most innovative companies in the world. Their success was largely due to the supportive environment that stimulated innovative ideas and experiments.

4. Angelina Jolie: The famous actress and humanitarian activist, Angelina Jolie, created a supportive environment that helps her combine a career in film with charitable work. She actively collaborates with the UN and various charitable organizations, enabling her to implement projects aimed at helping refugees and protecting human rights.

Practical Tips and Solutions

To successfully build a supportive environment in your life, it is essential to adhere to certain principles and apply specific methods. This section provides practical advice to help you create and maintain positive and healthy relationships.

1. Analyze Your Environment

Description: The first step in building a supportive environment is to analyze your current circle of communication. It's important to understand who in your life positively influences you and who may be causing more harm than good.

Example: A person decides to spend a day reflecting on their environment. They write down the names of friends, colleagues, and family members they interact with the most. Next to each name, they note the feelings and emotions that arise after interacting with that person. Through this analysis, they realize that a few acquaintances constantly criticize their ideas, leading to feelings of discouragement. At the same time, there are a few people who always support, motivate, and share helpful advice. Realizing this, the person decides to reduce interactions with those who negatively impact their mood and focus on nurturing relationships with those who contribute to their growth.

Solution: Regularly analyze your environment to understand who brings positivity and who brings negativity into your life. This will help you consciously choose the people you want to spend more time with and reduce interactions with those who do not contribute to your development.

2. Choose Positive People

Description: Focus on those who support your goals and aspirations. It's important to actively seek opportunities to connect with people who inspire and motivate you to grow.

Example: A person striving to advance in their career decides to expand their professional network. They start attending industry conferences and seminars, where they meet experts in their field. During these events, they meet several individuals who share their interests and are willing to share their experiences. They actively maintain contact with these people, inviting them for coffee, discussing new ideas, and receiving valuable advice. This new positive environment not only helps them grow professionally but also brings more satisfaction from their work.

Solution: Actively seek opportunities to connect with positive people. These could be professional events, volunteer organizations, or even interest clubs. It's important not just to find such people but also to maintain contact with them, building strong and trusting relationships.

3. Develop Healthy Relationships

Description: Building strong and healthy relationships takes time and effort. This involves effective communication, mutual respect, and support in challenging situations.

Example: A person notices that their relationship with a close friend has started to deteriorate due to a lack of time for communication. To improve the situation, they decide to schedule regular meetings and activities together. Additionally, they begin to communicate more openly with their friend, discussing their thoughts and feelings and actively listening to what concerns their friend. As a result, the relationship begins to improve, with more mutual understanding and support emerging.

Solution: Work on developing healthy relationships. This includes regular communication, mutual support, and respect. It's important to be open in communication and ready to listen to the other person to build strong and trusting relationships.

4. Mutual Support

Description: A supportive environment involves mutual support. This means not only receiving support from others but also being ready to help and support those you care about.

Example: A person working in a large company notices that one of their colleagues often stays late to finish tasks. They decide to offer their help, knowing that the colleague has some difficulties with time management. They start working together on tasks, and thanks to mutual support, both employees manage to complete their work on time and even begin to exchange ideas for process improvements. This not only improves their work results but also strengthens their professional relationship.

Solution: Be ready not only to receive support but also to offer it to others. Mutual support strengthens relationships and creates an atmosphere of trust. Help your friends and colleagues in difficult moments, and you'll notice how your relationships become stronger.

5. Recognize Toxic Relationships

Description: It's important to learn to recognize toxic relationships that can negatively impact your life and act accordingly. If a relationship causes more harm than good, consider distancing yourself or ending it altogether.

Example: A person notices that their coworker constantly criticizes their ideas in meetings, often doing so in a demeaning manner. Initially, they try to ignore these comments, but over time, they realize that it affects their self-esteem and work performance. They decide to talk to their supervisor and discuss the situation. The supervisor supports them, and together they develop a plan to minimize the negative impact of this coworker on the work process. Eventually, the person decides to reduce contact with this coworker and focus on interacting with more supportive colleagues.

Solution: Learn to recognize toxic relationships and make decisions to limit their impact on your life. If the situation doesn't improve, it may be worth considering ending such relationships to protect yourself and your emotional well-being.

6. Surround Yourself with People Who Encourage Development

Description: Your environment should encourage your personal and professional development. This could be a group of people with whom you exchange ideas, knowledge, and experiences. Such an environment helps you broaden your horizons, find new opportunities, and become a better version of yourself.

Example: A person working in the tech industry decides to join a professional club where regular meetings discuss new trends and technologies. They actively participate in these meetings, share their ideas, and receive feedback from other members. Through this, they learn about new technologies that help them improve their professional skills and successfully implement innovations in their work. This environment stimulates them to continually develop and provides new opportunities for career growth.

Solution: Look for an environment that encourages your development. This could be professional clubs, interest communities, or study groups. It's important to actively participate in such communities, exchange ideas, and learn from others to continually grow.

7. Develop Communication Skills

Description: Effective communication is key to building strong relationships. Learn to listen, express your thoughts and emotions, and resolve conflicts.

Example: A person notices that they struggle to express their thoughts during meetings, causing their ideas to often go unheard. They decide to work on their communication skills and enroll in public speaking courses. After a few sessions, they begin to feel more confident speaking in front of colleagues, their ideas become more structured and understandable to others. Over time, they notice that colleagues now often turn to them for advice and support, and their opinion in meetings is now considered.

Solution: Develop your communication skills to interact more effectively with others. This could include learning active listening, public speaking, or conflict resolution. The better you communicate, the stronger and healthier your relationships will be.

8. Be Open to New Connections

Description: Don't be afraid to expand your circle. Look for opportunities to meet new people who may become your like-minded friends.

Example: A person decides to expand their circle of acquaintances and enrolls in leadership development courses. During the courses, they meet people with similar goals and interests. They start communicating and sharing their experiences, discussing the challenges they face in their careers. Over time, these new acquaintances turn into strong professional connections, and the person finds new opportunities for career growth thanks to the support of new friends.

Solution: Be open to new connections and don't hesitate to step out of your usual social circle. This can open up new opportunities for growth and the creation of a supportive environment.

Common Mistakes to Avoid When Building a Supportive Environment

Building a supportive environment is a complex and lengthy process that requires a conscious approach and careful planning. There are several common mistakes to avoid to ensure the successful creation of healthy and strong relationships.

1. Ignoring Negative Influence

Description: One of the most common mistakes is ignoring the negative influence certain people may have on your life. Often, people are reluctant to change their environment, even if it hinders their development, due to fear of loneliness or conflict.

Example: A person has an old friend with whom they have been friends since childhood. However, this friend constantly criticizes their decisions and devalues their achievements. Despite this, the person continues to maintain close contact with them, fearing losing an old friend. Over time, they begin to notice that these interactions negatively affect their self-esteem and motivation, but they hesitate to change the situation.

Conclusion: It's important not to ignore the negative influence of others. If someone in your life constantly brings negativity, it's worth seriously considering whether it's beneficial to continue the relationship. Recognizing this will help you maintain emotional balance and promote personal growth.

2. Expecting Support Without Giving Back

Description: Another common mistake is expecting to receive support from others without being willing to give it. This can lead to one-sided relationships that eventually become superficial and unstable.

Example: A person always turns to their friends for advice or help, but when the friends need support, they often find excuses not to get involved in their problems. Over time, the friends begin to avoid interacting with them, and the person ends up alone with their difficulties, not understanding why the relationships deteriorated.

Conclusion: A supportive environment is based on reciprocity. It's important not only to receive support but also to be ready to provide it to others. Mutual support strengthens relationships and makes them more resilient.

3. Choosing the Wrong Environment

Description: It's important to approach the choice of environment consciously. Often, people find themselves in an environment that doesn't contribute to their development simply because they don't make an effort to seek out like-minded individuals or those who share their values and goals.

Example: A person starts working at a new company and immediately joins a group of colleagues who spend most of their time discussing personal problems and complaining about work. Over time, they begin to notice that these conversations negatively affect their attitude toward work and reduce their motivation. They spend a lot of time participating in such conversations but don't receive support for their professional development.

Conclusion: Choose your environment consciously. It's important to be among people who support your aspirations and values, not those who distract you from achieving your goals. This will help you stay focused and motivated.

4. Lack of Adaptability in Relationships

Description: In the process of building a supportive environment, it's important to be flexible and ready for change. Life circumstances can change, and relationships must adapt to new conditions. Lack of adaptability can lead to conflicts and relationship breakdowns.

Example: A person has a group of friends with whom they maintain close relationships. However, when one of the friends changes jobs and moves to another city, the person doesn't take the initiative to maintain the relationship long-distance. They don't try to organize meetings or communicate online, and over time, their connection weakens, even though the relationship could have remained strong under new circumstances.

Conclusion: Be ready to adapt relationships to new conditions. Changes in life don't have to mean the end of relationships if you're willing to work on maintaining and developing them.

5. Maintaining Toxic Relationships Out of Obligation

Description: Many people continue to maintain toxic relationships out of a sense of obligation or guilt. This can lead to emotional exhaustion and loss of motivation.

Example: A person maintains a relationship with an old acquaintance who is always negative and constantly demands attention. Despite the stress these interactions cause, they hesitate to end the relationship out of fear of offending the acquaintance. Over time, they notice that these relationships lead to emotional burnout and negatively affect other aspects of their life.

Conclusion: It's important not to maintain toxic relationships out of a sense of obligation or guilt. Your emotional well-being should be a priority. If a relationship isn't beneficial and causes negativity, it's worth considering ending it.

6. Overvaluing Quantity Over Quality in Relationships

Description: Another common mistake is believing that more relationships mean more support. However, a large number of superficial relationships don't always provide as much benefit as a few deep and meaningful ones.

Example: A person tries to expand their circle of acquaintances as much as possible, attending many social events and making new contacts. However, these relationships remain superficial, and they rarely turn to these people for support or advice. Over time, they notice that despite having many acquaintances, they feel lonely and lack genuine support.

Conclusion: Instead of trying to expand the number of relationships, focus on their quality. Deep, trusting, and reciprocal relationships are much more valuable than just a large circle of acquaintances. This will help you create an environment that truly supports you in difficult times.

Practical Tips for Building a Supportive Environment

Building a supportive environment requires a conscious approach and systematic work on relationships. Below are practical tips that will help you create and maintain such an environment.

1. Spend More Time with Positive People

Description: Actively seek opportunities to interact with those who inspire and support you. This can include meetings with friends, participating in joint projects, or attending events where you can find like-minded individuals.

Example: A person who decides to spend more time with positive people begins participating in charity events, where they meet new friends who share their values. These new acquaintances inspire them to start new projects and help maintain motivation even in difficult situations.

Solution: Schedule regular time for meetings with positive people. This could be a regular lunch with friends, joint sports activities, or attending cultural events. Focus on interacting with those who support your aspirations and motivate you to develop.

2. Be Open to New Connections

Description: Don't be afraid to expand your circle. Look for opportunities to meet new people who can become your like-minded friends.

Example: A person decides to expand their circle of acquaintances and enrolls in leadership development courses. There, they meet people with similar goals and interests. Over time, these new connections develop into strong professional relationships that contribute to their career growth.

Solution: Attend events, courses, or seminars where you can meet like-minded individuals. Don't hesitate to make the first move in meeting new people-this can open up new opportunities for development and creating a supportive environment.

3. Develop Your Communication Skills

Description: Effective communication is key to building strong relationships. Learn to listen, express your thoughts and emotions, and resolve conflicts.

Example: A person notices that they struggle to express their thoughts during meetings, causing their ideas to often go unheard. They decide to work on their communication skills and enroll in public speaking courses. After a few sessions, they begin to speak more confidently in front of colleagues, and their ideas become more structured and understandable to others.

Solution: Develop your communication skills through learning and practice. The better you communicate, the stronger and healthier your relationships will be.

4. Foster Mutual Support in Relationships

Description: A supportive environment is based on reciprocity. It's important not only to receive support but also to be ready to offer it to others.

Example: A person notices that their colleague often stays late after work to finish tasks. They decide to offer their help, and together they complete the tasks more quickly. This not only improves the work process but also strengthens their relationship.

Solution: Be proactive in providing support to others. Help your friends and colleagues in difficult moments-this will strengthen your relationships and create an atmosphere of mutual trust.

10-Day Implementation Plan for Building a Supportive Environment

This plan outlines specific actions to help you gradually create a circle of people who will support your growth and success.

Day 1: Analyze Your Current Environment

Task: Spend the day reflecting on your environment. Make a list of the people you regularly interact with and assess how each person impacts your life.

- **Example:** A person analyzes their environment and notices that one colleague constantly expresses pessimistic views, reducing their motivation at work. At the same time, they realize that another colleague always supports and inspires them. This analysis helps them understand who they should spend more time with and who to distance from.

- **Challenges:** It may be difficult to objectively assess who brings positivity and who brings negativity into your life.

- **Solution:** After making the list, recall your recent interactions with each person. What emotions did they evoke? This will help you better understand their impact.

Day 2: Choose Who to Spend More Time With

Task: Identify 2-3 people from your list who bring the most positivity into your life. Plan a meeting or joint activity with them.

- **Example:** A person decides to spend more time with a colleague who always provides support. They organize a meeting at a café where they discuss new ideas and plans. This meeting strengthens their interaction and promotes better collaboration at work.
  - **Challenges:** You might feel that you don't have time for additional meetings.
  - **Solution:** Review your schedule and make time for these meetings. This is an important investment in your emotional and professional well-being.

Day 3: Work on Developing Healthy Relationships

Task: Dedicate time to learning the principles of effective communication. Study the basics of active listening and ways to express your thoughts constructively.

- **Example:** A person reads a book on communication and tries to apply what they've learned during a conversation with a friend. They focus on active listening and notice that their conversation becomes deeper and more productive. The friend also feels more heard and appreciates this approach.
- **Challenges:** You might feel that you already know how to communicate, making this task seem unnecessary.
- **Solution:** Remember that even experienced communicators continually work on their skills. This will help you strengthen relationships and avoid misunderstandings in the future.

Day 4: Help a Friend or Colleague in a Difficult Moment

Task: Show initiative and support to those close to you. Help someone solve a problem, offer advice, or simply spend time together, providing support during a difficult moment.

- **Example:** A person learns that their colleague is going through a tough time at work due to personal issues. They offer their help with a joint project to ease the colleague's workload. The colleague appreciates the support, strengthening their working relationship.
- **Challenges:** You might not know who needs help or be unsure how best to support them.
- **Solution:** Ask your friends or colleagues if you can help them, even if they haven't directly reached out to you. This demonstrates your willingness to support them and strengthens your relationships.

Day 5: Learn to Recognize Toxic Relationships

Task: Spend the day analyzing your interactions with people who might negatively impact your life. Work on the skill of recognizing toxic relationships.

- **Example:** A person reflects on interactions with a friend who constantly criticizes their ideas and decisions. They realize that after each meeting with this person, they feel discouraged and lose motivation. After discussing the situation with a close friend, they decide to gradually reduce contact with this person.
- **Challenges**: You may feel guilty or unsure about distancing yourself from someone.
- **Solution:** Remember that your emotional well-being is a priority. Toxic relationships can harm you, so it's important to learn how to recognize and limit them.

Day 6: Spend More Time with Positive People

Task: Organize a meeting or join an event where you can interact with people who inspire and support you. Explore new opportunities for interacting with these people.

- **Example:** A person decides to organize a picnic for their closest friends, with whom they feel the best. During the picnic, they share their plans and dreams, discuss the challenges they face, and experience a sense of community and support.
- **Challenges**: It may be difficult to find time or events that interest you.
- **Solution:** Plan your participation in events or meetings in advance. This can be as simple as a shared meal or a walk with those who matter to you.

Day 7: Be Open to New Acquaintances

Task: Attend an event or gathering where you can meet new people who share your interests or values.

- **Example:** A person enrolls in a webinar related to their professional specialization and during the chat, meets several interesting people with whom they decide to keep in touch and exchange ideas.
- **Challenges:** You might feel uncomfortable at new events or in new environments.
- **Solution:** Don't pressure yourself; approach networking naturally. Remember, new acquaintances can open up new opportunities and perspectives for you.

Day 8: Develop Your Communication Skills

Task: Dedicate this day to practicing your communication skills. Practice active listening, expressing your thoughts clearly and constructively, and learning to resolve conflicts effectively.

Chapter 9: Building a Supportive Environment

- **Example:** A person records themselves during a short speech they are preparing for work. They analyze where their thoughts were expressed clearly and where the structure of the speech needs improvement. After several practices, they feel more confident in their ability to communicate effectively.

- **Challenges:** You may not know how to properly develop these skills or which specific ones need improvement.

- **Solution:** Use online resources, books, or courses to develop your communication skills. Regular practice and self-reflection will help you improve these skills.

Day 9: Review Your Relationships and Decide If Changes Are Needed

Task: Evaluate your relationships over the past 8 days. Think about whether there are people in your environment with whom you should interact more, and conversely, whether there are those with whom you should reduce interaction.

- **Example:** A person evaluates their relationships with colleagues and friends, noticing that several of them constantly support and inspire them to achieve new goals. At the same time, they decide to reduce interaction with those who criticize them or create conflicts.

- **Challenges:** You may doubt the necessity of changes or feel uncertain about your decisions.

- **Solution:** Approach this process carefully but decisively. It's important that your environment aligns with your needs and supports your development.

Day 10: Evaluate Your Progress in Building a Supportive Environment

Task: Assess the results of your efforts over the past 9 days. Note any changes in your well-being, motivation, and the level of support you receive from your environment.

- **Example:** A person analyzes their progress, noticing that their interactions with friends and colleagues have become more productive and enjoyable. They feel more motivated and satisfied with their environment, contributing to their overall well-being.

- **Challenges:** You may not immediately see significant changes, which could lead to frustration.

- **Solution:** Remember that building a supportive environment is a long-term process. Even small changes in your environment and relationships can have a significant impact on your life in the long run.

Reflection and Conclusions

Evaluating the success of building a supportive environment is a crucial step in your development process. Self-analysis and reflection will help you understand how your environment influences your achievements, stress levels, and overall well-being. This section focuses on how to properly assess your progress and make necessary adjustments to continually improve your support network.

The Importance of Reflection

Reflection is a key tool for analyzing how effectively your environment is working for you. It allows you to pause, look back, and assess your experiences. Through reflection, you can understand which relationships truly contribute to your growth and which may require adjustment or even termination.

- **Example:** After a month of working on building a supportive environment, a person reflects and notices that they have become more productive and emotionally stable by spending more time with supportive colleagues. At the same time, they realize that interactions with certain acquaintances are not beneficial and even cause stress.

Feedback

Feedback from others is an important part of the reflection process. By communicating with friends, colleagues, or mentors, you can gain an objective assessment of your actions and see the situation from another perspective. Feedback helps you better understand how others perceive your actions and what can be improved in your relationships.

- **Example:** A person asks close friends to share their impressions of their interactions over the past month. They mention that they've received more support and see that the person is also open to helping others. This feedback confirms that their efforts in building a supportive environment have been successful.

Reviewing and Adjusting Relationships

Life is constantly changing, and your environment must adapt to new circumstances. Regularly reviewing and adjusting your relationships is essential to ensuring your interactions remain healthy and supportive. It's important to be open to changes in relationships and to embrace new challenges.

- **Example:** After reflecting, a person realizes that one of their friends, who was once an important part of their support network, has started to distance themselves. They decide to discuss the situation with the friend to understand the reasons for the change. This helps them either restore closeness in the relationship or gradually reduce communication while maintaining mutual respect.

Continuous Improvement

Building a supportive environment is a process that requires constant attention and improvement. Life circumstances can change, and it's important to be ready to adapt your relationships to new conditions. Instead of taking your environment for granted, regularly review your relationships, assess their quality, and look for opportunities to improve.

• **Example:** A person decides to analyze their relationships monthly and evaluate whether they align with their current goals and needs. They set a rule to seek advice from a mentor or colleague at least once a month to keep their personal and professional development on track.

Final Recommendations

1. Develop Self-Analysis Skills: Self-analysis helps you better understand yourself and your environment. Set aside time to reflect on your relationships, analyze their impact on your life, and be ready to draw conclusions.

2. Seek Feedback: Regularly ask for feedback from those around you. Their input can be a valuable source of information for improving your relationships.

3. Be Open to Change: Life is dynamic, and your environment should meet your current needs. Don't be afraid to change or adjust relationships to keep them healthy and supportive.

4. Set Goals for Improving Relationships: Regularly set goals for developing your relationships. This might involve improving communication, finding new acquaintances, or working on specific aspects of your interactions.

5. Balance Quantity and Quality of Relationships: Ensure your environment consists not only of a large number of acquaintances but also of deep and trusting relationships that truly matter.

6. Develop Emotional Intelligence: The ability to understand and manage your emotions will help you better perceive the emotions of others and build stronger, healthier relationships.

Evaluating Success

It's important to regularly assess your success in building a supportive environment. This will help you determine if you're moving in the right direction and if your interactions align with your life goals and values.

● **Example:** A person conducts a comprehensive analysis of their relationships a year after starting to work on building a supportive environment. They find that their social circle has become smaller but more meaningful. They feel more confident and motivated, confirming the effectiveness of their approach.

Reviewing the Plan

Regularly reviewing your plan for building a supportive environment allows you to stay in control and make timely adjustments. This ensures flexibility and readiness for change.

● **Example:** A person reviews their plan for building a supportive environment every six months, analyzing successes and making adjustments. They pay attention to new challenges and opportunities that have arisen during this period and adapt their plan accordingly.

Final Thoughts

Building a supportive environment is a complex but incredibly important process. It not only helps you achieve your life and professional goals but also provides emotional and psychological comfort. Reflection and regular review of relationships will help you maintain an environment that supports your growth and well-being.

Additional Reading and Resources

To gain a deeper understanding of the importance of building a supportive environment and to receive practical advice on this topic, consider exploring the following books and resources:

1. Books

♦ "Connected: The Surprising Power of Our Social Networks and How They Shape Our Lives" by Nicholas A. Christakis and James H. Fowler

■ This book explores how our environment influences our habits, beliefs, and achievements. The authors offer practical advice on creating a supportive environment that helps you succeed.

♦ "The Tipping Point: How Little Things Can Make a Big Difference" by Malcolm Gladwell

■ This book examines how small changes in your environment can lead to significant outcomes, with insights on how to build a positive support network.

♦ "Emotional Intelligence" by Daniel Goleman

■ This book will help you understand how emotional intelligence affects our communication and interactions with others. It offers advice on developing emotional intelligence to build strong and healthy relationships.

- "How to Win Friends and Influence People" by Dale Carnegie

  - A practical guide to effective communication, this book will help you develop the skills necessary for building strong and trusting relationships.

2. Articles and Research Papers

- "The Impact of Social Networks on Well-Being" (2015) by Felix Elie and Sarah Goldberg

  - A research paper that examines the impact of social networks and relationships on psychological well-being, with recommendations on creating supportive social connections.

- "Building a Supportive Social Network: Strategies for Success" (2018) by Richard Carson and Emily Lindsay

  - This article provides practical advice on creating and maintaining a supportive environment based on psychological research.

3. Online Courses and Resources

- Coursera: "Social Psychology" (University of Michigan)

  - An online course that helps you understand how social interactions shape our behavior and how to create a supportive environment.

- TED Talks: "The Power of Vulnerability" by Brené Brown

  - A talk by Brené Brown exploring the importance of authenticity and vulnerability in building strong relationships.

- YouTube: "How to Build a Strong Support Network"

  - Various videos on this topic that offer practical advice on creating a supportive environment.

4. Communities and Forums

- Reddit: r/selfimprovement

  - An active community where users share their experiences in building a supportive environment and discuss different approaches to personal development.

- Meetup: Interest-Based Communities

  - Use Meetup to find groups of interest in your area. This is a great way to find like-minded individuals and build a new environment.

Chapter 10: Principles of Continuous Learning

Introduction and Context

Continuous learning is the foundation of personal and professional development in the modern world. We live in an era where knowledge and technology evolve at an unprecedented pace. Skills that were relevant yesterday can quickly become obsolete, and new demands arise daily. In such an environment, the ability to learn continuously is not just an advantage but a necessity for survival. Continuous learning is the process of actively acquiring new knowledge and skills throughout life. It helps us stay relevant, adapt to changes, and reach new heights in our careers and personal lives.

Continuous learning is not limited to formal education. While traditional education lays the foundation of knowledge, true learning begins when we take the initiative to explore new topics independently, participate in training sessions, seminars, webinars, read books and research papers, and learn from colleagues, mentors, and even students. Today, access to knowledge is almost limitless: online courses, podcasts, video lessons, digital libraries, and forums offer endless opportunities for self-development. This ongoing process helps maintain intellectual flexibility, develop critical thinking, and remain open to new ideas and approaches.

The significance of continuous learning extends beyond professional growth. It contributes to overall personal development, boosts self-esteem, and fosters a sense of constant growth. Through continuous learning, a person can better understand the world they live in and themselves within it. This understanding enables informed decision-making, impacting all aspects of life-from career to health, from personal relationships to financial stability. Continuous learning also helps build positive self-esteem, as each new piece of knowledge or skill increases one's sense of competence and readiness to face challenges.

In an era where change is the norm, the ability to learn becomes one of the most important skills for anyone. People who continually learn have more opportunities for career advancement, adapt more quickly to changes around them, and find new solutions to old problems. Continuous learning helps maintain intellectual activity, improves quality of life, and promotes overall well-being. It broadens horizons, allows for new perspectives, and opens doors to new opportunities.

It's important to understand that continuous learning is not just a set of tools for professional development but a way of life that fosters personal growth and self-realization. It enables you to stay relevant in a world where changes happen faster than ever before. Those who continuously learn can not only keep up with the times but also anticipate future trends, staying one step ahead. This helps maintain competitiveness in the job market and keeps life interesting, developing new hobbies and passions, and increasing overall happiness.

The goal of this chapter is to teach you how to apply the principles of continuous learning in your life to achieve professional and personal development. We will explore the key principles of continuous learning, provide tips on how to implement them in your life, and help you create a plan for ongoing growth and development. The ability to learn continuously will allow you to remain competitive in the job market, maintain interest in work and life, and ensure your constant progress in the rapidly changing modern world.

Continuous learning is the key to your success and well-being. Whether you aim to achieve professional heights or simply want to better understand the world around you, this process is an integral part of your life. Developing these skills will open new opportunities, enable you to achieve your goals more effectively, and ensure continuous progress in all areas of your life.

Core Theory

Continuous learning is a lifelong process that involves actively acquiring new knowledge and skills in various fields. In a world where changes occur daily, this process becomes critically important for achieving success and self-realization. However, for continuous learning to be effective, it is essential to understand and apply several key principles that help structure this process and make it as productive as possible.

Key Principles of Continuous Learning

1. Initiative

Initiative is the driving force behind continuous learning. It involves your ability to independently identify and seize opportunities for development. This means not waiting for someone to provide you with new knowledge or learning opportunities but actively seeking them out yourself. Initiative allows you to go beyond the familiar, discover new horizons, and continually grow.

Example: A person working in marketing decides to learn the basics of programming to better understand the technological aspects of digital marketing. They search for online courses, study materials on YouTube, practice on small projects, and gradually integrate their new knowledge into their professional activities. This not only enhances their competence but also opens up new career opportunities that were previously inaccessible.

2. Goal-Orientation

Goal-orientation means that learning should be focused on achieving specific objectives. This could involve developing professional skills, broadening your horizons, or mastering new technologies. Clearly defined goals help structure learning, set priorities, and use time and resources more effectively.

Example: A financial analyst decides to master a new method of analyzing financial reports that is becoming increasingly popular in their field. They set a goal to reach a high level of proficiency in this method within the next six months. To achieve this, they develop a detailed plan that includes reading literature, attending seminars, and applying their new knowledge in practice. This not only helps them master the new method but also positions them as a leader in their field.

3. Flexibility

Flexibility in learning means the ability to quickly adapt to new conditions, the willingness to learn in various formats and from different sources. This skill involves being open to new knowledge, even if it falls outside your primary field of activity. Flexibility allows you to remain relevant in a rapidly changing world and effectively apply new knowledge in different contexts.

Example: A surgeon decides to learn the basics of management to more effectively run their clinic. They combine their medical practice with studying management fundamentals, which not only helps them better organize the work of their team but also improves the quality of patient care. Flexibility in learning allows them to expand their professional capabilities and better adapt to changes in the healthcare field.

4. Critical Thinking

Critical thinking is a key component of effective learning. It enables you to analyze the information you receive, assess its reliability, and apply it in practice. Developing critical thinking helps avoid superficial learning and allows for a deeper understanding of the subject matter. It also helps filter out unnecessary or outdated information, focusing on what truly matters.

Example: An engineer working on developing a new product regularly analyzes the information they receive and checks its reliability. They do not take information at face value but question accepted approaches, allowing them to find innovative solutions. Critical thinking helps them develop new approaches to product development and ensures high-quality work.

5. Practical Application

Knowledge must be put to practical use, so it is important not only to acquire new knowledge but also to apply it immediately. Practical application helps reinforce new knowledge, make it part of your professional toolkit, and increase your effectiveness. The sooner you start applying new knowledge in practice, the better it will be retained, and the more benefits it will bring in the long term.

Example: An IT specialist decides to learn a new programming language. Instead of limiting themselves to theoretical study, they immediately begin using the new language in real projects. This not only helps them solidify their knowledge but also quickly see the results of their work, which further motivates them to continue learning.

Scientific Basis for Continuous Learning

Continuous learning has a solid scientific foundation that confirms its importance for personal and professional development. Various studies show that continuous learning not only enhances professional competence but also contributes to overall well-being, increases life satisfaction, and helps maintain cognitive functions at a high level.

1. Development of Brain Neuroplasticity

One of the key scientific aspects of continuous learning is the development of brain neuroplasticity. Neuroplasticity is the brain's ability to change and adapt in response to new experiences. When we learn something new, new neural connections are formed in our brains, which increases our ability to adapt to changes and solve complex problems. This is confirmed by numerous studies in the field of neurobiology.

Research: Scientists from the University of California, Los Angeles, conducted a study that showed that continuous learning of new skills stimulates the development of new neural connections in the brain. The study involved people aged 20 to 65 who regularly studied new topics and engaged in intellectual tasks over six months. The results showed that those who actively learned significantly improved cognitive functions, such as memory and problem-solving abilities, compared to the control group.

2. Increased Motivation

Continuous learning also helps maintain motivation. Learning new topics and mastering new skills activate the brain's reward center, increasing dopamine levels and providing a sense of satisfaction from learning. This is an important aspect that helps maintain interest in life and avoid burnout.

Research: Scientists from the University of Pennsylvania conducted a study that showed that people who regularly engage in learning have higher levels of motivation and life satisfaction. Study participants who took part in educational programs showed increased dopamine levels in the brain, accompanied by positive emotions and a heightened interest in further learning. The study also showed that regular learning helps maintain motivation even during difficult periods in life.

3. Improved Cognitive Functions

Learning new things helps maintain cognitive functions at a high level throughout life. This is especially important for preventing age-related changes in the brain, such as memory decline and cognitive abilities. Continuous learning stimulates the brain, keeping it in shape, which reduces the risk of developing diseases such as dementia.

Research: The University of Toronto conducted a long-term study involving over a thousand participants aged 30 to 80. The study showed that those who actively engaged in continuous learning had better memory, higher problem-solving abilities, and overall intellectual capabilities compared to those who did not focus on self-education. These results confirmed that continuous learning is an effective way to prevent age-related cognitive decline.

Scientific data confirms the importance of continuous learning for personal and professional development. It promotes the development of brain neuroplasticity, supports motivation, and helps maintain a high level of cognitive functions throughout life. Continuous learning is the key to maintaining competitiveness, flexibility, and adaptability in the modern world.

Problem Situations and Examples

In life, situations often arise where the lack of new knowledge and skills can lead to career stagnation, loss of interest in work, or even professional burnout. Continuous learning helps address these issues by ensuring a stable level of intellectual and professional growth. Let's explore a few typical situations where continuous learning can significantly improve the situation.

Situation 1: Feeling Stuck in Your Career

Problem Description: A person has been working in the same position for several years and sees no opportunities for further development. They feel that their professional growth has stalled and don't know how to change the situation. This can lead to demotivation, loss of interest in work, and even the desire to change careers.

Example: You have been working as a sales specialist for five years. Initially, the job was interesting and engaging, but over time, the tasks became routine. You feel that you've exhausted your potential in this position and see no paths for further career growth. This causes a sense of dissatisfaction and demotivation.

Solution: One way to overcome career stagnation is by acquiring new skills and knowledge. For instance, you might decide to learn the basics of digital marketing to expand your competencies and participate in developing new strategies for your company. Start by looking for online courses or training programs that match your interests. After gaining new knowledge, you can propose to your management the implementation of new methods in the sales department, which will not only invigorate your work but also help you climb the career ladder.

Situation 2: Loss of Interest in Work Due to Routine

Problem Description: You feel that your job has become routine and no longer brings satisfaction. Your duties have become predictable, and daily tasks don't spark interest. This leads to decreased productivity, dissatisfaction with the job, and even burnout.

Example: Your job as an engineer, which you once performed with enthusiasm, now seems monotonous. Every day, you perform the same tasks, and you feel that you're not growing. This causes fatigue and a loss of interest in work.

Solution: To regain interest in your job, it's worth focusing on opportunities for professional development. For example, you could participate in a qualification enhancement program that includes learning the latest technologies in your field. Afterward, you can apply the new knowledge in your work, developing new projects and implementing innovative solutions. This will help you restore enthusiasm and interest in your job, as well as increase your value to the company.

Situation 3: Insecurity in Your Knowledge and Skills

Problem Description: A person feels insecure about their knowledge and skills, leading to doubts about their abilities. They constantly compare themselves to colleagues and believe that their knowledge is outdated, which negatively impacts productivity and self-esteem.

Example: You're a young specialist who recently started working at a law firm. You notice that many of your colleagues have much more experience and knowledge. This makes you doubt your own competence and fear making complex decisions. You feel inadequate compared to more experienced colleagues.

Solution: Regular learning and participation in professional events can significantly boost your confidence. Enroll in advanced training courses, attend professional seminars and workshops, where you can not only expand your knowledge but also exchange experiences with colleagues. This will help you not only improve your competence but also strengthen your self-esteem, positively impacting your career.

Situation 4: Job Loss Due to Lack of New Skills

Problem Description: A person loses their job due to a lack of new skills and an inability to adapt to the demands of the modern job market. This can happen because they have worked in the same company or position for a long time and haven't engaged in self-education. Losing a job can be a severe blow to self-esteem and financial stability.

Example: You've worked in manufacturing for a long time, but your position was automated, and now you've been laid off. Your skills no longer meet the requirements of the modern job market, and you feel lost and unnecessary. You understand that you need to retrain but don't know where to start.

Solution: Acquiring new skills through continuous learning is key to successful retraining. You can explore new career opportunities that interest you and enroll in courses that will help you master a new profession. For example, you might decide to become a web developer or designer and start by learning the basics of programming or graphic design. After completing your education, you can find a job in a new field that is relevant in the job market.

Situation 5: Burnout Due to Routine and Lack of Development

Problem Description: A person experiences professional burnout due to constant routine and a lack of opportunities for development. They feel tired and demotivated, which negatively affects the quality of work and life in general.

Example: You're a middle manager who has been working at the same company for over ten years. You feel that your job has become too predictable and no longer brings satisfaction. The absence of new challenges and development opportunities causes you to feel tired and professionally burned out.

Solution: To avoid burnout, it's worth focusing on professional development opportunities. Start by acquiring new skills or knowledge that will help you implement innovative solutions in your work. For example, you could study project management or leadership, which will help you take a fresh look at your responsibilities and find new opportunities for development. This will not only renew your interest in work but also allow you to become a more effective leader.

Examples of Successful Application of Continuous Learning

Continuous learning is a key factor in the success of many well-known individuals across various fields. Here are a few examples of how continuous learning has helped them achieve remarkable results:

1. Serena Williams (Tennis Player)

Serena Williams is one of the most famous and successful tennis players in sports history. Her career has spanned over two decades, and she remains one of the most influential athletes of her generation. However, Serena's success lies not only in her physical abilities and natural talent but also in her continuous learning and commitment to self-improvement.

From the beginning of her career, Williams understood the importance of learning and constantly improving her skills. She has always been open to new approaches and techniques that could enhance her game. Over the years, Serena has worked with some of the world's best coaches, who have helped her develop new tactics, techniques, and game strategies. She constantly studied her opponents and sought ways to leverage her strengths on the court.

One of Serena's most crucial attributes is her ability to learn from her mistakes and adapt to new conditions. Throughout her career, she has faced numerous challenges, including serious injuries that could have ended her sports career. But instead of giving up, Serena used these challenges as opportunities for learning and improvement. She continually worked on returning to the court stronger and better prepared.

Serena Williams is also known for her curiosity and desire to learn beyond the tennis court. She engages in business, fashion, philanthropy, and even studies art. This broadening of interests has helped her maintain a balance between her sports career and personal life, as well as develop new skills and knowledge that she can apply in various areas of her life.

Thanks to her continuous pursuit of learning and improvement, Serena Williams has been able to stay at the top of professional sports for many years, becoming a role model for other athletes and people worldwide. Her story demonstrates that continuous learning is one of the key elements of success in any field.

2. Satya Nadella (CEO of Microsoft)

Satya Nadella, who took over as CEO of Microsoft in 2014, is a prime example of a leader for whom continuous learning has been the foundation of career success. When he became the company's CEO, Microsoft was at a crossroads. The company, which had once been a leader in the technology market, began to lose ground amid stiff competition. Nadella faced the challenge of not only bringing Microsoft back to the top but also adapting the company to the new challenges of the digital age.

From day one of his leadership, Nadella emphasized a culture of continuous learning. He believed that only through continuous learning and adaptation could the company remain competitive in the long term. One of his first steps was to introduce a "growth mindset" culture, which encourages employees to continuously develop, learn new technologies, and seek innovative solutions.

Personally, Satya Nadella has always been open to new knowledge and approaches. For example, he actively studied cloud technologies when it became evident that the future of the industry was in cloud services. He not only supported but also initiated many projects in this area, allowing Microsoft to become one of the leaders in the cloud services market with the Azure platform.

Nadella also paid attention to developing his leadership qualities. He constantly studied new approaches to management and leadership, learning from his colleagues and mentors. His ability to quickly learn and adapt helped him build an effective leadership team that could implement the company's ambitious strategies.

Under his leadership, Microsoft shifted its focus from software production to cloud services, artificial intelligence, and quantum computing, ensuring the company's steady growth and return to a leading position. Satya Nadella has become a symbol of how continuous learning can change not only an individual's career but an entire company, helping it adapt to new challenges and achieve success.

3. Angela Merkel (Former Chancellor of Germany)

Angela Merkel, who served as Germany's Chancellor from 2005 to 2021, is known for her ability to quickly acquire new knowledge and adapt to change. Trained as a physicist, Merkel has always placed great importance on learning and self-development, which helped her effectively govern the country for 16 years.

Merkel understood that to effectively govern a country, it was necessary to constantly update her knowledge and stay informed about the latest trends in politics, economics, and science. She actively participated in international conferences, meetings with scientists, and experts from various fields, which helped her make well-informed decisions in complex situations. For example, during the 2008 financial crisis, Merkel regularly consulted with leading economists and experts, allowing her to make effective decisions to stabilize Germany's economy.

In addition, Merkel continuously studied new approaches to management and diplomacy. Her ability to learn helped her effectively negotiate with leaders of other countries and find compromises in the most challenging international issues. For example, during the Eurozone crisis, she actively studied issues of economic integration and interaction between EU countries, which allowed her to help resolve conflicts and maintain the unity of the European Union.

Continuous learning also helped Merkel remain flexible and adapt to the changes that occurred throughout her political career. Her openness to new knowledge and willingness to learn from others made her one of the most influential political leaders of modern times.

4. Mary Barra (CEO of General Motors)

Mary Barra, the CEO of General Motors, exemplifies how continuous learning can help a leader successfully manage a large international company

Chapter 10: Principles of Continuous Learning

and implement significant industry changes. Barra began her career at General Motors as an engineer and worked her way up from technical positions to become the head of one of the world's largest automotive companies.

Throughout her career, Barra has always placed great emphasis on her professional development. She regularly attended courses in management, marketing, and finance, which helped her expand her knowledge and competencies. Moreover, Barra was always open to new ideas and approaches, which allowed her to effectively manage the company in a rapidly changing automotive industry.

One of the key elements of her success was her continuous study of innovative technologies and market trends. Barra understood that the future of the automotive industry depended on the development of electric vehicles and autonomous vehicles. She actively studied these technologies, attended industry conferences, and engaged experts to understand how General Motors could integrate these innovations into its products.

Thanks to her continuous learning and strategic thinking, Mary Barra was able to transform General Motors, making the company one of the leaders in electric vehicles and cutting-edge automotive technologies. Her example demonstrates that a constant pursuit of knowledge and development is a crucial factor in success in modern business.

Practical Tips and Solutions

To successfully implement the principles of continuous learning in your life and achieve maximum results, it is important to follow several key steps. These tips will help you systematically approach learning, make it a part of your daily routine, and achieve personal and professional goals.

1. Setting Learning Goals

Description: Without clear goals, learning can become chaotic and ineffective. The first step towards successful continuous learning is setting specific goals. These can be short-term or long-term goals related to your professional activities, personal development, or other areas of life.

Example: Imagine you work in marketing, and your task is to increase the effectiveness of digital advertising campaigns. However, you realize that you lack knowledge in analytics and working with big data. Set a goal to master the basics of web analytics and data analysis tools such as Google Analytics or Power BI. This is a specific goal that you can work towards by gradually acquiring new knowledge and applying it in practice.

Solution: Write down your goals in a separate document or journal. It is important that these goals are specific, measurable, achievable, relevant, and time-bound (SMART). Regularly review and adjust them according to changes in your needs and circumstances.

2. Planning Your Learning

Description: After defining your goals, it is important to create a clear learning plan. This will help you systematize the process and ensure consistency in achieving your goals. The plan should include sources of knowledge such as books, courses, training sessions, podcasts, and other resources.

Example: If your goal is to master web analytics, create a learning plan that includes the following steps: enroll in an online course on the basics of web analytics, find relevant literature, and subscribe to several data analytics podcasts. Schedule these activities in your calendar, dedicating an hour each day to study materials and complete practical tasks.

Solution: Use digital tools for planning your learning, such as Google Calendar or Trello. Set clear deadlines for each stage of learning and stick to them. Planning also includes regular periods of reflection to assess progress and make adjustments to your plan.

3. Self-Learning

Description: A crucial aspect of continuous learning is the ability to independently acquire new knowledge. This involves developing the skill of self-directed information search, analysis, and application. Self-learning helps develop self-discipline and responsibility for your growth.

Example: You decide to learn a new programming language, such as Python. Start by studying the basic concepts through online courses and books available for free on the internet. Set small tasks for yourself, such as writing simple programs or scripts. Regularly complete these tasks and check your knowledge through practical projects.

Solution: Use various sources of knowledge to ensure a comprehensive approach to learning. Combine reading literature with watching educational videos and completing practical tasks. Develop a habit of self-learning by dedicating specific time daily or weekly.

4. Learning Through Practice

Description: One of the most effective ways to acquire new knowledge is by applying it in practice. Learning through practice helps solidify the acquired knowledge and make it part of your professional toolkit. It also allows you to see the results of your learning faster and increases motivation for further development.

Example: After studying the basics of web analytics, you start applying your knowledge in practice by analyzing the effectiveness of advertising campaigns in your company. You use Google Analytics to collect data on user behavior on the website and draw conclusions about the effectiveness of various marketing channels based on this data. This knowledge helps you optimize campaigns and increase conversion rates.

Chapter 10: Principles of Continuous Learning

Solution: Look for opportunities to apply new knowledge in your daily activities. If you are learning a new technology or tool, find a way to integrate it into your work. For example, if you have learned a new approach to project management, apply it to a current project and analyze the results.

5. Developing Critical Thinking

Description: Critical thinking is an important component of continuous learning as it allows you not only to memorize information but also to analyze, evaluate its reliability, and apply it in practice. Developing critical thinking helps avoid superficial learning and enables you to use the acquired knowledge more effectively.

Example: You read an article about a new marketing trend, but instead of immediately implementing it in your work, you decide to research the topic further. You analyze the sources of the information, compare it with other studies and expert opinions. Only then do you decide whether it's worth applying this trend in your work.

Solution: Develop a habit of analyzing the information you receive. Before making decisions or implementing new approaches, assess their feasibility and potential risks. This will help you avoid unfounded decisions and focus on methods that truly bring value.

6. Using Diverse Learning Resources

Description: To ensure comprehensive development, it is important to use diverse sources for learning. These can include books, online courses, training sessions, podcasts, seminars, as well as personal experiences and mentorship. The variety of sources helps you gain a multifaceted understanding of the topics that interest you.

Example: You decide to study financial management for small businesses. To do this, you enroll in an online course, buy several books on financial management, subscribe to podcasts on economic issues, and attend a financial planning seminar. This comprehensive approach helps you gain both theoretical knowledge and practical skills.

Solution: Create a list of different learning resources you plan to use. For example, identify several books you want to read, find online courses that align with your goals, and enroll in them. Subscribe to podcasts or blogs by experts in your field to stay updated on new trends and ideas.

7. Developing a Network of Contacts and Team Learning

Description: One effective way to learn is by interacting with other people who share your interests or have experience in the area that interests you. Team learning allows for the exchange of knowledge and provides support from colleagues or mentors. Developing a network of contacts helps you stay informed about new developments in your field and find new opportunities for growth.

Example: You work in a software development team and decide to learn a new programming language. Your team organizes a study group where each member shares their knowledge and experience. You also start communicating with other developers through online communities, where you exchange ideas and solutions.

Solution: Create or join study groups where you can share knowledge and experience with others. Regularly participate in professional events, seminars, and conferences to expand your network of contacts. This will keep you connected with leading experts in your field and provide access to the latest knowledge and technologies.

8. Engaging in Professional and Learning Communities

Description: Professional and learning communities are valuable resources for continuous learning. In such communities, you can discuss current topics, receive advice from experienced colleagues, and share your own experiences. Communities can also provide access to exclusive materials, courses, and webinars.

Example: You decide to develop in the field of UX design. You join an online community of designers where weekly webinars and discussions of new trends and best practices in UX take place. Interacting with other community members gives you new ideas and tools to improve your skills.

Solution: Explore professional communities in your field and join those that align with your interests and goals. Actively participate in discussions and events organized by the community. This will help you not only expand your knowledge but also gain support from like-minded people.

9. Using Technology for Learning

Description: Modern technologies offer numerous opportunities for effective learning. Online platforms, mobile apps, virtual classes, and other technological tools allow you to learn anytime and anywhere. Using technology helps make the learning process more convenient and interactive.

Example: You decide to learn the basics of programming in Python. To do this, you download a learning app to your smartphone that allows you to take courses during your commute or between meetings. The app also provides interactive exercises and tasks that help you reinforce the knowledge you've gained.

Solution: Explore available technological tools that can facilitate your learning. Choose those that suit your needs and learning style. Use mobile apps, online platforms, video courses, and other technological resources to make the learning process more effective and flexible.

Chapter 10: Principles of Continuous Learning

10. Constant Progress Evaluation

Description: It is important to regularly evaluate your progress in learning to ensure you are moving in the right direction and achieving your set goals. Constant progress evaluation helps identify problems in time and make adjustments to your learning plan.

Example: You are studying a new programming language and evaluate your achievements monthly by checking how well you have mastered new concepts and whether you can apply them in practice. If you notice that you are having difficulty with a particular topic, you decide to spend more time studying it or seek help from a mentor.

Solution: Create a system for evaluating your learning progress. Regularly test your knowledge and skills through tests, assignments, or practical projects. Record your achievements and the challenges you face to make timely adjustments to your learning plan.

Final Recommendations:

1. Be Consistent: Continuous learning requires regularity. Set aside specific time for learning and stick to this schedule.

2. Don't Be Afraid to Make Mistakes: Learning involves making mistakes. Learn from them and use them as opportunities for growth.

3. Remember Your Motivation: Identify what motivates you and use it to maintain your enthusiasm in the learning process.

4. Share Knowledge: Helping others learn reinforces your own knowledge and develops teaching skills.

These practical tips will help you systematize the process of continuous learning and make it an effective part of your life, contributing to your personal and professional growth.

10-Day Implementation Plan

To successfully implement the principles of continuous learning in your life, it is essential to develop a clear action plan for the next 10 days. This plan will help you systematize the learning process, define specific steps, and ensure that you achieve your set goals.

Day 1: Define Your Learning Goals

Description: The first step in continuous learning is to define specific goals you want to achieve. These can be short-term or long-term goals related to professional development, personal growth, or acquiring new skills.

Example: A person working in marketing might set a goal to learn the basics of web analytics to improve the performance of advertising campaigns. Another person might aim to learn a new programming language to expand their professional opportunities.

Task: Set aside time to analyze your needs and define specific learning goals. Write them down in your journal or a digital document. Ensure that these goals are Specific, Measurable, Achievable, Relevant, and Time-bound (SMART).

Day 2: Create a Learning Plan

Description: After defining your goals, you need to create a learning plan that will help you achieve them. The plan should include sources of knowledge, the time you will allocate for learning, and specific steps for mastering the material.

Example: A person aiming to master web analytics might create a learning plan that includes an online course, books on analytics, practical tasks, and weekly progress evaluations. Another person might plan to learn a new programming language by dividing topics weekly.

Task: Develop a learning plan that considers your goals, resources, and available time. Set clear deadlines for each learning stage and record this plan in your journal or digital document.

Day 3: Self-Directed Learning

Description: Self-directed learning is a crucial component of continuous development. It allows you to flexibly approach the acquisition of new knowledge and skills using various information sources.

Example: A person might start self-directed learning in web analytics by watching video tutorials, reading articles, and completing practical tasks. Another example is learning a programming language through online resources like Codecademy or Coursera.

Task: Begin self-directed learning in the direction you have chosen. Allocate daily time for learning and stick to your plan.

Day 4: Apply Knowledge in Practice

Description: Applying new knowledge in practice is a key stage in the learning process. It allows you to solidify the acquired knowledge and make it part of your professional activities.

Example: A person studying web analytics might start analyzing data from their advertising campaigns and making changes based on the results. Another example is creating a simple project using the programming language they have learned to solidify their knowledge.

Task: Use your new knowledge in your daily activities. Look for opportunities to apply what you've learned in real projects or tasks.

Day 5: Develop Critical Thinking

Description: Critical thinking helps analyze information, evaluate its reliability, and make informed decisions. This is an important aspect of continuous learning that allows you to use the acquired knowledge more effectively.

Example: A person studying new marketing strategies might analyze their pros and cons before implementing them in their company. Another person might verify the reliability of the information sources they use for learning.

Task: Practice critical thinking by analyzing the information you receive during learning. Ask yourself questions, evaluate the reliability of sources, and think about how the knowledge can be applied in your work.

Day 6: Attend a Professional Event or Webinar

Description: Attending professional events such as conferences, seminars, or webinars allows you to gain new knowledge, expand your network of contacts, and stay updated on the latest trends in your field.

Example: A person in marketing might register for a webinar on new web analytics tools. Another example is attending a programming conference where new programming languages and frameworks are discussed.

Task: Find and register for a professional event or webinar that aligns with your learning goals. Schedule your participation in the event in the coming days and note down the new knowledge you gain during the event.

Day 7: Join a Professional or Learning Community

Description: Joining professional or learning communities allows you to exchange knowledge and experience with others who share your interests. It also provides opportunities to receive support from colleagues and mentors.

Example: A person studying web analytics might join an online community of marketers or analysts discussing new trends and tools. Another example is participating in a software development group where members share experiences and offer advice.

Task: Find a professional or learning community in your field and join it. Participate in discussions, ask questions, and share your experiences.

Day 8: Evaluate Your Learning Progress

Description: Evaluating your progress helps determine how successfully you are moving toward your goals and what still needs to be done to achieve them. This is an important step that allows you to adjust your learning plan and use your time more effectively.

Example: A person studying web analytics might assess how well they have mastered new tools and whether they can apply them in practice. Another example is checking their knowledge of a new programming language by completing practical tasks.

Task: Evaluate your learning progress. Identify which goals you have already achieved and which still need additional attention. Record your conclusions and adjust your learning plan according to the results.

Day 9: Review and Adjust Your Learning Plan

Description: Reviewing and adjusting your learning plan is necessary to ensure its relevance and alignment with your needs. This allows you to adapt the learning process to changing circumstances and new challenges.

Example: A person studying web analytics might decide to add new tools to their plan that have recently become available. Another example is adjusting task deadlines due to new priorities at work.

Task: Review your learning plan and make the necessary adjustments. Consider the results of your progress evaluation, new needs, and circumstances. Ensure that your learning plan remains relevant and aligned with your goals.

Day 10: Summarize and Reflect

Description: Summarizing and reflecting helps you understand what you have achieved during this period and what steps you need to take next. It also allows you to assess how effective your approach to learning has been and what changes should be made.

Example: A person studying web analytics might summarize their achievements, problems, and conclusions. Another example is setting new goals and directions for further learning based on the experience gained.

Task: Write down your achievements and conclusions in a journal or document. Analyze what worked well and what could be improved. Set new goals and develop a plan for further learning based on the results of your reflection.

This 10-day plan will help you make continuous learning an integral part of your life, contributing to your professional and personal growth. Regularly review and adjust your plan to stay on track toward achieving your goals.

Reflection and Conclusions

Reflection is a crucial step in the process of continuous learning. It allows you to pause, evaluate your achievements, understand what is working well and what needs improvement, and make the necessary adjustments. Reflection helps you maintain high motivation and stay on track to achieve your goals.

Importance of Reflection

Reflection is a key tool for deep understanding of your own experience and learning outcomes. It helps you better comprehend how you absorb new knowledge and skills, which approaches were most effective, and which need adjustment. Reflection also allows you to focus on successes, boosting your confidence and stimulating further development.

For example, if you are learning a new professional skill, reflection will help you assess how well you have mastered it, how it applies to your work, and whether additional training is necessary. This will help you plan your time and resources more effectively and avoid future mistakes.

Feedback

Receiving feedback from colleagues, mentors, or friends is an essential part of the reflection process. An objective perspective can help you identify aspects of your learning that might otherwise go unnoticed. Feedback provides valuable advice and recommendations that can contribute to further improving your skills.

For example, you might ask your mentor to evaluate your learning results and offer recommendations on how you can improve your knowledge or approaches to learning. This will help you understand what you are doing right, what needs correction, and provide you with new ideas for development.

Reviewing and Adjusting Plans

The learning process is not static; it requires constant review and adjustment. Life circumstances may change, new challenges and opportunities arise, and it is important to be ready to adapt your learning plans accordingly. Regularly reviewing your learning plans helps ensure their relevance and effectiveness.

For instance, if you find that a particular topic is more challenging than expected, you may need to allocate more time to master it. In this case, adjusting your learning plan will allow you to focus on the topic and ensure deeper comprehension.

Evaluating Achievements

Reflection allows you to evaluate your achievements and see how far you have progressed in your learning. This is important for maintaining motivation and enthusiasm for further learning. Evaluating your achievements helps you understand which goals have already been met and what new tasks you should set for yourself.

For example, if your goal was to learn new software, evaluating your achievements might reveal that you have mastered the basic functions and can start working on more complex tasks. This gives you confidence in your abilities and motivates you to continue developing.

Identifying Problem Areas

Reflection helps identify aspects of your learning that may require additional attention. This allows you to make timely adjustments to the learning process to avoid stagnation or uncertainty in your knowledge. Identifying problem areas is key to ensuring effective learning and achieving high results.

For instance, if you notice that you keep postponing the study of a particular topic, it may indicate the need to change your approach or find other sources of information. This enables you to respond promptly to difficulties and maintain progress in your learning.

Final Recommendations

Based on reflection and the results obtained, it is important to draw the appropriate conclusions and formulate recommendations for further learning. This will help you maintain a high level of efficiency in learning and achieve new goals.

1. Continue Developing Your Continuous Learning Skills: Regularly analyze your successes and challenges to continuously improve your learning approaches. This will allow you to stay at the forefront of professional and personal development.

2. Be Flexible and Open to Change: Life circumstances and requirements may change, so it's important to be ready to adapt your learning plans to new conditions and challenges.

3. Utilize Feedback: Regularly seek advice and recommendations from colleagues, mentors, or friends. This will help you discover new opportunities for growth and avoid mistakes.

4. Review and Adjust Your Plans: Regularly review your learning plans and make the necessary changes to ensure their relevance and alignment with your goals.

5. Remember to Rest and Maintain Balance: Continuous learning is important, but don't forget the importance of rest and maintaining a balance between work and personal life. This will help you preserve energy and motivation in the long term.

Summary

Reflection and conclusions are integral parts of the continuous learning process. They help you gain a deeper understanding of your experience, evaluate achievements, and make necessary adjustments for further development. Regularly reviewing and adapting learning plans, utilizing feedback, and maintaining a balance between learning and other aspects of life will help you achieve high results and stay on the path to success.

Continuous learning is a process that has no end. It requires constant attention and effort, but the results are worth it. Keep learning, developing, and applying new knowledge to achieve your goals, and you will undoubtedly succeed.

Additional Literature and Useful Links

For an in-depth study of the principles of continuous learning and their effective implementation in your life, it is recommended to familiarize yourself with the following resources:

Books

1. "Mindset: The New Psychology of Success" by Carol S. Dweck

♦ This book explores the concept of a "growth mindset" and how it influences success in life. The author explains why continuous learning and openness to new knowledge are key factors in personal and professional growth.

2. "Atomic Habits: An Easy & Proven Way to Build Good Habits & Break Bad Ones" by James Clear

♦ This book discusses how small changes in daily life can lead to significant results. It provides specific strategies for forming habits that promote continuous learning and personal development.

3. "The Power of Habit: Why We Do What We Do in Life and Business" by Charles Duhigg

♦ The book reveals the mechanisms behind habit formation and explains how these mechanisms can be used to improve learning and achieve success in career and life.

4. "Deep Work: Rules for Focused Success in a Distracted World" by Cal Newport

♦ This book offers strategies for deep, focused work, which is the foundation for effective learning and developing new skills. It will help you better concentrate and achieve higher results in learning.

5. "Lifelong Learning: A Key to Competitiveness in Europe" by the European Commission

♦ This collection of research and analytical materials emphasizes the importance of continuous learning in the modern world. The book provides examples of successful programs and strategies for lifelong skill development.

Online Courses and Resources

1. Coursera (www.coursera.org)

♦ Coursera offers a wide range of online courses from leading universities and organizations worldwide. You can find courses on various topics, including personal development, professional skills, management, and more.

2. Udemy (www.udemy.com)

♦ Udemy provides courses on various disciplines, including programming, business, design, and personal development. Courses are available in video format with the option to take tests and receive certificates.

3. LinkedIn Learning (www.linkedin.com/learning)

♦ LinkedIn Learning offers professional development courses, including leadership, project management, programming, and more. The platform is also integrated with LinkedIn, making it easy to add completed courses to your profile.

4. edX (www.edx.org)

♦ edX offers courses from leading universities such as MIT, Harvard, Berkeley, and others. You can find courses on various fields of knowledge, including science, business, technology, and the humanities.

5. Khan Academy (www.khanacademy.org)

♦ Khan Academy is a free educational platform offering courses in math, science, programming, and other disciplines. It also provides tools for assessing your progress and developing skills.

Articles and Blogs

1. Harvard Business Review (www.hbr.org)

♦ Harvard Business Review publishes articles on continuous learning, career development, leadership, and more. It is a valuable source of knowledge for professionals in various fields.

2. The Learning Scientists Blog (www.learningscientists.org/blog)

♦ This blog is dedicated to scientific research in the field of learning and education. It offers articles, tips, and resources to help you better understand how to learn and develop effectively.

3. MindTools (www.mindtools.com)

♦ MindTools provides tools and resources for skill development, including time management, problem-solving, career development, and more.

4. The Learning Lab Blog (www.learninglabblog.com)

♦ The blog offers articles on various aspects of learning, including skill development, productivity enhancement, and effective use of learning resources.

These resources will help you deepen your knowledge of continuous learning and find new tools to achieve success in your career and personal life. It is important to constantly develop your skills, utilize available resources, and be open to new learning opportunities.

Epilogue

As we conclude this book, it's important to emphasize that each of the ten methodologies we've explored is not merely a standalone tool for improving quality of life but also a part of a holistic approach to personal and professional development. They complement each other, forming a powerful system that helps achieve balance, productivity, and inner peace.

Throughout your reading, you may have noticed that many of the described methodologies, such as goal setting, daily planning, morning rituals, or journaling, share a common trait-they are all aimed at enhancing mindfulness in your life. Mindfulness means understanding what you truly want and confidently moving toward it through the right actions, enriching your skills, and developing emotional resilience.

You've learned not just to set goals but to formulate them correctly using the SMART principle. This transforms abstract desires into clearly defined tasks that can be realistically achieved. Morning rituals, in turn, help set a positive tone for the day, while the Pomodoro Technique sustains efficiency throughout the day, helping you avoid burnout.

Visualization and meditation open up possibilities for deep immersion into your dreams and desires, helping you focus on them with renewed strength. These methods strengthen your self-belief, fueling your confidence and providing motivation for further actions. Journaling helps organize your thoughts, track progress, and analyze results, which is a crucial aspect of personal growth.

One of the main themes of this book is the importance of energy management. This aspect is often overlooked, but it is key to maintaining high productivity and life balance. Understanding when and how to use your resources most effectively allows you to work at your best without exhausting yourself.

Social support and learning are also important components of success. The environment and the people you interact with greatly influence your development. By choosing the right surroundings, you create conditions for continuous growth and achieving new heights. Continuous learning, in turn, ensures the ongoing improvement of your knowledge and skills, opening new opportunities for self-realization.

It is important to understand that these methodologies are not one-time tools but a way of life. Their success depends on regular and consistent implementation. Just as physical training becomes effective only with consistent practice, these methods work best when integrated into your daily life.

This book does not just offer you a set of tips and techniques-it provides a roadmap for creating your own self-development strategy. Regardless of where you are on your life journey, everyone can find something useful among these methodologies. You may have already achieved certain successes and only need minor adjustments, or you might be seeking a complete overhaul of your approach to life-either way, these ten methodologies will help you become a better version of yourself.

Epilogue

Remember, self-development is a journey, not a destination. There will always be new goals, new challenges, and new opportunities for growth. Every day is a chance to take another step toward success. Use these tools wisely and persistently, and you will surely achieve your highest ambitions.

May this book serve as a reliable companion on this journey, helping you overcome difficulties, strengthen your strengths, and inspire you to new achievements. Your success story begins here and now-with the realization that you have all the resources needed to create the life you dream of.

About the Author

My name is David Cross, and over the course of my 42 years, I have navigated a challenging path from a novice entrepreneur to a successful business owner selling decorative items worldwide. Like many, I faced numerous challenges that accompany the growth of one's own business: stress, overload, sleeplessness, and a sense of losing control over the situation.

One day, during an especially tough period when the number of tasks exceeded the capacity to accomplish them, I realized that I needed to find new approaches to managing my life and business. My first step was implementing meditation and visualization techniques, which I had previously read about but had not taken seriously.

Morning rituals became my first step on this path. Every morning, I started meditating, dedicating 10-15 minutes to calm my mind and prepare for the day. Meditation not only brought me peace but also helped develop inner discipline and the ability to focus. Visualization, which I practiced immediately after meditation, allowed me to clearly imagine the desired outcomes. This helped me not only to dream but also to define concrete paths to achieving my goals.

One example of how these practices genuinely helped me occurred during the expansion of my business into a new market. It was a challenging period that required a lot of important decisions and courage. I used meditation to maintain calm in difficult situations and visualization to create a positive scenario for the development of events. Thanks to this, I was able to make strategically important decisions that led to success.

Over time, I began to study psychology and self-development more deeply. This helped me better understand both my own needs and those of my team. Studying these topics allowed me to build an effective business management strategy based on harmony between work and personal life.

These techniques not only helped me achieve success but also provided resilience in the face of stress and the pressures of the modern business world. Today, I can say that this approach is an integral part of my life, helping me stay focused, motivated, and successful.

Additional Materials

This section contains useful resources and materials that will help you delve deeper into the practices described in this book. Here you will find recommendations for further reading, useful tools and apps, and templates to help you implement new habits and methodologies into your daily life.

1. Recommended Reading

- "The Power of Habit" by Charles Duhigg – A book about how habits are formed, changed, and influence our lives.

- "The Miracle Morning" by Hal Elrod – A practical guide to implementing effective morning rituals.

- "Think and Grow Rich" by Napoleon Hill – A classic guide to setting your mind for success.

- "Atomic Habits" by James Clear – A book about how small changes can lead to significant results in life.

- "Deep Work" by Cal Newport – A study on how to focus on important tasks in a world of constant distractions.

- "Daring Greatly" by Brené Brown – A study on vulnerability and courage, which will help you discover new ways to self-development.

- "Focus" by Daniel Goleman – A study on how concentration skills can change your life and work.

2. Useful Tools and Apps

- Headspace (meditation app) – Helps you start practicing meditation and mindfulness.

- Todoist (task management app) – An effective tool for planning and prioritizing tasks.

- Toggl (time tracking app) – Allows you to track the time spent on various tasks, which can be useful for implementing the Pomodoro Technique.

- Calm (meditation and sleep app) – Provides practices for stress relief and better sleep.

- MyFitnessPal (healthy eating app) – Helps you track your diet and physical activity.

- Notion (organization app) – A versatile tool for note-taking, project management, and creating personal databases.

- Habitica (habit tracking app) – A gamified approach to forming new habits.

• RescueTime (time management app) – Analyzes how you spend time on your computer and helps improve productivity.

3. Templates and Workbooks

• Reflection Journal Template – Helps you regularly reflect, evaluate progress, and make adjustments.

• Morning Ritual Planner – A handy tool for implementing and structuring your morning habits.

• Gratitude List – A template for daily gratitude practice, which helps focus on the positive aspects of life.

• Habit Tracker – A convenient tool for tracking new habits you want to implement.

• Pomodoro Technique Planner – A special template for planning and tracking work time using the Pomodoro Technique.

• Daily Planner – Helps you structure your daily tasks by setting priorities.

4. Videos and Courses

• Course "Foundations of Meditation" on Coursera – A deep dive into meditation practice for beginners.

• YouTube Video "How to Start Journaling" – A practical guide to journaling and reflection.

• Webinar "Energy Management for High Productivity" – Helps you better understand how to manage your energy throughout the day.

• Course "How to Set and Achieve Goals" on Udemy – A training course on implementing the SMART methodology and other effective approaches to goal achievement.

• TED Talk "Morning Rituals for Success" – An inspiring lecture on the importance of morning rituals.

• Course "Productivity: From Science to Practice" on Coursera – Learning productivity through scientific approaches.

These resources will help you deepen your understanding of continuous learning and find new tools for success in your career and personal life. It is important to continuously develop your skills, use available resources, and be open to new learning opportunities.

www.ingramcontent.com/pod-product-compliance
Lightning Source LLC
Chambersburg PA
CBHW052147220526
45471CB00004B/1568